The Dilemma
of Enquiry and
Learning

Hugh G. Petrie

The Dilemma of Enquiry and Learning

The University of Chicago Press

Chicago and London

The University of Chicago Press, Chicago 60637
The University of Chicago Press, Ltd., London

Library of Congress Cataloging in Publication Data

Petrie, Hugh G.
    The dilemma of enquiry and learning.

    Bibliography: p.
    Includes index.
    1. Learning. 2. Learning and scholarship.
I. Title.
LB1060.P47   370.15′23   81-3381
ISBN 0-226-66349-3   AACR2

Hugh G. Petrie is Dean of the Faculty of
Education Studies, and Professor of
Education, State University of New York
at Buffalo. [1981]

Contents

To Carol

Acknowledgments

The ideas for this book have come from a variety of sources. It would be impossible to acknowledge my debt to everyone who has in one way or another stimulated my thought, challenged an idea of mine, or given me encouragement when I needed it. Nevertheless, there are a few people whom I would like to single out for special thanks.

I would first like to mention Donald T. Campbell, who, when I was a newly minted assistant professor at Northwestern University, took me under his wing and gave me perhaps the finest postdoctoral experience anyone could have. I began by sitting in on Don's course in knowledge processes and arguing vehemently with him. I ended by coteaching the course with him and fully accepting his emphasis on evolutionary epistemology and the processes of knowing as opposed to the stress on static knowledge structures with which I had begun.

Several years later I met William T. Powers at an informal luncheon group and found his ideas on control system theory both intriguing and perplexing. I invited Bill to be the sole lecturer at a seminar I held the next year, and that experience provided the insights I needed to begin bridging the gaps I had long deplored between philosophy and psychology.

During my time at Northwestern I also met Stephen Toulmin. After I moved to the University of Illinois, I had several long and fruitful discussions with him. In addition, several of his works formed the basis for a series of important graduate seminars I held at Illinois during the early seventies. My intellectual debt to Toulmin will be obvious in the pages which follow.

The final intellectual stimulus came, however, from a group of graduate students the likes of which come along once in a lifetime. During the early and mid-seventies we read and talked and wrote and argued, and most of the ideas in this book had their genesis in those encounters. I particularly want to mention Robert Halstead, Bruce Haynes, Felicity Haynes, Graham Oliver, Ralph Page, Martin Schiaralli, Ron Szoke, and Eric Weir. Without the yeasty intellectual ferment of those days, this book would likely not have been written.

For all the ideas bubbling around in my head, however, I also needed the calm emotional encouragement provided by my wife, Carol Hodges.

She listened patiently as I tried out first one, then another formulation. She understood and accepted all the days and weeks and months of revising and rewriting. She kept me at the task, and she took me away from it when I needed the respite.

In the end, of course, the book is my responsibility. Its successes and failures are my successes and failures. My hope, however, is that it will stimulate others to take a fresh look at some of the epistemological problems of education. I sense a resurgent interest across the country in the epistemological foundations of a variety of fields, from sociology of knowledge, to cognitive science, to organizational behavior. If this book can contribute to these new directions I will be more than satisfied.

1 | The Meno Dilemma

Perhaps the greatest crisis currently facing education, especially in its institutional guise of schooling, is one of conscience. Education seems to have lost its way. It has, fairly obviously, lost its way demographically and financially. The main problem facing elementary and secondary school administrators has changed in the past ten years from how to build and staff new schools to how to close schools. The problems of the next several decades for higher education will be fiscal reduction, budgetary reallocation, and faculty retrenchment. The population bulge has passed the elementary and secondary schools and will soon be past the colleges and universities. Financial support for education measured in real terms has dropped even faster than enrollments, owing to society's disenchantment with education and the increased competition from other social services for funds.

Such financial setbacks would be easier to bear if somehow there existed a sustaining vision of the purpose and worth of education. But that vision has also been lost. Advocates of a general and common education in the schools are fighting a losing battle with the proponents of cultural pluralism on the one hand and the proponents of career education on the other hand. Even liberal education in the colleges and universities is in retreat before a fresh onslaught of careerism. Attempts to combat the new vocationalism, such as the curricular reforms at Harvard and Berkeley, are criticized for being elitist.

One of the fundamental questions underlying these educational issues is whether it is possible to pursue coherent, reasonable educational policies without succumbing to an elitist dogmatism on the one hand or giving in to the radical subjectivism so recently rampant in our society on the other hand. Without question there have been educational policies and practices in the past which, posing as the deliverances of objective reason, have masked discrimination and class bias. Outmoded subjects and instruction have had a dehumanizing influence on students. Such policies and practices are deserving of our critical scorn. But equally disturbing is the fact that in many cases uninformed whim has been substituted for a standard compulsory curriculum. It is one thing to be tolerant of others' opinions. It is quite something else to disclaim any ability to judge rationally between competing subjective claims. The "back to basics" movement is already reacting against a perceived looseness in the curriculum. Are we to be condemned constantly to alternate between the chaos of unbridled subjectivity and the tightly reined influence of dogmatic orthodoxy? Is there no middle ground?

More specifically, why can our educational theory not be put into practice? Should we not hold the schools accountable for what they do? But by what criteria? Do not students learn more when they are taught to memorize the facts? But what do they learn? Do we not have to take account of the individuality of each student? But what of the common store of the knowledge of mankind? "I teach arithmetic." "*I* teach children." Why can we not open up our classrooms to a more humane and fulfilling way of teaching and learning? Why can Johnny neither read *nor* write *nor* do arithmetic?

The frequent pendulum swings in educational practices, policies, and principles are notorious. No doubt there are multiple causes for the comings and goings of all of these fads and fancies, and it is certainly not my purpose in this book to examine all of the many facets of the educational problems and issues I have alluded to. Yet all of these issues share one concern in common. They are concerned with learning. It is not so much that the nature of learning is the focus of our many practical educational concerns; it is rather that particular views of the nature of learning are always presupposed, however implicitly, by the disputants in most educational issues. Is learning a process of transmitting that which is readily at hand, or must learning be conceived of as an achievement by the individual? If the former, why are we not significantly more successful; if the latter, by what criteria do we judge the learning successful? I will argue in this book that the reason we are unable to answer these questions is that our understanding of the concept of learning is caught up in an ancient dilemma, and that a whole host of educational disputes can be seen as ways of alternating between one extreme and another in an attempt to meet the challenge of this dilemma of enquiry and learning.

1. The Dilemma of Enquiry and Learning

You argue that a man cannot enquire either about that which he knows or about that which he does not know; for if he knows, he has no need to enquire; and if not, he cannot; for he does not know the very subject about which he is to enquire.

Plato, *Meno,* 80 E (Jowett translation)

This passage is one of the few instances in the Platonic dialogues in which Socrates' "yes-men" pose what seems to the reader a real problem for Socrates. Indeed, as I shall try to show, the problem is with us today. Plato's answer in terms of recollection of a previous existence is inadequate, and nothing in intellectual history since then has constituted much of an improvement on Plato's response. Meno's question is a paraphrase of the foundational question of educational theory, "How is learning possible?" This book is an attempt to answer this ancient, yet enduring, question.

For, if a person can enquire neither about what the person knows nor about what the person does not know, then it would seem that learning is either trivial or impossible. Yet, we all know that learning is neither trivial nor impossible. Every day we witness the struggles of our students to learn rewarded at least occasionally. When a paradox about something as common as learning can be so easily raised, it would seem that our implicit presuppositions about learning, enquiry, knowledge, teaching, and related concepts are perhaps not all in order. How is it that we all know that learning and enquiry do occur, even if less often than we would like, and yet we all understand the apparently compelling argument of the *Meno* showing that learning and enquiry are either trivial or impossible?

The problem raised by the *Meno* is not, strictly speaking, a logical paradox. A logical paradox is a statement such that both it and its denial lead to a contradiction. Rather, the puzzle raised in the *Meno* contradicts a basic belief that we have concerning the possibility of learning; namely, that it is the simple acquisition of new knowledge. The problems raised by the *Meno* are akin to the intellectual perplexities raised during the Copernican revolution by the increasing argument and evidence that the sun did not revolve around the earth as was then commonly believed. The arguments and evidence, in themselves seemingly incontrovertible, contradicted the basic belief that the earth was stationary at the center of the universe. Although many at the time thought the problem was not a real one, in the end we were forced to give up the basic belief about the earth's centrality in the universe. At the time no one knew how the issue would be resolved. Perhaps the arguments for the earth's movement would have proved in error. When such arguments contradict basic beliefs, however, the whole intellectual setting in which such problems can be raised needs to be carefully examined.

There is another puzzle, from the ethical sphere, which is directly relevant both to education and to the problem of enquiry in the *Meno*. This is the paradox of moral education (Peters, 1974b). Briefly, the paradox is this: Most theories of moral judgment and action require such judgment and action to be informed by reason, intelligence, and critical thought. Yet the facts of human development seem to show that at certain crucial developmental stages of a child's life we cannot appeal to the child's reason, intelligence, and critical capacities, for the child cannot understand such appeals. At these early stages we must inculcate mere habits of "moral" behavior. Yet how is it possible that these habits can be transformed into the reflective thought and action that are necessary for truly moral behavior? How are we to find the pathways from the courtyard of habit to the palace of reason? I shall later return to the paradox of moral education in an effort to show its close structural affinity with the puzzle of the *Meno,* but for now I offer it as yet another example of the sorts of puzzles and problems which generate intellectual discomfort. We *know* people do, sometimes, learn to behave morally, but the question is, How?

My purpose in the foregoing examples has been to illustrate that to dismiss such puzzles and paradoxes out of hand as silly and sophistical is wholly unwarranted. The puzzle *may* turn out, on investigation, to be nothing more than an intellectual trick, but that is a judgment to be arrived at by a careful examination of the issues involved, and not by a snap appeal to our intuitions that the puzzle must be silly. Commonsensical beliefs can sometimes be combined in ways that create puzzles and paradoxes that we cannot immediately understand. We know *something* is wrong, but what? Historically our philosophical and intellectual efforts to say what is wrong have led to a deeper and more profound understanding of the world, the human condition, and our attempts to cope with ourselves and our relations in the world.

Yet, even if one is convinced that such puzzles as the one propounded in the *Meno* ought to be taken seriously, there are two responses which might tend to halt my enquiry, and your learning, before either one begins. First, it might be objected that learning must be distinguished from enquiry, i.e., an individual's coming to know must be demarcated from the general human acquisition of knowledge represented by science and scholarship. The puzzle of the *Meno* may be appropriate to enquiry, it will be said, but it is inappropriate to learning. What one does not know can be learned by being taught it by someone who does know it. On this view the *Meno* puzzle would not be a problem for the transmission of knowledge in education, however much it might be a problem for the acquisition of knowledge through scholarly and scientific enquiry.

The distinction between enquiry, conceived as processes leading to the growth of human knowledge in general, and learning, conceived as processes leading to the growth of an individual's knowledge, is, I think, a useful one. However, I do not believe the distinction can be used to dismiss the puzzle of the *Meno* with regard to learning. Indeed, it is part of the purpose of this book to draw out the numerous parallels between learning and enquiry. Because the connection between the two is crucial to much of this book, I shall devote a good portion of chapter 7 to exploring the relations between them. For now, it will suffice to note that enquiry itself has important educational implications, in the area of curriculum, for example; and that the situation facing the scholar or scientist on the frontiers of knowledge is very similar to the problems facing the student confronted with a totally new body of knowledge. Thus, prior to my explicit consideration of the relations between enquiry and learning I shall, for purposes of exposition, speak primarily of enquiry, that is, the processes involved in the growth of human knowledge in general, rather than of an individual's learning.

The second immediate objection concerns the initial sense of the question, "How are enquiry and learning possible?" If one views learning as do many psychologists as simply changes in behavior due to environmental causes, one might be tempted to answer the problem posed in the *Meno* by attempting to lay bare the mechanisms of such behavior change. Such a move completely misses the point of the problem raised in the *Meno*. The learning referred to in the *Meno* is aimed at coming to know. That is, we must be concerned that the changes in behavior be *reasonable* and *appropriate* ones. Not just any changes of behavior will count as learning in this sense. There must always be a very general judgment that the learning or enquiry will be valid.

This normative judgment of validity distinguishes the epistemological problems with which I shall be concerned in this book from the more general problems of psychology proper. I am not concerned with the general mechanisms of changes in behavior and belief. Such mechanisms, if they were known, would presumably account for the acquisition of false beliefs, bad habits, and improper skills. While such descriptive knowledge of how and why such changes occur may be tremendously important, it would not answer the normative question of which beliefs, habits, and skills we believe to be knowledge and, therefore, ought to acquire. It is to this latter normative question that the *Meno* puzzle is directed.

A time-honored example of the distinction between a descriptive and a normative study is that of the difference between psychology and logic as applied to deductive argument. Both are concerned with argument, but the former, psychology, is as much concerned with the causes and mechanisms of sloppy, inadequate, mistaken, and invalid argument as it is with the causes and mechanisms of clear, adequate, valid argument. On the other hand, logic is concerned with what constitutes the difference between valid and invalid modes of deductive argument. Psychology is descriptive, logic is normative. Both disciplines are important, but their aims are different. For a complete understanding of argument, one would need both psychological and logical results, and at some level these bear important relations to each other as I shall later show. But none of this affects the fact that the aims and initial methods of the two disciplines with respect to the same subject matter, deductive argument, are fundamentally different. Henceforth, I shall always use "learning" in the normative sense unless I explicitly note otherwise.

So it is with the *Meno* paradox. We do not now possess the kinds of theoretical results in psychological learning theory which adequately describe the mechanisms of behavior change, but even if we did, such descriptive results would not solve the paradox of enquiry to be found in the *Meno*. For obviously enough, if *any* behavior change, valid or not, reasonable or unreasonable, counted as learning in the normative sense, then it would not matter that one did not know the subject about which one was enquiring. *Any* behavior change would count as a proper end of enquiry, and that conclusion is obviously absurd. Neither Socrates nor we can say, "Enquiry is unnecessary. You may believe whatever you wish."

Descriptive cognitive psychology attempts to remain neutral with respect to the validity of behavior change; education, however, cannot avoid entering the fray. Education is essentially concerned with changes in belief which are at least thought to be justifiable, with skills which are held to be useful, and with habits believed to contribute to the good life. In short, education may use descriptive psychology as part of its arsenal, but education's aim is unavoidably normative. That is why the *Meno* paradox is so crucial for education.

I need to forestall one possible misapprehension at this point. In committing myself to investigating a normative notion of learning rather than a descriptive one, I am not thereby committed to some notion of absolute or eternal truth. Such doctrines have, of course, sometimes emerged as the results of normative investigations of the kind I am undertaking, but they need not, and, indeed, will not in this study.

There is another narrowing of my area of concern that should be noted here. Even within a normative investigation into learning, there are a number of different kinds of questions one might ask. One might, for example, pursue the policy question of how best to organize institutional and individual efforts to promote learning. Although my results may have some implications for such questions, they are not my major concern. Alternatively, one might ask for an analysis of the varying concepts of learning. What, in other words, does "learning" in its various senses mean? Although I shall be doing some conceptual analysis in the course of this work, that will not be my primary aim either. Again, one might ask for fairly specific criteria for deciding when something has been learned. Although some guidelines may be suggested by what I shall say, it is not my specific purpose to develop such criteria.

Rather, I shall take the question, "How is learning possible?" in a Kantian sense. That is, "What are the presuppositions we have to make about the world and our attempts at knowing the world in order to render possible and intelligible our learning and our failure to learn?" I am not looking for sufficient conditions guaranteeing that learning will take place, although such conditions would be welcome to educators. Rather I am looking for those conditions rendering the human activity of learning, where this includes successes *and* failures, intelligible. I take the ease with which Plato has generated the *Meno* paradox as an indication that we probably do not as yet understand learning as well as we might, and to that extent, we do not understand what we are about in our educational enterprises. And *this* lack of understanding is not a value disagreement about the ends of education, although it is clear there is plenty of that in contemporary educational discussion. Rather it is a lack of understanding of the epistemoligical conditions which render the central task of education, namely learning, possible.

2. A Formal Characterization of the Dilemma

Having shown the importance of the *Meno* dilemma for education, I shall now exhibit the paradox by means of a formal model. This will enable me to structure various philosophical positions in terms of the ways in which they are, or can be seen as, attempts to overcome the problems of learning and enquiry raised by the *Meno* dilemma. Such a formal structuring will also enable me to show in a general way the various conditions and constraints which operate on any proposed solutions. Finally, the formal structure will also enable me to interpret several important and perennial educational issues in terms of the dilemma.

The *Meno* paradox is not a logical paradox, but rather an argument which seems to lead to the conclusion that learning or enquiry is unnecessary or impossible. Such a result is paradoxical in that it contradicts what seems to be absolutely certain—namely, that learning takes place all the time. Is the argument correct and we have been mistaken all this time about learning? Or is the argument faulty somewhere?

If so, where? Or do we need to reassess and reinterpret some of our basic concepts regarding enquiry, learning, knowledge, and so on?

Logically, the argument takes the form of a simple constructive dilemma, which can be presented schematically as shown in figure 1.

MAJOR PREMISE	If we already know that about which we are to enquire, enquiry is unnecessary (because we would have no need to enquire). *and* If we do not know that about which we are to enquire, enquiry is impossible (because we do not know the very subject about which we are to enquire).
MINOR PREMISE	Either we know that about which we are to enquire or we do not know that about which we are to enquire.
CONCLUSION	Therefore, enquiry is either unnecessary or impossible.

Figure 1. The Meno Dilemma

Or, if we leave out the parenthetical background arguments for the two halves of the major premise, and make the following symbolic substitutions:

p: We know that about which we are to enquire.
q: Enquiry is necessary.
r: Enquiry is possible.

we get,

$$(p \rightarrow \text{not-}q) \text{ and } (\text{not-}p \rightarrow \text{not-}r)$$
$$\frac{p \text{ or not-}p}{\text{Therefore, not-}q \text{ or not-}r}$$

which is a perfectly valid argument form. Thus, unless we can refute the argument, enquiry and learning will, to use the colorful language of ancient logic, be impaled on the horns of the dilemma.

Now the only ways to refute a formally valid constructive dilemma are either to deny one or more of the premises or to show there is an equivocation in the sense of one of the crucial terms. To take the latter tack, it might be claimed that "knowledge" is being used in different senses in the major and minor premises. This would dissolve the dilemma. With respect to the former move, one could grasp either of the horns of the dilemma by arguing against the appropriate part of the major premise. Arguing that the minor premise is false is said to be going between the horns of the dilemma. I shall briefly sketch each of these moves for the *Meno* dilemma.

The first move would be to grasp the first, or, as I shall call it, the "old-knowledge" horn of the dilemma. That is, it could be denied that if one already knows that about which one is to enquire, enquiry is unnecessary. This denial is usually buttressed by attacking the argument given for the "old-knowledge" horn. This attack tries to show that even though there is a sense in which we know that about which we are enquiring, there is another sense in which we do not. It is in this second sense, the sense in which we do not yet know, that enquiry will be necessary and nontrivial. It might be argued, for example, that the student does not know, but the teacher does, and that is how learning can take place. But the question remains, How does the student learn in the first place to rely on the teacher as a source of learning? Compare the situation with that of the scientist on the frontiers of knowledge. How does the scientist learn which of "nature's" lessons to believe? Similarly, how does the student learn which of the teacher's lessons to believe? The student does learn, of course; that is not the point. Rather the question is whether the student is justified in such initial "learning."

I shall critically investigate attempts to grasp the old-knowledge horn in chapter 2. Interestingly, those two arch rivals in Western epistemology, empiricism and rationalism, will both turn out to be somewhat different attempts to grasp the old-knowledge horn of the dilemma. Basically, I shall argue that there are two main problems with any attempt to grasp the old knowlege horn. First, the dilemma can apparently be raised once again about the source of the old knowledge which is postulated as grounding enquiry and learning. Second, there seems to be no way of accounting for the attainment of truly new knowledge. All attempts to grasp the old-knowledge horn seem to claim that any apparently new knowledge is simply illusory; yet historically it seems we do sometimes obtain radically new knowledge.

Another move would be to grasp the second, or, as I shall call it, the "new-knowledge" horn of the dilemma. That is, it could be denied that if one does not know that about which one is to enquire, enquiry is impossible. This denial is rendered plausible by attacking the argument given for the new-knowledge horn. The attack on the new-knowledge horn sketches ways in which one could know the subject of enquiry, and, even more importantly, could have some idea when such enquiry into new areas was successful. Examples of attempts to grasp the new-knowledge horn are relatively infrequent in Western philosophy, although radically progressive educational movements which tend to emphasize an individual's construction of knowledge bear a close affinity to epistemological attempts to grasp the new-knowledge horn of the *Meno* dilemma.

I shall critically investigate attempts to grasp the new-knowledge horn in chapter 3. Such attempts, of course, emphasize the radically new nature of knowledge which can be obtained by means of enquiry. There are typically two main problems with attempts to grasp the new-knowledge horn. First, no account seems to be given of the fact that our first fumbling attempts in new areas of enquiry are seldom completely misplaced. That is, attempts to grasp the new-knowledge horn seem unable to account for the historical continuity of knowledge that we find. Second, the necessity for evaluating putative new knowledge as successful, both in terms of initial plausibility and in terms of later justification, seems to be ignored, and yet we do critically assess new knowledge claims in terms of what we currently know.

A last tactic would be to slip between the horns of the dilemma by denying the minor premise that either we already do or do not know that about which we are to enquire. Such a denial would appear to be denying a logical tautology and, therefore, not a very promising move. Nevertheless, that is essentially the path I shall take in this book. I shall not, however, be denying a tautology because the claim that we either know or do not know that about which we are to enquire presupposes that knowledge is a particular *state* which people either are or are not in. Now while a "static" view of knowledge may be intelligible in a derivative sense, I shall argue in chapter 4 that knowledge, at least for purposes of educational epistemology, is most fundamentally conceived of as a *process*. The argument for this view will take the form of attempting to demonstrate that there is such a thing as rational conceptual change that cannot be explained away by traditional accounts. If this is so, then knowing must be conceived of as a continuing *process* of shaping our conceptual, perceptual, and representational schemes in response to the twin constraints of the general purposes of human activity on the one hand and the indirect editing effects of "the world" on the other hand.

It is the existence of rational conceptual change which will give point to the reinterpreted ways of grasping the two horns to be discussed in chapters 5 and 6. However, since knowledge will be conceived of as a process of adaptation, a continual historical shifting back and forth between the horns of the dilemma actually constitutes the way in which we both do and do not know that about which we are to enquire. This reciprocal and iterative process will be discussed in chapter 7 along with the problem of the interrelations between the growth of human knowledge in general and the growth of an individual's knowledge. It is, of course, the latter that is the primary concern of education. Up until chapter 7 I shall, as I have indicated, be concerned with the growth of human knowledge in general, with enquiry, although, as will be evident, much of what I say about the growth of human knowledge will obviously be related to an individual's learning. I shall not look specifically at the relations between the two, however, until chapter 7.

The basic processes of the acquisition of knowledge, both in general and on an individual level, that I shall defend give a kind of epistemological legitimacy to an individual student's way of looking at and dealing with the world. That is, according to the view I shall develop, educators cannot simply assume that it is always appropriate to induct the young into our collective modes of knowledge and understanding without taking into account the students' autonomy. The burden of proof is on the educator to convince the student *in the student's terms* that a change in cognitive structure is appropriate. Now sometimes this burden can be carried, and when it can, the question arises as to how, pedagogically, such learning is possible. Thus, the *Meno* dilemma of the theoretical possibility of learning is reproduced on the practical level of pedagogy. In chapter 8 I shall suggest that a triangulation of thought and action on the material to be learned is the key pedagogical notion needed to bridge the gap between the student's konwledge and modes of understanding at any given time and the general konwledge and modes of understanding into which we wish to induct the student. So the *Meno* dilemma will receive both a philosophical and a practical pedagogical solution.

The educational concerns of this book will be interspersed throughout it. I do not believe that one can philosophize about education by simply substituting educational terms into general philosophical formulas. Rather one must philosophize within educational contexts, and that view dictates that the educational and philosophical concerns interact continuously. It will, therefore, not be possible for the philosophical reader to skip over the educational parts nor for the educator to ignore the philosophy. Perhaps that will be good for the souls of both of them.

2 | Grasping the Old-Knowledge Horn

1. Conceptual and Factual Knowledge

Consider the following argument for the superficiality of the *Meno* dilemma. Suppose a school has been faced with steadily declining enrollments in the past few years and the superintendent of the district wants to determine how many children of kindergarten age currently live in the district. There is clearly something the superintendent does not know, the number of kindergarten-age children in the district. It also seems clear that the superintendent can enquire into the answer to this question. A survey can be designed to find out how many such children there are, and surely the superintendent will recognize what will count as an answer. Indeed this situation is common. There are literally an infinite number of such things that people do not know, can enquire into, and for which they recognize what would count as an answer. "Is there any hamburger in the freezer for dinner tonight?" I don't know, but all I have to do is go look. "What is the weather going to be tomorrow?" I will listen to the forecast on the radio and find out. "What kind of gasoline mileage did I get on my trip last month?" I can determine the miles traveled and the gallons of gasoline used and compute it. And so on and on. What could possibly be the problem with enquiry and learning in such situations?

Not only can innumerable examples of such everyday enquiry be cited, but a simple analysis of why such enquiry is successful is also available. In considering the question, "How many children of kindergarten age live in the district?" the problem is understood as well as the general outlines of what would count as an answer. We understand the *concepts* involved, what is being asked, and how an investigation like a survey could provide an answer, but it is not yet known just how the world sorts itself with respect to the concepts "children of kindergarten age" and "in the district."

However, it could be asserted, this kind of example shows the old-knowledge horn of the dilemma to be false. The old-knowledge horn is: If we already know that about which we are to enquire, enquiry is unnecessary. However, on the view under consideration we do know, in the sense of understanding the question, what would count as an answer, yet we do not know the actual answer to the question, and so need to enquire. The antecedent of the old-knowledge conditional is true, the consequent is false, and so the conditional is false.

This same example could also be used to show that the new-knowledge horn can be construed as false as well. The new-knowledge horn is: If we do not know that about which we are to enquire, enquiry is impossible. Again the antecedent is true in the sense that we do not know the actual answer to the question, but we do know, i.e., understand, the general outlines of the subject about which we are to enquire, namely, the children in district. Thus the consequent is false, and the whole conditional false.

According to this line of argument the dilemma is dissolved once we distinguish two senses of "knowing." First, there is the sense of knowing what it is the question asks, and in general what would count as an answer. This is a knowledge of the concepts involved in the question. Second, there is the sense of knowing the actual answer to the question, what in fact is the case. This is a knowledge of the facts. The whole force of the dilemma comes from equivocating between these two senses of "knowing" in the horns of the dilemma. If we stick with knowledge of concepts, then the old-knowledge horn is false. That is, we can know, i.e., understand, the concepts in terms of which we are enquiring and yet still need to determine how, in fact, the world sorts itself into these concepts. On the other hand, if we stick with knowledge of facts, then the new-knowledge horn is false. That is, we may not know the answer to our question, but can still enquire about it, for we do at least understand what would count as an answer.

For the sake of argument at this juncture, I wish to accept the rough distinction between knowledge of facts and knowledge of concepts outlined above. Provisionally, a knowledge of concepts is the ability to order and classify experience into meaningful categories. We know the concept of a dog when we can recognize dogs. We know the concept of eating when we can recognize organisms engaged in the process of eating. A knowledge of facts is a knowledge of how the world, natural and social, actually is. If my dog is eating and I know it, that is a knowledge of fact. Knowledge of facts can be of objects, events, and situations. Facts can be particular or general. They are expressed by propositions which in turn contain concepts as constituent parts. Typically a sharp distinction is drawn between concepts and propositions. I shall later argue that no such hard and fast distinction is possible. For now, however, I shall accept the rough distinction and content myself with noting that one can scarcely be said to know the concept of dog if one knows no facts or true propositions about dogs.

There are two main reasons, however, for not resting content with the claim that the *Meno* dilemma evaporates on noting the distinction between knowledge of facts and knowledge of concepts. In the first place, the solution to the dilemma by means of the distinction clearly presupposes the preexistence of a knowledge of concepts such that enquiry is solely concerned with determining the facts. Recall that the proposed solution reads: "If we already know the subject about which we are to enquire (understand the concepts), then enquiry (coming to know the facts) is still necessary, and if we do not know the facts about which we are to enquire, enquiry is still possible, for we do know (understand the concepts in) the general area of enquiry." Thus in both cases knowledge of the concepts is presupposed. So this "solution" of the paradox actually proceeds by grasping the old-knowledge horn of the dilemma, because the claim is that there is a sense in which we already do know that about which we are to enquire, namely, we know the concepts which structure our enquiry.

But it seems to me that the dilemma can simply be raised anew about this sense of knowledge. In other words, suppose I grant for the moment that enquiry into facts is nonproblematic. What about an enquiry into concepts? The first premise of the dilemma can be restated as: "If one already knows the subject about which one enquires (possesses the concept), enquiry into that concept is unnecessary, and if one does not already know (possess the concept), enquiry is impossible (for one will not know the very concept about which one is to enquire)." The dilemma as reformulated concludes that *enquiry into concepts* is unnecessary or impossible.

But this is also paradoxical for we do believe that we can enquire into and learn concepts. Once again it might be urged that enquiry and learning must be sharply distinguished. Learning concepts is surely possible, it will be said, while enquiring into them does not make sense. The detailed discussion of the relation between learning and enquiry will be given, as I have already noted, in chapter 7. For now, it will suffice to note that insofar as the development of human understanding in general occasionally requires the alteration or abandonment of existing concepts and the creation of new ones adequate to our knowing activities, it would seem to make sense to speak of an enquiry into concepts. For example, we no longer have the concept of aether in physics, but we do have the concept of a black hole in astrophysics.

A second reason for continuing to worry about the *Meno* dilemma—even if we do accept the distinction between knowledge of concepts and knowledge of facts—is an educational one. It may, indeed, be true that a goodly portion of ordinary adult enquiry is of the sort exemplified by the superintendent determining the number of kindergarten students in the district. The conceptual background which structures such enquiry can simply be taken for granted. But surely such is not always the case in education. Children plainly do *not* possess such conceptual frameworks, at least at a young age, and a part of the task of education is precisely to help them acquire the requisite concepts. The case is abundantly clear when we consider subjects such as chemistry or engineering in which, as an integral part of learning the facts of the subject matter, the student must also acquire the concepts in terms of which those facts are expressed (Hirst, 1965). Education, as opposed to informed common sense, cannot ignore the source of our knowledge of concepts.

2. Conditions of Conceptual Knowledge

In contemporary times knowledge of concepts has typically been taken to be the same as knowledge of the definitions of terms. There are, however, deep and profound questions surrounding such an assimilation of questions concerning the nature of things to questions concerning the definitions of terms (Rorty, 1967; Veatch, 1969). There is a temptation to dismiss problems of the adequacy of concepts by such remarks as, "Oh, that's just true by definition," or, "It all depends on how you define your terms." Such remarks make it appear as if definitions were more or less arbitrary and anyone were entitled to any definitions desired. The counter to such a trivialization of the problem of conceptual knowledge is that in transforming questions of how experience is to be categorized into questions of definition we are still seeking "real" definitions of terms, i.e., those definitions which state how things really are and not merely how we use words. To speak of real definitions emphasizes the point that definitions of terms are not arbitrary and must be adequate to the way the world actually is.

   This point is important precisely because it is so little understood in contemporary thought. Take a current controversial example. We are interested as educators in the nature of intelligence. It enters crucially into any number of educational problems—competence levels, instructional design, individualized instruction, differential educational opportunity, and so on. But what is it? Suppose we give the question its linguistic formulation and instead of asking what is the nature of intelligence, we ask what is the definition of the word intelligence? The most common reply at this point is for testers to define intelligence "operationally" in terms of the concrete notions of scores on intelligence tests. Intelligence is what intelligence tests say it is. Laymen do, but social scientists often do not, recognize the blatant circularity and arbitrary use of language involved in such an operational definition. In one sense the social scientist is vaguely honoring the idea that (real) definitions must be about the world and thus is defining intelligence in concrete observable terms—test scores. But in another sense the relevance to the world depends solely on the apparently arbitrary stipulation of the social scientist. Why, we can legitimately ask, do you think test scores have anything to do with intelligence?

In this case the linguistic shift to considering definitions instead of the nature of things seems to have perverted the language-world link. Real definitions must not only make contact with the world (operational definitions do that, all right), but they must also be concerned with the way the world really is. And except in a totally arbitrary and unmotivated way, operational definitions tend not to take this latter requirement seriously. It may be true that the world really does contain such and such test scores (marks on a piece of paper), but the question remains, what do these scores or marks have to do with intelligence?

It can be seen from this discussion that "concepts" seem to perform a mediating function between language and the world. Concepts are ways of categorizing our experience of the world, yet they are the sorts of things that are paradigmatically expressed by means of language. We can define linguistic terms and in that sense we show our knowledge of concepts. At the same time the question is open as to whether or not any given definition really does express the nature of things in the world. We can agree that people do in fact define their terms in such and such a way and still question the adequacy of those definitions. Therefore, when I speak of a knowledge of definitions as providing a knowledge of concepts, it will be in the context of judging the adequacy of the definition as a real definition.

One of the main problems with treating a knowledge of concepts as equivalent to a knowledge of definitions is the so-called "paradox of analysis" (Weitz, 1967). Indeed, we might view this paradox as a near relative of the *Meno* paradox, although the exact bloodlines are unclear. Basically the paradox of analysis arises because of the condition that the concept being analyzed, the analysandum, be synonymous with the concept(s) giving the analysis, the analysans. On virtually any theory of meaning, two synonymous expressions can be substituted one for the other in any context. This leads to the following paradoxical result: If "A brother is a male sibling" is treated as a successful analysis, we can derive, by substitution of synonymous terms, "A brother is a brother." The original putative analysis is intuitively informative, whereas the result one gets by synonymy substitution is not. In particular, the latter is *not* an analysis and is blatantly circular, yet it was obtained by an unobjectionable synonymy substitution.

To state the problem in a manner analogous to the *Meno* dilemma, it appears to be impossible to give an analysis of any concept. For either we already know the meaning of a term or we do not. If we do, analysis is unnecessary. If we do not, we could never be certain of the correctness of any putative analysis, for to be certain of the correctness would require knowing the very synonymy relation in question!

One very natural way of attempting to meet the problem of the paradox of analysis would be to try to determine a special class of antecedently understood terms which must be used in any appropriate analysis. An analysis given in these terms would be informative and nontrivial in that it would utilize the building blocks of language, namely, these basic terms, thus blocking the dangerous circularity of the paradox of analysis. The old-knowledge horn would also have been successfully grasped in that an analysis with the aid of these basic terms would constitute a nontrivial enquiry into concepts. Furthermore, we would be able to recognize an appropriate analysis when we came across one. It would be given in terms of the antecedently understood concepts.

There is, however, yet another condition in operation here. The way in which the antecedently understood class of terms is to be picked out cannot allow the *Meno* dilemma to be raised at *that* level, too. Otherwise, we would be in danger of generating an infinite regress. In short, our knowledge or understanding of these basic terms must be of a type which cannot itself admit of enquiry. Our knowledge of them must be direct and unimpeachable.

Let me recapitulate this section. The suggestion was that the *Meno* dilemma could be solved by distinguishing knowledge of facts from knowledge of concepts. A knowledge of concepts is something we already have and such knowledge would enable us to enquire into the facts. However, the *Meno* dilemma can be raised again at the level of the knowledge of concepts. Knowledge of concepts is understood as the analysis of concepts or as real definitions of terms. The necessary constraints on such knowledge involve having to specify a special class of concepts in terms of which the analysis or definition can be given. This follows from having to overcome the paradox of analysis. But such a special, basic class of concepts must be known in such a direct way that the concepts in that class do not admit of enquiry in this or in any sense. Otherwise we would be faced with an infinite regress of *Meno* dilemmas. To illustrate how actual accounts of the acquisition of concepts attempt to satisfy these conditions, I now turn to some examples.

3. Platonism and Conceptual Knowledge

A number of commentators argue that Plato himself believed that the only "real" knowledge was conceptual knowledge, which turns out to be equivalent to knowledge of the Forms. The Platonic Forms are absolute, eternal, unchanging, nonsensible universals, such as The Good, or The Chair. Sensible things, such as this particular chair, are considered knowable insofar as they model the *truly* knowable Form of Chair. What we call empirical knowledge, or knowledge of particular things, was, for Plato, a matter of mere belief and opinion. F. M. Cornford (1952, p. 110) writes:

> Plato was not seeking a basis for any science of the sensible world; he was, in the first instance, seeking to give an account of that knowledge which must direct the conduct of human life. The objects he discovered were not laws of nature, if by that we mean formulas describing the sequence of sensible phenomena, or anything of that sort. The theory grew upon his hands into a doctrine of an intelligible 'nature of things,' consciously opposed to the materialism which identified reality with the elementary components of tangible bodies.

To give the "intelligible nature of things" is, at least to a first approximation, to give the concept of the things under investigation.

As Bernard Phillips (1948–49, p. 79) says:

> Meno's objection is not directed against the whole of human knowledge or against the cognitive enterprise as such. Meno is not expressing a general scepticism; what he questions is the possibility of achieving the sort of knowledge which they are pursuing in the dialogue. It is the Socratic type of inquiry which forms the target of Meno's paradox, and in relation to the sort of investigation which Socrates was wont to pursue, Meno's question formulates a genuine problem. For how are we to construe the question, What is virtue? Presumably it is not simply an empirical question of fact. It does not ask what is the current usage of the term 'virtue'; neither does it seek to determine what any particular individual may choose to denote by the term. It is by intention an inquiry into the real inner nature of that which is designated by the conventional label 'virtue'; it seeks the 'essence' of virtue.

To give the "essence" of virtue is, at least to a first approximation, to give the concept of virtue, although the notion of "essence" already presupposes a Platonic theory of concepts in terms of the Forms.

For Plato a knowledge of the essence of things came to be seen as an acquaintance with the Forms. Somehow, we had true knowledge of the nature of things when we had intuitively and directly apprehended the Forms. This process was exceedingly difficult and was tied up for

Plato with his doctrine of the immortality of the soul. Basically, our souls had direct acquaintance with the eternal Forms before birth, and it was our having taken on a body which clouded and distorted true knowledge of the Forms. Learning thus became for Plato a process of recollection, and this process is generally taken to have been well illustrated in the *Meno* by the slave boy episode. In this episode, Socrates, by means of a series of brilliant questions, elicits the proof of a somewhat difficult geometrical theorem from a slave boy who has never before been tutored in geometry.

A careful examination of Plato's doctrines will reveal that they are not nearly so absurd as they often first appear to the contemporary mind. But the importance of the doctrine of the Forms for my purposes is rather that it illustrates a whole class of attempted solutions to the *Meno* dilemma of conceptual knowledge. The Forms are the class of basic concepts, and our knowledge of them is direct and unimpeachable—a kind of primitive knowledge by acquaintance. The search for real definitions, which is a hallmark of the Platonic dialogues, involves recollecting our knowledge of the Forms and of how they are connected. Nor is enquiry appropriate at the original level of knowledge of the Forms, for at that stage our souls and the Forms coexist as equals. Such an approach, no matter that one objects to the details, is indicative of what I shall call a rationalistic view of conceptual knowledge.

Now obviously there are serious objections to the Platonic formulation of a rationalistic approach to the knowledge of concepts. The original acquaintance of the soul with the Forms is mysterious, to say nothing of postulating such questionable entities as souls and Forms. Furthermore, the history of thought amply demonstrates divergent beliefs as to the nature of the Forms of Goodness, Right, Truth, Knowledge, and so on. Such diversity seems wholly incompatible with the requirement that knowledge of the Forms be direct and unimpeachable. There is also the suspicion that the basic, direct knowledge of the Forms is merely postulated and never really shown. That is, the potential infinite regress of *Meno* dilemmas applied to the "basic" class of concepts is blocked by arbitrary fiat. Finally, there seems to be no way on this approach to account for conceptual change. The problem of conceptual change is so central that I reserve a fuller discussion of it to chapter 4.

4. Associationistic Empiricism

Because of such difficulties with a variety of forms of rationalism, there has arisen in the history of thought a more empiricist account of the nature of conceptual knowlege. Some sort of empiricism informs most of contemporary social science, and yet, as I shall argue, the empiricist approach is also inadequate. Not only is it inadequate, but the reasons for its inadequacy suggest a return to a Platonic account (Weimer, 1973). But if Platonism breeds empiricism and empiricism breeds Platonism, and neither is adequate to account for conceptual knowledge, then there will be good reason to believe that grasping the first horn of the *Meno* dilemma will not be successful.

If we object to the notion of a transcendent soul communing with a world of abstract, unchanging Forms, then associationistic empiricism provides another way of picking out the basic items which are needed to ground conceptual knowledge. The basic direct knowledge is taken to be of concrete particulars rather than of abstract universals (e.g., Russell, 1956). Our intuition of universals is mysterious and uncertain; our acquaintance with the immediate data of experience is certain and direct. People are forever disagreeing about the Forms, but surely, empiricism claims, we can reach agreement about the basic particulars of experience. Nor will knowledge of these basic particulars be open to the charge of a regress of *Meno* dilemmas. We do not need to enquire into our knowledge that this is a page in front of us; we directly observe it.

These concrete particulars (whether they are physical objects, sense data, or whatever, makes no difference to my purpose) are taken by empiricism to be organized in the mind by laws of association. Typically such principles include similarity, contrast, and contiguity. The operation of such principles is believed to account for all the ways in which concrete particulars are connected with each other, and such laws must enable us to explain our knowledge of general terms and concepts and the acquisition of such concepts. "Kindergarten children" as a general term is simply the similarity of people with respect to a certain age. "People" is just the similarity of objects with respect to "rationality" and "animality." And so it would go. Concrete particulars group themselves into natural kinds with respect to the similarity relations among them.

Thus, according to the associationist account of general concepts, we have a direct experiential access to basic concrete particulars, and by the laws of association these particulars group together to form our general concepts. The *Meno* dilemma is to be solved by grasping the first horn. With respect to conceptual knowledge, we do know directly that which we seek (the concrete particulars are the constituents of our conceptual knowledge), but we can still enquire into the ways in which these particulars are combined and recombined to give us our concepts. This view of concept formation is widespread in the psychological literature from early work on concept formation (Bruner, 1956) to more recent computer simulation investigations in cognitive psychology (Anderson and Bower, 1973).

In order to provide a solution to the *Meno* dilemma, however, these basic elements must be basic in both a psychological sense and an epistemological sense. The elements must be basic psychologically to enable the learning of concepts to get some kind of toehold with children who are not aware of and do not sense the more complex concepts of adult thought. The elements must also be epistemologically basic because they must be directly known if they are to stop the threatened regress of *Meno* dilemmas. But neither of these requirements seems to be met.

The Gestaltist ambiguous figures provide one of the most striking illustrations of the inability to find psychologically basic elements given in experience. Consider, for example, figure 2, the famous duck-rabbit (Hanson, 1969). The point here is that we are not directly given basic elements which we put together into a figure falling under the concept of a duck, for example. We are not given the duck's bill which is then combined with the head and eye until we recognize a duck. Rather the bill is a bill only insofar as we already see the figure as a duck. Indeed that same part of the figure becomes ears when the figure is seen as a rabbit. Associationism holds that we are given elements out of which we construct more complex concepts. The plain fact of the matter seems to be that the concept determines what the elements are. And this phenomenon, although particularly striking in the ambiguous figures, is extremely widespread (Petrie, 1974b).

Nor will it do to argue that really the lines are the basic elements and that we infer a duck or a rabbit. For one thing, the lines seem not to determine the inference one way or the other; we already need the concept for that. But if we must presuppose the concept, then the "basic

Figure 2. The "Duck-Rabbit." Redrawn from N. R. Hanson, *Perception and Discovery* (Cambridge University Press, 1969).

elements" explanation of concept learning would be clearly question begging. Furthermore, it takes effort to see *just* the lines. One has to work on it, psychologically, and that is an embarrassing consequence for an account which was supposed to have given us psychologically basic phenomena.

Furthermore, the "basic elements" view seems inadequate epistemologically as well. Our observation of or acquaintance with any concrete particular of experience is always of the particular as a particular of a certain kind. Particular experiences, by definition, never recur. It is only those experiences as classified that can be a foundation of commonsense and scientific knowledge. The best that I could say of a totally particular experience is that I had it. If a particular experience of a kindergarten child is to serve as the basis for propositional knowledge claims about, e.g., kindergarten-aged children, it must be because of the classification of that experience as similar to other experiences all of which fall under the concept of kindergarten children. Thus, knowledge structures deal essentially with the abstract and the general, and the particular in its full-blown particularity will be unable to serve as a grounding of conceptual knowledge.

And so the attempt to substitute empirical particulars for Platonic forms as the basic elements in the grounding of conceptual knowledge has led back to the requirement for something abstract such as Platonic Forms. Platonism seems unable to grasp the old-knowledge horn of the *Meno* dilemma, and so does empiricism. They both postulate basic elements which are somehow directly known and thus not in need of enquiry or learning but which form the basis for further enquiry and learning. They differ in the nature of the postulated basic elements, and they both fail to give a plausible account of how their basic elements are known. Empiricism fails in this regard because the basic elements must be abstract. Yet abstract elements appear not to be directly knowable. There is in the history of human knowledge a diversity in the abstract elements accepted as basic both at a time and over time, diachronically and synchronically. And, even more importantly for education, there seems to be a diversity of basic conceptual elements over the life span of the individual. The cognitive structures of individuals undergo development.

5. Conceptualism

The failure of both Platonism and empiricism to give us an explanation of the acquisition and knowledge of concepts has recently led to a number of positions reminiscent of Kant. Weimer (1973), also starting from the *Meno* paradox, has argued that transformational linguistics with its emphasis on deep structures and innate linguistic universals is Platonic in spirit. However, Weimer believes that innate linguistic universals promise an advance over Platonic Forms in that linguistic universals are knowable through individual language learning. That is, since these universals are believed to structure and be exemplified by the particular language any individual learns, they appear not to form a set of mysterious entities like Platonic Forms.

The revival of what has been called "schema theory" (Anderson, et al., 1977) in cognitive psychology is another indication of the dawning recognition that empiricism without abstract concepts is blind. Anderson (1977, p. 429) and his associates say, for example, "Without some schema into which it can be assimilated, an experience is incomprehensible and, therefore, little can be learned from it." A schema is a cognitive structure that gives meaning to sensory inputs.

These "schema" approaches attempt to solve the problem of the abstract nature of conceptual knowledge by building some a priori concepts into the very nature of our sensory and empirical experience. It just would not be *experience* without the operation of such presupposed a priori concepts. Once we are secure in the knowledge that our basic manner of experiencing is legitimately bound up with the abstract concepts appearing in our judgments about experience, we can proceed with a clear conscience to construct other a posteriori concepts and judgments much in the way empiricists believe we do. That is, the "old-knowledge" presupposed in attempts to grasp that horn of the *Meno* dilemma is not knowledge of substantive elements, be they concrete particulars or abstract universals, but rather knowledge that our ways of thinking are a priori legitimate. This is a shift, from locating the grounds or guarantee of knowledge in direct acquaintance with basic elements, to locating the guarantee in the procedures of knowledge gathering or enquiry. I shall call such approaches variants of conceptualism.

Note that such a move renders this position distinct from Plato's. Plato recognized the primacy of the abstract but in a way which made it necessary for us to have a kind of direct access to his basic abstract elements, the Forms. Conceptualism, on the other hand, does not require such a direct knowledge, but rather says that the presupposition of experience as we have it is that experience is structured by concepts. If we cannot ground our knowledge in basic incorrigible elements, perhaps we can ground it in knowing that the processes of enquiry can occur only in ways that correspond to the forms of experience. The turn is made from questions concerning *what* is known to questions concerning *how* we know, and thus although still clearly an old-knowledge approach to the *Meno* dilemma, this alternative is significantly different from Platonism or empiricism.

Does conceptualism succeed in grasping the old-knowledge horn? Yes and no. The crucial objection to Platonism and empiricism is that the source of and access to the basic "known" elements is mysterious and seems incapable of accounting for divergences and changes in what are considered basic elements at different times and by different people. Conceptualism does seem to solve the problem of our access to the basic elements, by suggesting not that these basic features are elements of knowledge but rather that they structure whatever can be taken to be knowledge. On the other hand, the problem of the validity of our conceptual knowledge remains.

Both Platonism and empiricism seek to guarantee validity by means of a theory of incorrigibility of their basic elements; neither is particularly successful. It might be thought that by pointing out that certain concepts structure our very experience as knowable we solve not only the problem of the abstract nature of knowledge but also the problem of how we can understand and give theoretical reasons for the empirical facts we do observe. But these are two separate problems (Toulmin, 1972, pp. 420–36); and although we may agree that concepts structure our experience, we need not believe that these concepts are exempt from historical change. Conceptualism is still faced with the problem of how the process of coming to know is intelligible and rational. One way of looking at the program of this book is as an attempt to give an account of the pragmatic, historical, and evolutionary ways in which our concepts structure our experience and how changes in these structures—our collective structures of understanding and knowledge—can rationally take place. Once that is done, however, it will be apparent that the result is quite different from ordinary versions of conceptualism.

6. Old Knowledge in Educational Thought

I believe that a very old and hoary controversy in educational thought can be given an interesting illumination by being viewed through the lenses of the *Meno* dilemma. I refer to the age-old dispute between subject-centered and child-centered instruction. To state the dispute in a somewhat oversimplified way, subject-centered modes of instruction regard the subject matter to be learned as providing the guiding principles for educational decisions. Proponents of subject-centered approaches recognize the autonomy of the student but tend to view that autonomy as subservient to the demands of the subject matter being considered. Child-centered approaches to instruction, on the other hand, treat the development of the student as an individual as the highest goal. Proponents of child-centerd education recognize that you cannot teach just the student without teaching some subject matter; however, they tend to view such subject matter as subservient to the development of the student's autonomy.

Subject-centered approaches seem to emphasize that knowledge must in some sense be present to form the conditions under which further enquiry and the gaining of new knowledge are possible. Child-centered approaches, on the other hand, assert that each conceptual advance for the child is radically new from the child's perspective and in the name of human autonomy is to be cherished. Thus, at least in a rough sense, subject-centered approaches can be seen as connected with attempts to grasp the old-knowledge horn of the *Meno* dilemma, whereas child-centered approaches are closely associated with attempts to grasp the new-knowledge horn. In this section I shall briefly examine one recent formulation of the subject-centered tradition, namely, the attempt of Paul Hirst to argue for the concept of a liberal education in terms of "forms of knowledge."

In an influential article Paul Hirst (1965, p. 123) has argued that a modern interpretation of liberal education must be "one concerned with the development of the mind as that is determined by certain forms of knowledge." This development is possible because of a kind of harmony between knowledge and the mind. Hirst specifically rejects the harmony of knowledge and mind implicit in the Platonic theory of recollection which I have already considered. He does not believe that any such metaphysical argument is persuasive. Rather, he holds "that the 'harmony' is a matter of the logical relationship between the concept of 'mind' and the concept of 'knowledge,' from which it follows that the achievement of knowledge is necessarily the development of mind— that is, the self-conscious rational mind of man—in its fundamental aspect."

What is the nature of this logical relationship according to Hirst? He claims that to have a rational mind is to have one's experience structured by a conceptual scheme. And the basic conceptual schemes which can perform this task of structuring experience are the forms of knowledge which have emerged in the history of human thought. The forms of knowledge are thus the ways in which human experience has become intelligible to man. Tentatively, Hirst believes that the basic forms of knowledge include mathematics, physical sciences, human sciences, history, religion, literature and the fine arts, philosophy, and morals.

What is important here is the set of criteria Hirst uses to pick out the forms of knowledge. In the initial formulation there are four. First, each form of knowledge has central concepts peculiar, although not necessarily exclusive, to that form. Second, each form has a distinctive logical structure for these concepts. Third, the criteria of "truth" (or whatever is analogous to "truth" in the given form) are distinctive. That is, each form has distinctive tests for the correctness of statements formulated in that form. Fourth, each form has particular techniques and skills developed for exploring and testing the experience and statements structured by that form.

Note that Hirst's view is clearly in the tradition of grasping the old-knowledge horn of the *Meno* dilemma and is a variety of conceptualism. The forms of knowledge structure our experience and make possible enquiry into new knowledge. The goal of education (at least liberal education) is in some sense to induct students into the forms of knowledge so that they can further pursue their intellectual aims. The subject-centered view of education comes to be seen as the logical precondition of learning and enquiry. We cannot learn anything except insofar as what we learn is structured by the forms of knowledge.

In a later article Hirst (1974) clarifies and expands on his thesis. Much of what he says there takes account of the lines of criticism I have been urging against attempts to grasp the old-knowledge horn. Yet, in a fundamental way, Hirst does not fully appreciate the demands placed by the *Meno* dilemma on a concept of learning. His account, even with the clarifications and amendments, remains firmly wedded to the notion that we must assume some valid knowledge as given in order to enquire about further knowledge. Let me try to show how this is so.

Because Hirst believes that the actual activities of enquiry are irrelevant for determining the criteria for a form of knowledge, he is driven to claim that the domain of knowledge is part of the domain of true propositions. The forms of knowledge themselves serve to partition this domain by means of the distinctive concepts, structures, and truth criteria of the forms. Now "truth" for Hirst is a very general notion which is primarily a demand for objective judgment. In some areas the judgment is as to what is the case, our more familiar notion of truth. In other areas it might be concerned with what ought to be the case, or with what is beautiful, and so on, depending on the form of knowledge to which the specific "truth" criterion belongs. Furthermore, the criteria of application for concepts are identical with the truth criteria for the propositions in which such concepts appear.

All of this helps to overcome the objections to empiricism. Hirst explicitly recognizes that abstract concepts structure the particulars of our experience and seems to give full recognition to what I have called the primacy of the abstract. This much can be granted to Hirst even though he continues to speak of a "given" element in experience. This given element is to be judged only by means of socially constructed concepts, but somehow it is also to provide the ground of objectivity and, hence, truth. This requirement sounds suspiciously like the requirement that there be certain directly known basic elements in order to allow enquiry to proceed and is characteristic of the attempts to grasp the old-knowledge horn of the *Meno* dilemma. However, Hirst is apparently not eager to saddle the given element in experience with the responsibility for providing a nonproblematic basis for enquiry.

If Hirst's given is not intended to play the role of basic elements in an empiricist epistemology, what about the forms of knowledge, the concepts, structures, and truth criteria? Are these meant to play the role of Platonic basic elements? Hirst explicitly denies that the forms have the kind of unchanging permanence which necessarily structures our experience. He grants that the forms may well be changing and that they are simply the best we have in an evolving scheme of knowing. At the same time he denies that they are arbitrary or idiosyncratic to a given society. This move, too seems to avoid the difficulties surrounding the absolutism of the Platonic approach.

The problem here is that by allowing for changeable concepts and developing forms of knowledge, Hirst seems to have reopened the door to a new application of the *Meno* dilemma at the level of the concepts basic to the forms of knowledge. Once again we find ourselves unable to acquire knowledge of these concepts. For either we know them and hence cannot learn them, or else we do not know them and enquiry is again impossible because we will be unable to recognize the concepts were we to run across them. By loosening the absolute nature of the concepts in the forms of knowledge, Hirst has reopened the question of where they can rationally come from and how they can justifiably change. Hirst's problem is not so much making room for the *fact* of change; he recognizes that concepts do change. His problem is rather the *rationality* of conceptual change. Not only do we in historical fact see conceptual diversity, but we also see a conceptual continuity. Put another way, conceptual change seems just to happen on Hirst's account. The standards of reasonableness are contained within the forms of knowledge, and so it appears we cannot ask how those standards themselves could reasonably change. Yet Hirst admits they do indeed change. If one denies the absolute character of basic concepts, one must give an account of the rationality of changes in them.

Hirst also grants that there need be no direct pedagogical or curricular implications from the forms of knowledge thesis. That is, even if we could describe the logical form of knowledge of, say, the physical sciences, with its distinctive concepts, structures, and truth criteria, it does not mean that we have any direct information about how best to present that form to students. As has often been noted, the logical structure of a discipline may well not be the best pedagogical structure. Still we must certainly ask whether the goal of any particular curriculum from elementary school through a university graduate program ought to be to reproduce the logical forms of knowledge in the student. Must the ways in which the forms of knowledge structure experience and contribute to the development of rational mind be taught explicitly in order to do their job? (See, for example, Halstead, 1977.) The connection between the logical structures of the forms of knowledge and the cognitive structures present in students' minds engenders difficulties with respect to the *Meno* dilemma. For certain purposes and at certain stages in the educational process, one may want precisely to ask the question, "How are such changeable forms of knowledge connected with the changeable structures of knowing to be found in individual students?" This question will be treated in some detail in chapter 7. It is sufficient here to note that Hirst is, unfortunately, silent on these points.

What emerges from the discussion of Hirst as an example of the subject-centered approach to learning is that such approaches tend to make one of two errors. Either they fall into the category of grasping the old-knowledge horn of the *Meno* dilemma by claiming that enquiry and learning are possible only in terms provided by static disciplines or forms of knowledge. Or, if they allow for a change in the forms of knowledge, just how those forms of knowledge are first acquired by anyone is left problematic, and the questions of how and when they can be justifiably changed and challenged remain open.

Grasping the New-Knowledge Horn

1. The Structure of New-Knowledge Approaches

Attempts to grasp the old-knowledge horn of the *Meno* dilemma involve one in a kind of fruitless alternation between rationalist and empiricist approaches to the learning of concepts. As one examines rationalism, its defects seem to call for something like empiricism; whereas the elucidation of empiricism seems to demand a recognition of the conceptual primacy of the abstract, and around the circle one goes. The important point is that these two competing philosophical doctrines are actually siblings when it comes to solving the *Meno* dilemma. Both attempt to grasp the old-knowledge horn, and both fail because they presuppose a static, nondevelopmental view of knowledge. Somehow basic knowledge is supposed to be just "there," either in universals or in particulars, and "process" questions of its source, its change, and its development seem to be obscured. If, however, diachronic or historical problems could be dealt with successfully, it may be that some of the insights generated by conceptualist theories could be interpreted so as to give a reasonably adequate account of what knowledge and coming to know are like at a given time.

The new-knowledge horn of the *Meno* dilemma, on the other hand, is precisely concerned with *changes* in knowledge, and, therefore, with a historical approach to questions of knowledge acquisition. Approaches to grasping the new-knowledge horn do not assume that we already know that about which we are to enquire, but rather attempt to explain how we can generate "knowledge variants" concerning brand-new areas and test the validity of these variants to see whether or not they deserve to be called knowledge.

Generally I shall reserve the term "knowledge" for those claims which are both true and justified in some suitably broad interpretation of "true" and "justified." Thus, strictly speaking, of various competing candidates for knowledge only one at most will deserve in the end to be called knowledge. One might call such candidates "hypotheses" except that that term is closely associated with the propositional side of the concept-proposition distinction. Similar considerations hold for "*conceptual* variant," since sometimes the crucial variations involve precisely some amorphous mix of concept and proposition (or hypothesis). Furthermore, I wish to emphasize the *processes* of knowing. I shall, therefore, often use "knowledge variant" (along with hypothesis and conceptual variant), to indicate candidate variations in the knowing process.

It should be noted here that I am still operating under the assumption that we can draw a distinction between conceptual knowledge on the one hand and factual knowledge on the other hand. That is, if our basic conceptual schemes are not at issue, obtaining new knowledge seems simply to consist of putting ourselves in the position of observing new facts. That may be tremendously difficult in some cases. We may, for example, have to build complex atom smashers to observe the facts of subatomic interactions, but the general shape of the domain is given; we just have not explored it all yet. The difficulty comes only when we shift our attention to concepts and conceptual schemes and ask how radically new knowledge of them is possible.

It is the requirement of validating the knowledge variants which partially explains the relative paucity of attempts at grasping the new-knowledge horn. Western thought has generally had a powerful concern with the justification of knowledge claims, and this emphasis has tended to lead fairly naturally toward attempts to grasp the old-knowledge horn. In such approaches basic knowledge is by hypothesis justified and can, therefore, ground our enquiry. Without such basic knowledge, the justification problem for proposed variants looms very large indeed.

These problems can be seen through a brief examination of the recent resurgence of the sociology of knowledge. (See Keat and Urry, 1975, for a good recent example of a discussion of these and related issues in the social sciences.) Since philosophical approaches that attempt to isolate an incorrigible foundation for knowledge appear to have failed, it is more and more often being suggested that we should look at how knowledge is actually acquired by people who are in that business, e.g., scientists and scholars. Such a look might involve historical, psychological, and sociological elements. We might, for example, trace the way in which a certain scientific theory developed through history. We might talk about the ways in which a given scientist went about conceiving, testing, and developing a given theory. Or we might describe the sociological arrangements that allow scientists to check each other's work thereby advancing knowledge in their area. All of these influences, it is claimed, will influence our knowledge of the world at any given time and will condition what we are likely to accept as new knowledge.

There is, of course, no doubt that we can learn a good bit about science, society, and our knowledge-gathering processes from such studies. The problem is the one raised in the first chapter regarding the confusion between a descriptive study and a prescriptive study of the acquisition of knowledge. The descriptive studies mentioned above all seem to presuppose that we already know in principle what *knowledge*, as opposed to mere belief, is like. At a bare minimum, the historian, psychologist, or sociologist of science must have some idea of the criteria for calling something a piece of knowledge or science. Without such an idea, the historian, psychologist, or sociologist does not even know where to begin.

If one were to object at this point that knowledge simply is what knowledge seekers, i.e., scientists and scholars, say it is, a radical relativism is but a step beyond. For throughout history knowledge seekers have said incompatible things about what is knowledge. Galileo believed the earth moves; many of his contemporaries did not. Turn-of-the-century physicists believed in the aether; current physicists do not. Some psychologists believe in a strong inheritability of intelligence; others do not. But either the earth moves or it does not; there is an ether or there is not; and intelligence is strongly inherited, or it is not. Knowledge seekers do not agree on what they choose to call knowledge, either across time or at a given time. How then are we to appeal to their beliefs in order to judge what knowledge really is?

Notice that this question need not be a problem for the historian, psychologist, or sociologist of science if the goal is merely to describe what people have taken to be knowledge. But the suggestion I am examining is that what knowledge seekers call knowledge determines prescriptively what knowledge *is*. And it is the latter, prescriptive area that is the province of the *Meno* dilemma. Grasping the new-knowledge horn involves showing we can generate knowledge variants in new fields and recognize which of these variants deserve to be called knowledge. If knowledge variants are to be judged on the basis simply of what one chooses, and these choices can be incompatible, we can justifiably ask for reasons for choosing one over the other variant. Yet the choice itself is supposed to be the criterion of reasonableness, and we are trapped in a very small circle.

The typical move at this point is simply to deny that there is any sense in which the basic choices of knowledge seekers can really be understood as compatible or incompatible. Since the choice serves to ground reasonableness, we cannot say that the choices themselves are either reasonable or unreasonable. However, such a move seems inadequate to the human condition. Our choices do make a difference in our lives, and, to the extent that we are concerned about such differences, that we would prefer to live this life rather than that one, that it would be better to live this life rather than that, so are our choices conditioned by considerations of reasonableness. It is, of course, true that, once made, these choices do themselves provide the framework for judging lower-level choices, but the basic choices themselves seem unable to escape the potential relevance of considerations of reasonableness. Once scientists decided to treat the movements of the heavenly bodies as part of mechanics, the theories and explanations that are acceptable were constrained by this choice. But, equally, it seems sensible to ask what are the reasons for celestial mechanics in the first place. Given certain ends, what will count as reasonable means are to some extent relative to those ends. But surely we can ask about the reasonableness of the ends themselves, even if these are the basic ends of human existence.

There is another serious problem with the thesis that at bottom a mere choice or commitment serves to ground all criteria of reasonableness or rationality. The problem is that the claim seems to be in some way self-defeating. For if this claim is seriously asserted in an effort to gain assent, then we can ask whether that claim is itself a reasonable one to hold. And it follows from the nature of the claim that we shall find it reasonable only in the case in which we have already made just that choice. If we have not, we cannot be convinced that we ought to make that choice by appealing to our reason. In fact, some thinkers accept this conclusion and the concomitant abdication of social responsibility it appears to entail. As individuals we might do likewise, but what we could not coherently do, for the reasons just noted, is to argue that educational systems as social entities be organized in such an anarchic way.

What this brief discussion has underlined with respect to the *Meno* dilemma are the problems with grasping the new-knowledge horn. By emphasizing human freedom, activity, and choice in a historical context, these doctrines bring forth the necessity of considering knowledge variants and changes in our conceptual schemes. Our knowledge does seem, at least in part, due to our changing purposes and goals. And this "due to" not only reflects the causal effects of our purposes but also is itself partly constitutive of our knowledge, as I shall argue in more detail in the next chapter. At the same time, the knowledge variants emphasized by new-knowledge approaches seem not to be completely justified by means of simple choice or commitment. How is it that the variants have the initial plausibility they do? How is it that we can reasonably choose among initially plausible variants? To respond that we simply choose seems simply inadequate, and that inadequacy is the main problem in grasping the new-knowledge horn. To illustrate how these questions are answered in concrete cases I turn now to two examples from the philosophy of science and from education.

2. Paul Feyerabend's Philosophy of Science

One of the current debates in the philosophy of science concerns the growth of scientific knowledge. Discussions of theory change in science have a direct bearing on the question of the *Meno* dilemma, namely, "How is enquiry possible?" The so-called received view in the philosophy of science (Suppe, 1974) interprets scientific theories as (ideally) partially interpreted logical calculi which are tested against observational experience for their validity. The generation of such theories and the hypotheses in them are viewed as falling within the psychological context of discovery; whereas, the elaboration and testing of the theories are viewed within the logical context of justification. Theory growth is taken to occur both by the more or less additive extension of well-confirmed theories to cover new domains and by the reduction of special theories to more basic ones. Such a view has obvious affinities with empiricist attempts to grasp the old-knowledge horn of the *Meno* dilemma in its implicit separation of theory from empirical fact, its reliance on basic concrete observations as the source of validity for theories, and its presupposition of old knowledge (the existing theories) to account for new knowledge (extension and reduction of theories). This hypothetico-deductive account of scientific method, with its use of empirical observation as a touchstone of justification, underlies, implicitly or explicitly, the views of science held by a majority of educational researchers today.

This view of the growth of scientific knowledge is sharply challenged by Paul Feyerabend (1970). He holds, following Popper (1965), that theories are *not* confirmable by observation, but at best falsifiable; that the terms of science do *not* summarize observations in an inductive manner, but are rather dispositional in that they tell us what we *would* observe under certain conditions; and that the road to the growth of scientific knowledge is through the proliferation of theories, which can then be exposed to potential falsification through editing effects of the world. In a manner reminiscent of schema theories in current psychology, Feyerabend solves the problem of the conceptual priority of the abstract by claiming that abstract theories are what give intelligible structure to our experience. At the same time he takes seriously both the problem of knowledge variants by insisting on the proliferation of theories, and the problem of the validity of those variants by insisting on the potential falsifiability of these variants by means of the editing effects of the world.

There are two problems here, however. First, how are we to understand the proliferation of plausible alternative theories; and, second, just how does the world edit our knowledge variants? Let me take the second question first. According to Popper there is a neutral observation language in which we report our shared, unproblematic, neutral observations. This observation language edits out false theories. For any two competing theories, we can always deduce contradictory observational implications and then design an experiment which consults neutral observation to see which theory is falsified. This is the doctrine of the "crucial experiment" and is rejected by Feyerabend for reasons originally given by Duhem (1954). Whenever we derive an observational consequence from a theory we utilize not only the restricted theory in question but also a whole system of supporting theories— theories of perception, of instrumentation, of measurement, and other such auxiliary hypotheses. Thus a falsifying instance falsifies the theory under consideration *or* one of the innumerable supporting theories. The experiment tells us something is wrong, but not what is wrong.

But the situation is even worse than this. Exactly the same considerations which lead to believing that the terms of science are dispositional and theory-laden also imply that observation itself is theory-laden. This point has already been made in discussing the conceptual primacy of the abstract and will be further amplified in the next chapter. The supposition of a nonproblematic neutral observation language is highly suspect. Our concepts and theories infect even our basic observations. Thus it is possible, even likely, that the observational consequences derived from one theory will be incommensurable with the observational consequences derived from a competing theory. If this happens in the so-called crucial experiment, then, as Hanson (1958) puts it, competing theorists may well be looking at the same thing but seeing two different things. The influence of the world on our knowledge variants suddenly becomes highly mysterious.

This view of both meanings of concepts and observational categories as highly theory dependent seems to imply that everything depends on our world view. Competing theories are not consistent with each other in their use of observational categories, nor is there a meaning invariance of the terms which function in various theories. In the sense that Feyerabend is espousing such a position, he is clearly concerned with conceptual diversity and conceptual change and can be construed as an advocate of grasping the new-knowledge horn of the *Meno* dilemma.

But the question then becomes, "Can we reasonably decide among apparently incommensurable theories?" Feyerabend suggests three possibile ways of making such decisions. First, we might develop a more general theory which encompasses the competitors and, therefore, allows for shared observations. Second, we can examine the theories internally to see how well they connect with their own observations. Third, we can invoke a "pragmatic theory of observation" which instructs us to accept that theory whose observation language most successfully matches the ways in which we actually do observe. The problem is that each of these methods of validating knowledge variants seems to presuppose a denial of the radical position developed thus far. If there really were a more general theory encompassing two "incommensurable" theories, they would actually *be* commensurable in terms of that general theory. Second, the way a theory hooks up with its own proper observations is assessable only intratheoretically, and so it would be impossible to make a comparison between the ways of two different theories. Finally, at least without further specification, even the description of our observational behavior will be conditioned by our theories and thus incapable of serving as an independent test of knowledge variants in any proposed pragmatic theory of observation. I shall later consider whether human actions themselves, not descriptions of human actions, could serve to get a pragmatic theory of observation started.

In response to this kind of criticism, Feyerabend resorts to an explicitly Hegelian line. The theory is best which most accords with the freedom and spontaneity of the human mind. But how are we to determine *that?* It seems that either we are to judge on some yet to be elucidated grounds that a given variant accords with the freedom and spontaneity of the human mind, in which case Feyerabend has still not answered the reasonableness challenge; or else any choice which results from the free and spontaneous operation of the mind is, ipso facto, a reasonable one, in which case we do not know how to deal with conflicting choices.

It seems that Feyerabend wants to pursue the latter course. Anything that arises as a result of the playfulness of the human mind is appropriate to ground reasonableness. Indeed we are actively to seek theories which contradict the best-established theories we have. The grounds for this injunction are that accepted theories always inadequately account for their domains and are always encrusted over with "natural interpretations" of experience which need to be overthrown.

Feyerabend believes that this free generation of variants also accounts for the initial plausibility of the variants as well as for their later validation. His policy of "counterinduction" will generate plausible theories precisely because the established theories are bound to be inadequate. Moreover, this policy of playfully generating new and radically different variants requires us to learn to speak a "new language," the language of the proposed new "natural interpretations." This language must, of necessity, be learned directly and not by means of a translation into any existing language we may know. That this is so follows from the radical dissimilarity of competing theories. They really are incommensurable. In the end, basic theory choice becomes a function of our psychopolitical interest along with some esthetic judgments concerning the beauty of our theories. Nothing more reasonable is to be found.

Thus Feyerabend is left with an anarchistic view of knowledge which seems to most people unacceptable for precisely that reason. What he seems to have pointed out brilliantly is the pervasive influence of human interests and the spontaneous operation of the mind upon our theories and concepts, and especially the nature of the variants we can intelligibly countenance. We really can and do change experience to fit our preconceptions. What Feyerabend has failed to account for is the limits to such self-serving processes. The world may not be directly accessible to our observation, but neither is it infinitely pliable to our interests. Problems and difficulties do arise with our theories which seem to call for more than playfulness of mind and require more than a mere existential choice. Thus Feyerabend's positive account of the growth of scientific knowledge is faced with the same structural problems as the general attempts to grasp the new-knowledge horn of the *Meno* dilemma. How do we account for the historical continuity we do find in conceptual change? How do we judge the reasonableness of knowledge variants? How do we assess their initial plausibility and their later justification?

3. Open Education

Traditionally, the major alternative to a "subject-centered" approach in curriculum has always been a "child-centered" approach. In the last chapter I argued that Paul Hirst's forms of knowledge approach to curriculum represents a contemporary example of a subject-centered approach and is properly construed as an attempt to grasp the old-knowledge horn of the *Meno* dilemma. It will come as no surprise to find that child-centered approaches to curriculum can be fruitfully construed as attempts to grasp the new-knowledge horn. In particular I will examine that somewhat loose contemporary movement known as "open education." (The remainder of this section is an adaptation of Petrie, 1975.)

Anyone who assays to speak generally about even some limited aspect of open education is surely treading on dangerous ground. For here is a development in education where even the advocates feel universally constrained to comment on the lack of systematic, agreed-upon principles in their domain. Indeed, they make of this lack of coherence the virtue of flexibility. Nevertheless, from a sampling of the works of writers on open education and from the talk of those who engage in what they call open education, a general picture of the sort of thinking which ties this loosely knit field together begins to emerge.

Rathbone (1971, pp. 102–3), a typical source on open education, claims:

> knowledge is idiosyncratically formed, individually conceived, fundamentally individualistic. . . . Because knowledge is basically idiosyncratic, it is most difficult to judge whether one person's knowledge is 'better' than another's. . . . On the contrary, the child envisioned by open education faces a world of potential but unpredetermined knowledge that will admit to a plurality of interpretations.

The first principle of importance to be found in open education is, thus, that knowledge is an idiosyncratic, personal construct and cannot be "transmitted" in the usual standard sense. In one recent volume on open education, Spodek and Walberg (1974) speak of the attempts to break down standard boundaries between disciplines, the use of disciplines only as needed for a student-initiated project, the teacher as facilitator, and so on. Knowledge is felt to be attained only when the student makes it her or his own through seeing its importance and relevance. It cannot be handed over by the teacher. The interdisciplinary, problem-oriented mode of discovery learning replaces the disciplinary, subject-centered mode of instruction. I shall call this set of claims and observations the personal construct view of knowledge.

The second principle of importance to the *Meno* dilemma has to do with the central role of the student in open education situations. It seems to be generally held that students can and ought to play a much larger role in their own education than they traditionally do. It is believed that the students can profitably make significant decisions concerning what they will learn, when they will learn, and even how they will learn. The teacher's role never vanishes completely, but neither is it dominant. The students themselves must be actively involved in the learning process. Furthermore, it is important to note that such student involvement may, at least for some open educators, go beyond merely making choices within a teacher-structured context to participating in the choice of that very context itself. Put another way, it is assumed, at least by some, that children must help in choosing the ultimate ends of their education and not only the means. This principle, in all its variations, I shall call the principle of respect for student integrity.

The two principles are, of course, closely connected, but I do not believe they are identical—at least not in all senses. For one might believe that knowledge is a personal construct and yet maintain that some students are not intellectually capable of learning certain things. Likewise, one might respect a student's integrity and yet believe that knowledge is objectively to be found in the traditional disciplines; that is, one respects the student as a person but locates the authority of knowledge outside the student. On the other hand, there probably are interpretations of the two principles which are logically connected, but more of that later.

Although these principles could be interpreted in psychological, ethical, or affective ways, I shall interpret them as being concerned in an epistemological way with the acquisition of knowledge. Consider first the principle of knowledge as a personal construct. This can be taken as saying that no matter how true or well justified anything may be, until a given student has appropriated the materials, he or she cannot be said to know it. Commonsense examples abound. We often say that a rote-memorized lesson is not really known, or that a mere use of the jargon in a field does not demonstrate understanding. The point is a simple one but has profound implications for education. Various things may be known in the sense of having a place within the justificatory framework of some subject matter, but until the student places the thing within his or her own justificatory framework, the student does not know it. And the two frameworks may be quite different. Physics may have one justification for Einstein's theory of relativity; a student may justify it on the basis of the authority of the teacher. A well-known subject matter may be unknown to the student, and the problem is to say in what sense the student's grasp of the new knowledge is reasonable.

Within this general framework one can distinguish a strong and a weak epistemological interpretation of the view that knowledge is a personal construct. In the weak version the open educator is saying that a student does not possess knowledge until it has been appropriated into the student's justification scheme. Before then the knowledge may be "there" in some sense, but it is a useless sense as far as the learner is concerned. The strong epistemological version of the thesis, on the other hand, is that there really is no sense to be given to the notion of an objective justification to be found outside individual knowers. There would be no justification to be found in physics, for example. Such justification turns out to be merely the individual justifications of certain designated "experts" in the field. Thus, all justification, and hence all knowledge, would be fundamentally a personal construct.

Such a strong thesis can be seen to be compatible with the attempts already outlined in this chapter to grasp the new-knowledge horn of the *Meno* dilemma. To the extent that established knowledge is nothing more than the current personal knowledge constructs of the authorities in the field, to that extent does open education seem committed to grasping the new-knowledge horn. What counts as knowledge is determined by the commitments of a personal justification scheme. The analogies of a personal construct view of knowledge with Feyerabend's emphasis on the mind's freedom and on individual choice as epistemological principles are striking. Open education is expounding in an educational context the view of knowledge variants I have claimed to be characteristic of approaches to grasping the new-knowledge horn of the *Meno* dilemma.

The principle of respect for student integrity can also receive a strong and a weak epistemological interpretation. In the weak sense, respect for student integrity can simply be taken to mean respect for persons as a source for potential argument and reasons. Indeed failure to bestow this kind of respect for persons as a potential source of rationality leads to a particular informal fallacy in logic, the "ad hominem." This is the fallacy of attacking the person rather than the argument, and it is a fallacy just because any person might be the source of valid arguments and good reasons. The weak version of respect for the potential integrity of student reasons leaves open the possibility that although a student's reasons are potentially as valid as anyone else's, in fact we can and do have a standard of evaluation of these reasons. Thus, we could sensibly make comparative judgments as to which of two sets of reasons is better. Furthermore, it might be urged that most if not all of the time, the reasons contained in the disciplines are simply better than the student's reasons.

The strong version of the respect for student integrity would, however, deny that there is such a standard of comparison. That is, a student's reasons are taken to be intrinsically as good as any other reasons. If we add the strong view of knowledge as a personal construct, we can see that the student's reasons logically would have to be intrinsically as good as anyone else's because justification is radically idiosyncratic. Even what counts as a reason depends on the conceptual scheme of the individual knower. And, conversely, if any individual's coherent set of reasons is as good as any other individual's coherent set of reasons, then justifications for knowledge would have to be relative to the coherent sets of reasons. Thus, in its strong version, the principle of knowledge as a personal construct implies the incommensurability between justificatory schemes of teacher and student or between two different schemes in the same student's history of cognitive development. Conversely, the respect for student integrity in its strong form implies individual coherence as the only standard for the justification of knowledge.

Before we proceed to evaluate these positions, perhaps an example will help to illustrate the various differences. Consider the proposition that the black-white IQ score differences do not reflect racial differences in intelligence. Assume the proposition is true. Further assume that the student's personal reason for believing this is the belief in a conspiracy to falsify the IQ scores of blacks, and that the public "objective" reasons involve the belief that there are conceptual confusions surrounding the use of IQ tests to measure intelligence.

First, under the presupposition that both principles are to receive their weak interpretation, we get the following: We must respect the student's reason. It does, with some historical justification, fit into a coherent scheme. Racism is a deep feeling, and it would at least make sense to suppose a conspiracy. All of this can and probably should be granted to the student. On the other hand, if there really is no conspiracy, the student will not fully understand that black-white IQ scores do not reflect racial differences in intelligence because the reasons the student gives would not be appropriate. We need to bring the student's subjective justification into line with the objective justification. We might do this by challenging the student to show us the conspiracy; by pointing out studies where black experimenters themselves get the same differential results; and so on. We might also demonstrate the importance and subtle influence of differing conceptions of intelligence; how reliance on IQ scores as an operational definition of intelligence guarantees a status quo concept of intelligence; how such considerations as the foregoing explain the results better than the conspiracy theory; and so on. That is, we can appeal to old existing knowledge in the subject matter to criticize a student's justifications.

Under the supposition that both principles are taken in their strong sense, however, the scenario would look like this: The two explanations are simply incommensurable. Indeed, they structure experience of the world differently, for every concept is idiosyncratic. There is no conceivable evidence that would tend to show one position wrong and the other right. To assume that a socially relative analysis of intelligence could be given is to leave open, at least in principle, the question of the possibility of racial differences in intelligence. If, however, we really understand racism, we understand that such a question cannot even arise in a truly nonracist society. If you are not part of the solution, you are part of the problem. In this scenario there could be no rational way of deciding between the allegedly competing explanations because rationality is limited to the prior acceptance of one or the other of the schemes. The pedagogical task would at best be to make the individual schemes coherent.

What bearing do the strong and weak interpretations of the two principles have on the *Meno* dilemma? To begin with the weak version of the respect for student integrity, I have already indicated that to deny that a student's arguments and reasons are potentially valid and sound is to commit the fallacy of "ad hominem," or perhaps "ad studentum." The philosophical point is that to the extent that children do possess a form of rationality, then to that extent must they be treated as potential sources of argument. This is, however, a "burden of proof" kind of claim. We might be able to demonstrate psychologically and anthropologically that actually organizing a classroom to take each student's reasons and arguments completely seriously would lead to severe pedagogical problems of coverage and may serve to instill a sloppy and undisciplined mode of enquiry into the students. Thus, practices curtailing the unfettered promulgation of student reasons might be justified even though this occasionally could lead to ignoring an individual student's argument that turned out to be correct (Campbell, 1969). Practices limiting the consideration of student's reasons must be justified rather than requiring the students to justify exceptions to the practice, and this formal shift in burden of proof may have profound differences in the way schools are run. However, it is hard to see how open education would fare differently in this regard from any other mode of schooling. Indeed we could view the whole age-graded, subject-specific, lecture-oriented nature of today's curriculum as a rough attempt to take into account these kinds of problems by allowing the teacher to deal at appropriate times with arguments that are characteristic of the subject matter and the age and background of the students. But the weak version of the principle of student integrity says nothing about how new knowledge is acquired.

The weak version of the personal construct view of knowledge also seems to be perfectly correct. No proposition can be known by a student until the student believes and can justify it in terms of his or her own conceptual scheme. This result follows directly from a detailed analysis of the justification condition in the classical analysis of knowledge as justified true belief. At the same time, however, it remains an open question as to whether the personal idiosyncratic justification must be brought into line with the public objective justification before knowledge can be properly attributed to the student. This is more likely to be the case with integrated bodies of knowledge called subjects and less likely to be necessary for relatively isolated propositions. Again, open education methods such as discovery learning may happen to be more successful than other forms of schooling. But even here, a well-designed lecture that began with what the students currently know might be much more efficient (Petrie, 1970). Once again, nothing particular seems to follow concerning the acquisition of radically new knowledge.

But the strong versions of the two principles allow no such accommodation with alternative, more traditional, conceptions of schooling. If objective justification of knowledge is a myth, and if student reasons are intrinsically as good as any other reasons, then any method of schooling that failed to put the student front and center would not be justified on epistemological grounds. Concomitantly, the possibility that such an epistemology would be relevant to the *Meno* dilemma would be greatly increased. I turn, therefore, to a detailed consideration of the strong versions.

In the first place, insofar as the strong versions of the two principles imply a radical subjectivism, they must be wrong for the same reason already outlined. In their strong subjectivist formulations the principles are in some sense self-defeating or pointless. Their truth is inconsistent with seriously asserting them. Consider: If knowledge were really only a personal construct, then knowing that very assertion would be possible only for those who, personally, already have constructed it. Those who personally believed otherwise could not—logically could not—be rationally convinced that knowledge is a personal construct; for the requisite, independent, nonpersonal evidence or justification is not allowed. Or take the view that student reasons are as good as any other reasons as long as they belong to an individually coherent scheme of reasons. The reasons which are taken as justification for the personal construct view of knowledge cannot be as good as the reasons against the view, for the former are, I have just shown, incoherent. But even if they were coherent, since reasons are incommensurable, I could have no more reason for believing in the absolute autonomy of student reasons than for believing the opposite.

Second, the strong versions of the two principles lead to the same kind of anarchy in education that Feyerabend was led to in the philosophy of science. One of the motivations for the current "back to the basics" movement in education is the inchoate sense that there are intellectual standards independent of any student's conception of those standards. Since individual views of what constitutes knowledge do conflict, there must be some way of deciding which is most reasonable; we cannot allow a wholesale subjectivism. Nor will it do to turn over such decisions to a political process. We cannot legislate what will count as sound thinking and clear communication. What counts as knowledge depends in part on more than our personal choice and commitment. The very idea of education, let alone the institution of schooling, depends on our belief that disciplined thought and enquiry can be of some help to the human condition. Otherwise, we could all make our lives beautiful simply by wishing them so. The world is not the silly putty of our minds and hearts.

Thus the problems of giving a coherent formulation of the strong interpretation of the two epistemological principals of open education turn out to be identical with the problems of grasping the new-knowledge horn of the *Meno* dilemma. We must find a place in our epistemology for knowledge variants, but the source of these variants must be specified and the historical continuity with other conceptual and knowledge variants accounted for. Even more importantly the reasonableness of alternative knowledge variants must be explained both in terms of the initial plausibility of such variants and in terms of their later verifiability. There are strong arguments in open education for taking seriously the notion of knowledge variants, both the historical variations in human knowledge and the individual variations among students and teachers. At the same time, however, the source and reasonableness of such variation are left largely untreated by advocates of open education. To the extent that open educators advocate a totally free and unconstrained choice in matters epistemological, to that extent must we refuse as educators to take them seriously. To the extent that they might be able to suggest an account of grasping the new-knowledge horn of the *Meno* dilemma, to that extent can we incorporate the epistemological insights of open education into our educational theory. These insights are, first, that education cannot simply be the handing over of established bodies of knowledge without taking account of the ways in which students integrate such knowledge into their own cognitive frameworks, purposes, and activities; and, second, that the students' own cognitive frameworks, purposes, and activities have an individual integrity which must be accorded both ethical and epistemological respect.

Historically, neither attempts at grasping the old-knowledge horn of the *Meno* dilemma nor attempts at grasping the new-knowledge horn appear to have been successful. Indeed, upon analysis each of these attempts seems to require the other. I shall, therefore, examine the possibility of slipping between the horns in saying how enquiry and learning are possible.

4 | Conceptual Change

1. The Meno Dilemma and Conceptual Change

What I have argued so far is that in order to understand the possibility of enquiry, we have to take the challenge posed by the *Meno* dilemma seriously. If we attempt to grasp the old-knowledge horn, the challenge is to say how it is that we can already know that about which we enquire and yet engage in enquiry in a nontrivial way. If we attempt to grasp the new-knowledge horn, the challenge is to say how it is that in areas of which we know nothing we can yet generate knowledge variants and justify appropriate ones as knowledge. In both cases we are fairly quickly forced from a consideration of knowledge in general to a consideration of conceptual knowledge. That is, if it can be assumed that conceptual knowledge is already present in some sense, there seems to be no particular philosophical difficulty in pursuing factual knowledge about the way the world happens to sort itself in terms of our conceptual schemes.

I have urged that the insight seemingly grasped by those approaches which attack the old-knowledge horn is that our knowledge in some sense is conditioned by a reality which is independent of our manner of knowing it. In some fundamental sense we cannot "know" anything we choose. The world sets very definite and independent limits to what can be known. Both Platonism and empiricism honor this insight even though they differ dramatically in what they conceive reality to be and how they believe we have access to it. What they do agree on is that a kind of direct access to reality at some level or other is essential to objectivity and thus also essential to knowledge.

There are, as I have shown, serious problems associated with attempts to grasp the old-knowledge horn of the dilemma. In the first place, no philosophical account of the necessary basic contact with reality is fully adequate. Thus, the acquisition of concepts, at least the basic ones, appears ultimately mysterious. But the situation is not much better even if we assume we have a basic stock of concepts. For I will argue in this chapter that the "building block" picture of the acquisition of concepts is highly dubious. Concepts seem to be subject to Gestaltist-type changes rather than simple rearrangements of basic given elements, and that fact illustrates the second main difficulty with attempts to grasp the old-knowledge horn. There is a wide range of conceptual diversity and change. Different historical ages have different concepts and they change over time; different cultures at the same time possess varying concepts; and even an individual's conceptual scheme changes over time both developmentally and as a result of learning. Such diversity seems a product as much of differing individual and social goals and purposes as of different external ecologies.

On the other hand, I have granted that those approaches which attempt to grasp the new-knowledge horn of the *Meno* dilemma embody this last important insight, namely, that our knowledge is due to our human purposes and activities in pursuing knowledge as well as to an independent reality. There are an indefinite number of things one might come to know about the world. (I shall use the term "indefinite" to refer to cases where not only are there an infinite number of things we might come to know, but also there are no unambiguous ways of even deciding what things to count.) Which things we know and even how we come to know them—indeed, the very possibility of their being known—depends on our directed knowing activities as human beings. From Feyerabend to open education, human intention and commitment are seen as conditioning our knowledge.

But I have argued that new-knowledge approaches are subject to difficulties as well. By emphasizing human purposes, activities, and choices one may well be able to account for the source of concepts as well as for their diversity and change over time, but the continuity which also underlies conceptual change seems slighted. Furthermore, the justification for preferring one conceptual variant over another is not obvious. This question of justification arises both at the level of the initial plausibility of the variant or existential choice and at the level of its ultimate adequacy.

These difficulties bring us full circle back to the insight of those who would grasp the old-knowledge horn. Thus the two approaches can be seen as having complementary insights and weaknesses. The old-knowledge approaches emphasize the role of the external world in rendering knowledge justifiable, but such approaches fail to account for knowledge variation. The new-knowledge approaches emphasize the role of human purposes and activity in accounting for rational knowledge variation, but such approaches fail to account for the objectivity of knowledge.

The problem which remains is similar to that in contemporary discussions of conceptual change. Do concepts change? If so, how? If not, how do we account for the apparent conceptual diversity among cultures and among individuals at any one time, and across time, both historically for humanity at large, and developmentally for any given individual? If concepts change, how does that occur and how can such change be seen as rational? What I will do in this chapter is to investigate the general phenomenon of conceptual change in the acquisition of knowledge in an attempt to throw light on the solution of the *Meno* dilemma. Conversely, the complementary strengths and weaknesses of the old- and new-knowledge approaches will point the direction to what I hope will be a satisfactory account of conceptual change.

2. What Is Conceptual Change?

It would certainly be nice if I could give an account of a concept. It might be argued that I can scarcely talk about changes in concepts if I do not know what a concept is. However, no one else seems to know what a concept is either so I am no worse off than those who would solve the *Meno* dilemma in other ways. I hope I will be able to say something useful about conceptual change and the acquisition of concepts even if I cannot give an account of a concept itself. Plato never succeeded in defining virtue in the *Meno,* but still managed to say some very enlightening things about whether or not and how virtue might be taught. Indeed, it has recently been argued (Sternfeld and Zyskind, 1978) that the *Meno* represents a significant departure from the ordinary conception of Platonic method. Plato seems content to have brought Meno as far along the road to enlightenment as he could even though that distance fell short of a full definition of virtue. Sternfeld and Zyskind present a compelling argument in terms of Platonic scholarship for viewing the *Meno* as primarily concerned with right action— a perspective which will be amplified in educational terms in the present work.

What I shall do in the following is to discuss examples of conceptual change drawn from the history of science. Examples of conceptual change in areas such as political philosophy, or ethics, or ideology are often suspect. It always seems possible for those who would deny the reality of conceptual change to object that examples from such fields do not really involve different concepts, but rather different value or political judgments on the same concepts. Although this may sometimes be true, I do not believe that such value-laden cases are different in principle from scientific cases with regard to conceptual change. However, in choosing my examples from the prima facie value-free area of science, I hope to obviate such criticisms.

Conceptual change is a complex phenomenon which I cannot hope to cover completely. I shall instead identify and illustrate three aspects of this phenomenon: change of meaning, change of perception, and change of methodology. I suspect that each of these aspects is involved to a greater or lesser extent in every conceptual change, but it may be useful to point each example toward one of them. On the other hand, I am not claiming that these are the only aspects of conceptual change, merely that they are very important ones.

The first example involves the concept of combustion (see Butterfield, 1957). For a long time it was thought that in burning an object one was driving off something, so that the end product of combustion was something less and more elementary than that with which one began. Indeed, observation of common cases of burning appeared to confirm this notion. When wood burns, flames and smoke appear to escape and only ash is left. The substance driven off was thought to be a solid, fatty substance which came to be called phlogiston, and if figured in some very complex theories. However, scientists were unable to ignore or explain away the cases in which something was *added* in combustion. When mercury or iron was heated, for example, the resulting product weighed *more* than it did prior to the heating. Of course, such cases could be handled within the theory by suggesting that phlogiston had negative weight or by hypothesizing the existence of a secondary incidental process which added weight during combustion, but such emendations came to be considered more and more ad hoc. Following Priestley and Lavoisier the concept of combustion changed to account for these phenomena in ways that did not seem so arbitrary and which began to show promise of being able to cover other phenomena as well. The concept of a chemical element as we now know it began to emerge, and combustion came to be seen as a process of oxidation where oxygen or "dephlogisticated air" is added to materials. Thus, the concept of combustion changed from one in which something was lost to one in which something was gained. This example of conceptual change seems to me to illustrate a change in the *meaning* of the term "combustion," and the process of this change of meaning I call conceptual change.

Let me turn to the second example. We all, of course, know that the earth rotates on its axis, thereby causing night to follow day in a regular succession. People did not always know this, however, and even now our reasons for this belief are perhaps not as strong as we would like to think. Consider, for example, the following argument adapted from Feyerabend (1970): If the earth really moved, i.e., rotated on its axis, then a ball dropped from a high tower would not, indeed, could not, land at the base of the tower, but would land at some distance from the base. After all, if the earth is moving, and the tower is attached to the earth, then the tower must be moving too. Hence the tower will move some considerable distance during the time the ball is falling and the ball will land at some distance from the tower's base. The exact distance away could be calculated easily enough if we knew the supposed speed of the earth along with the time taken by the ball to reach the ground. But, plainly, as soon as one carries out such an experiment, one finds by observation that the ball drops vertically and lands at the foot of the tower after all. Since the hypothesis that the earth moves leads to a prediction which is clearly falsified in experience, the hypothesis must be false. The earth does *not* move.

I suspect that many will be just a trifle puzzled by this argument. We *know* it must be wrong, but, just how. . . ? At one time people had concepts of the earth and relative motion which rendered the "tower argument" plausible as a counter to the suggestion that the earth rotates, whereas now we have concepts of the earth and motion which render the "tower argument" clearly fallacious. What happened to the concepts between the two states? That process is conceptual change.

One reason the example is so engrossing is that our own concepts have changed so little that we can understand and appreciate the very real intellectual puzzle which the argument generates. We are not sure what concepts we should rely upon to refute the argument. Thus, the difference between the two cognitive states is highlighted for us. The process of moving from the concept of relative motion, in which the tower argument is taken as a persuasive reason against the movement of the earth, to the concept of relative composite motion, in which we can conceive of how the argument is invalid, involves, I think, a change of *perception*. Instead of imagining ourselves on top of the tower dropping the ball and then being carried away from the ball by the moving tower connected to the earth, we instead imagine ourselves out in space looking at the earth, the attached tower, and the ball all moving together. Once we attain this new perspective, we see that the ball and tower share an angular motion that carries the ball along with the tower and makes plausible what we actually observe, namely, the vertical fall of the ball to the foot of the tower.

The third example of the phenomenon I am calling conceptual change involves the teaching of science, in particular explaining Newton's laws of motion. For all of recorded history people have been interested in explaining physical motion and its changes. Why, for example, do various projectiles, rocks, arrows, cannonballs, and so on, fall to the earth? Now, according to Newton's first law every body continues in its state of rest, or of uniform motion in a straight line, unless it is acted on by an external force. We all know that, if we have taken even a high school physics course. Yet my colleagues in science education tell me that college students consistently seem not to understand Newton's law.

When asked, for example, how far a puck will travel on an infinite, frictionless air hockey table when hit with a certain force as against being hit with twice the force, almost all will say that the harder the puck is hit, the farther it will travel. When asked to explain why, they typically talk about the lesser force "wearing out" first, not being as strong, and so on. This way of talking is almost a paradigm case of the historical concept of impetus. Before Newton, most scientists treated projectile motion as due to the forward motion imparted to the projectile by the means of projection. That power then "resided" in the projectile and was "used up" during the flight of the projectile. Obviously the more power or "impetus" given to the projectile, the farther it would travel.

Clearly, not only can a concept of impetus handle projectile motion, at least on a gross level, but many contemporary college students who "know" the right (Newtonian) concepts still apparently retain large doses of the old impetus notion. Again the example is useful because it apparently gives a view of both sides of a conceptual change. I suspect that many would have to stop and consciously apply the Newtonian concepts to avoid falling into the same trap as the prospective science teachers. The process of giving up the concept of impetus and replacing it with the concept of Newtonian motion in a straight line unless acted upon by external forces is an example of what I mean by conceptual change, in this case primarily a change in *methodology*. What needs to be explained on the impetus view is how the motion starts and continues; the falling to earth is natural and requires no explanation. On the Newtonian view, what needs to be explained is the falling to earth; for, without gravitational attraction, the motion would simply continue. Toulmin (1963) calls such a shift a change in the *ideals of natural order*.

Now it is undoubtedly true that each of these examples has elements of all the aspects of conceptual change in it and is not limited to the aspect I tried to highlight. Thus, in addition to the obvious change of meaning in the concept of combustion, it was probably also necessary to adopt new ways of seeing ordinary burning, as well as new methods of measuring oxidation. Likewise, in addition to the new perspectives required for the tower argument, the meaning of "vertical fall" changed as well as the ways of measuring speed and acceleration. Finally, the change from impetus to Newtonian motion would be aided by the perspective given by the infinite air hockey table as well as by changes in meaning of the concepts of motion and change of motion.

One of the obstacles to appreciating the role of conceptual change in the development of knowledge is that sometimes earlier concepts are distorted in historical accounts to make them appear obvious precursors to current ways of looking at and dealing with the world. This gives the impression of a relatively straightforward accumulation of scientific knowledge in a building block sort of progress. On the other hand, if the differences between old and new concepts are very large, the earlier concepts are sometimes viewed by the history books simply as mistakes and clearly not worthy of study. Science textbooks often take one or the other of these approaches when they deign to talk about the history of science at all. In either case the history of science becomes more or less irrelevant to science; under the former view, because current concepts would already logically include their precursors; under the latter perspective, because the precursors would be logically unconnected with current concepts. In any case it is the phenomena that these examples illustrate to which I intend to refer when I speak of conceptual change.

3. The Current Status of Views on Conceptual Change

Recently, a number of historians and philosophers of science have raised serious doubts about the standard ways of accounting for the phenomenon of conceptual change, and about standard views of the growth of scientific knowledge (Kuhn, 1970b; Feyerabend, 1970; Hanson, 1958; Toulmin, 1972; Polanyi, 1962; Suppe, 1974; and Lakatos, 1970). Perhaps the besk-known work in this area is Thomas Kuhn's *The Structure of Scientific Revolutions* (1970). However, the critical introduction to *The Structure of Scientific Theories,* by Frederick Suppe (1974), provides a complete and illuminating picture of the current status of discussions on conceptual change and the growth of scientific knowledge in philosophy of science. I shall review this material briefly, supplementing it in certain areas to show how similar is the current predicament in philosophy of science to the predicament I have urged exists in trying to solve the *Meno* dilemma.

Suppe characterizes the "received view" of the structure of scientific knowledge as follows: scientific knowledge is to be understood as a theory formulated in a special language. This language contains essentially two disjoint kinds of primitive nonlogical terms, the observation terms and the theoretical terms. There is associated with this language a formal logical calculus of whatever power seems necessary (typically, it must be powerful enough to generate mathematics) to enable us to express all of the sentences or propositions of the theory.

In this special language the sentences which contain only observation terms are given a semantic interpretation. That is, the observation terms are associated with directly observable events, things, and relations. Thus, a sentence of the language which contains only observational terms will be able to be judged true or false by direct observation. At the other end of the spectrum, from the set of sentences which contain only theoretical terms (e.g., mass, force), a selection is

made of those sentences which are to be treated as theoretical postulates or axioms or laws (e.g., Newton's laws). The axioms are usually
chosen on a complex of grounds; they may be self-evident, fundamental,
highly confirmed, and so on. Finally, a subset of the sentences con-
taining both theoretical and observational terms is postulated as con-
taining the correspondence rules of the theory. These correspondence
rules link up, as it were, the strictly theoretical claims of the theory
with the strictly observational claims. The theoretical postulates together with the correspondence rules thus provide a partial interpretation of the theoretical terms and give form to the intuitive demand
that a scientific theory be *about* the empirically observable world. The
theory proper consists of the conjunction of the theoretical postulates
and correspondence rules, together, of course, with all the logical consequences of these sentences.

This picture of scientific theories has often been called the hypothetico-deductive model. Certain axioms and correspondence rules are
hypothesized which, together with observation sentences expressing
observable initial conditions, permit the deduction of other observation
sentences which can then be checked for truth or falsity by direct
observation of the world. If the predicted observation sentence turns
out to be true, the theory is to some extent confirmed, although in just
what sense is still highly controversial. Because theories purport to be
universal or at least probabilistic, it is difficult to see how one of an
infinite number of possible instances can confirm the theory (Carnap,
1962; Hempel, 1965). On the other hand, if the observation sentence
turns out to be false on direct observation, then the theory is falsified
(Popper, 1959), as a single instance *can* falsify a universal generalization. However, as I have already pointed out in discussing Feyerabend, just which among the myriad of sentences used in the derivation
is to be counted as false is indeterminate. So neither confirmation nor
falsification is without its problems in accounting for the way in which
scientific theories can be reasonably judged true or false by reference
to their empirical consequences.

I turn now to the doctrine of development and change of scientific
knowledge which seems to be held by most partisans of the received
view of the structure of scientific theories. Initially a theory is proposed
and is immediately tested empirically in roughly the manner noted
above. If it seems reasonably well confirmed, then only something like
fairly radical advances in the technology of measurement could ever
later disconfirm or falsify it. And presumably it would then be
superseded by another theory which fit the refined measurements. No
account is offered, however, of any connections between the two theories

in such a situation. That is usually taken to be a matter for the psychology of discovery and not the logic of justification.

A second case in which a later theory has a connection with an earlier one is when the earlier theory can be reduced to the later one in a fairly rigorous way. Kepler's laws of planetary motion, which were reduced to Newton's laws of motion, are often cited as an example. In this case, however, the original theory was never disconfirmed; it was simply seen as a special case of a more inclusive theory and derived from the inclusive theory, possibly with the aid of some additional assumptions. The derivability criterion ensures on pain of equivocation that there has been no change in concepts in this kind of development of scientific knowledge.

The third way in which there can be scientific development in a way compatible with the received view is that of the extension of a well-confirmed theory to cover a larger scope of phenomena than it was originally designed to cover. An example here is the extension of classical particle mechanics to rigid body mechanics. This kind of development probably comes as close as any to being able to capture at least a part of what I have illustrated as conceptual change. It could be argued that such an extension involves perceiving new areas as falling under the given concepts of the theory and, thus, does not involve some conceptual change of the perceptual type. I say "could be argued," for such argument is not typical, and, in any event, theoretical concepts are not thereby changed. Rather at most the new area into which the theory is being extended will require a change of observational concepts.

Can these three modes of the development of science account for the sort of conceptual change noted in my examples? Meanings change as one moves from, say, combustion as burning to combustion as oxidation, but in the received view these changes appear to be a case not of theory reduction or extension, but rather of one theory's being superseded by another. Because the change seems not to have been simply the result of better measurement (Butterfield, 1957, pp. 195–209), the motivation for the change seems quite mysterious. Concerns such as the initial plausibility of knowledge variants are simply pushed into the context of discovery and left for psychologists. However, such a sharp discontinuity is foreign to the actual historical development of knowledge. If they do nothing else, Kuhn's historical examples in *The Structure of Scientific Revolutions* make abundantly clear that the picture of the growth and change of scientific concepts painted by the received view is historically inaccurate.

To take another example, the historical record clearly indicates that at least on occasion there are fundamental changes in the methodological principles of any science—what Toulmin called ideals of natural order, and which I illustrated by considering the difference between impetus and Newtonian accounts of motion. None of the modes of change—disconfirmation as a result of better measurement, reduction, or extension to new domains—seems capable of handling such methodological changes, except perhaps by *refusing* to handle them by banishing them to the psychology of discovery.

Similarly, there is a significant clash between the kind of perceptual change countenanced by the received view and the kind of perceptual change involved in the example of the tower argument. As already remarked, the perceptual change allowed by the former seems at best to allow us to see some new area in terms of the concepts of a given theory. What the tower argument, on the other hand, seems to require is a quite different and new perspective on our basic experience.

Thus, the first kind of criticism that can be leveled against the received view is that it is historically inaccurate, a criticism that was simply brushed aside by early advocates of the position. What they were seeking was not a historically accurate descriptive account but a rational reconstruction of science which would exhibit in a perspicuous way the relations between observation and theory and between our scientific claims and the rational ground for those claims. In a word, the concern was for the justification of knowledge and an exhibition of how knowledge could be objective. As long as this goal seemed attainable, historical inaccuracies could be ignored as of little philosophical consequence. Note, too, that the received view is an empiricist account of the growth of conceptual knowledge, sharing with all such attempts at grasping the old-knowledge horn of the *Meno* dilemma the strength of taking seriously a reality independent of our knowledge of it and the weakness of paying scant attention to conceptual diversity and change.

However, since, as I shall show, there are structural problems with the received view as well, brushing aside historical inaccuracy by the use of the slogan of rational reconstruction seems much less justified. Furthermore, the nature of these problems casts considerable doubt on the distinction I have thus far accepted between conceptual knowledge and factual knowledge. It will be recalled that I have been assuming that if, somehow, we could account for conceptual knowledge, then enquiry into knowledge of the empirical world could escape the *Meno* dilemma. Once the hard and fast distinction between conceptual and factual knowledge is given up, however, the dilemma once more threatens all of our knowledge. At the same time, I think that blurring this distinction will open the way for the kind of historical, evolutionary, and developmental account of knowledge and enquiry which seems to be required to solve the dilemma.

It is clear that the received view depends on the distinction between conceptual knowledge and factual knowledge (or, as some contemporary cognitive psychologists would put it, between our knowledge of language and our knowledge of the world). If the empiricist rational reconstruction view is to be tenable, it must distinguish the basic terms which are immediately known through direct observation from the other terms to be defined with the use of the basic terms. The antecedently intelligible basic terms required by an old-knowledge approach to the *Meno* dilemma are the received view's observational terms. These observational terms are applied as a result of direct, unproblematic observation. The theoretical terms then depend for their meaning on the observation terms. In early formulations of the received view, the correspondence rules actually were to take the form of definitional analyses. This oversimple idea of the connection between the observational and the theoretical was soon abandoned, but the idea that the observational terms were still to provide the ultimate source of the meaning of the theoretical terms was retained. Thus the ability to distinguish our knowledge of how observational terms are related to theoretical terms (conceptual knowledge) is crucial for the received view.

It should be pointed out here that we can, in principle, draw the distinction between knowledge of concepts and konwledge of facts independently of an empiricist interpretation of concepts. Indeed, Kant's famous distinction between analytic and synthetic statements does just that. What we do in giving an empiricist interpretation of concepts is to specify that the basic antecedently intelligible concepts have an empirical source. This in turn means that for an empiricist if the analytic-synthetic distinction does not, in general, hold, the observational-theoretical distinction will likewise fall. Thus we can examine the tenability of the analytic-synthetic distinction in the received view and in so doing cast some light on the conceptual knowledge-factual knowledge distinction.

Kant claimed that a proposition was analytic if the predicate concept was contained in the subject concept; all other propositions were synthetic. More recent extensions and elaborations of the notion (Quine, 1962) define a proposition as analytically true if it is true in virtue of its logical form alone or can be reduced to a proposition true in virtue of its logical form alone by substituting synonyms for synonyms. Contrary to Kant, the new view no longer defines synthetic statements as the nonanalytic ones, but rather as those whose truth or falsity can be determined by factual information about the world.

Quine's classic paper, "Two Dogmas of Empiricism" (1962), has, however, cast considerable doubt on the analytic-synthetic distinction. After examining any number of ways of attempting to draw the distinction, he concludes that they all fail, and for some interesting general reasons. In the first place analyticity seems to depend on synonymy or vice versa, but both are equally problematic. Furthermore, we cannot characterize synthetic statements by reducing them to statements about immediate sensory experience. In other words, the empiricist version of the source of old knowledge cannot be located in sensible particulars. Thus the empiricist cannot meet the requirement of specifying nonproblematic, already-existing knowledge which is the basis for further enquiry.

Moreover, although there have been attempts to overcome Quine's arguments, such attempts seem not to have actually exhibited the requisite distinction between analytic and synthetic statements, or, if they have, it has been in a relativized version. That is, within a given structural framework we may be able to draw the distinction, but it cannot be generalized, and for the purposes of a different structure the distinction may get drawn in a different way. In short, the distinction is relative to a world view, and world views are distinguished by the different human purposes, choices, and activities they embody. Even within a given context or world view there may be a number of statements which are neither analytic nor synthetic. It would seem that the conceptual knowledge-factual knowledge distinction cannot be drawn in a hard and fast way and, therefore, the theoretical-observational term distinction is likewise imperiled.

But the theoretical-observational term distinction is directly untenable as well. The general reasons are the ones already given in chapter 2: the fact that actual attempts to draw it have failed; the Gestaltist point that what will even count as observational depends upon a theoretical or abstract whole which determines the significance of the parts; and the epistemological point concerning the conceptual primacy of the abstract. Once again we may be able to draw a relative theoretical-observational distinction, but that is all (Petrie, 1971a). The relativity will be to a given context or reasonably well-defined and accepted set of human activities. For example, within Newtonian mechanics the observational-theoretical distinction is fairly clear, but it gets drawn in quite a different way in quantum mechanics.

Another major difficulty for the received view is its inability to cope with the place of iconic models in the growth of knowledge. By iconic model, I do not necessarily mean a model which "pictures" the theory in any straightforward way, although I certainly wish to include models such as the billiard ball model of Newtonian mechanics. Rather I mean by "iconic" a model which is essentially nonlinguistic in any normal sense. As opposed to mathematical models, iconic models, or, as Kuhn (1970) calls them, exemplary problem solutions, tend to be treated as possibly of heuristic value in teaching science or communicating new theories but do not figure essentially in the received view's account of science. Rather, the distinction between the psychological context of discovery (or in this case, learning) and the logical context of justification is relied upon to rule questions of models out of philosophical court.

However, given the difficulties with the analytic-synthetic distinction and the theoretical-observational distinction, the discovery-justification distinction is probably not sustainable, except perhaps in a relativized form, relative once more to given systems of human activity. The argument for the epistemological necessity for such models is due to Wittgenstein (Petrie, 1971b), and I summarize it briefly here. On pain of infinite regress there must be either self-evident rules for interpreting a rule, or a way of interpreting the rule which is not itself a rule. That is, when we interpret the rules of the formal logical calculus which represents any scientific theory, we do it in terms of some language in use, say, English. As long as we need raise no problems about the language in use, all is well. Or if we could reduce that language to unproblematic observation statements which could be conclusively verified by direct observation, we could put an end to any potential regress. However, by now it is clear that such direct observational knowledge is not to be had. For certain purposes, and in certain contexts, the language in use, i.e., the rules for the application and use of English, can be questioned. This is, of course, to be expected on a view which takes conceptual change seriously.

Therefore, as Wittgenstein says, there must be a way of interpreting a rule which is not itself a rule and which can bring the whole process to an end. This way of interpreting the rule is to be found by reference to language games as they are played and forms of life as they are lived. In other words, the foundation for interpreting any cognitive activity lies in the models to be found in training and education. We get people to behave as we do by having them *act* in the world—both the physical and the social world. *The grounding of epistemology is learning!* This is Wittgenstein's behaviorism; it is not a reductive behaviorism at all, but rather a recognition that it is our purposes and activity in the world as well as the brute givenness of the world itself which ground our knowledge of the world.

Kuhn (1974) shows clearly the role of iconic models in the epistemology of science. He argues that it is not by means of linguistic rules that science attaches its language to nature, but rather by means of exemplars, a scientific community's standard examples. And although he admits that added precision may sometimes be obtained by formulating such exemplars in linguistic rules, nevertheless, such a move subtly changes the preformulated similarity relations. It is, as he puts it, the ability to see resemblances between apparently disparate problems which enables the scientist to attach the theory to the world.

Kuhn's argument is mainly by means of historical examples, but one area he discusses is particularly instructive for education. He considers the age-old pedagogical question of how a science student learns to do the problems at the end of the chapter (see also Petrie, 1976b). How does the student "apply" the theory he or she has learned in the chapter to the problems at the end? How do we account for the common experience that a student will understand the chapter in the sense of being able to derive the formulas, see how the chapter fits with the rest of physics, be capable of discussing it with the teacher, and so on, but will have not a clue as to how to attack the problems at the end?

The common view of scientific pedagogy seems to be that the student needs to learn the (linguistic) rules of application which link the theory learned in the chapter with the problems at the end. And, of course, this presupposes that the problems at the end are independently intelligible and accessible—an analogue of observation terms, if you will. And so the educational problem is posed in terms of a search for rules of application of theory to practice (correspondence rules). Education's perennial failure to answer the question of how we "apply" theory to practice while at the same time quite often successfully getting students to make just such "applications" suggests that perhaps we have misformulated the problem.

Kuhn's view of scientific pedagogy is that the student does not "apply" theory to practice, but rather acquires a nonlinguistic, nonexplicitly rule-governed way of seeing similarity relations among problems, thus providing a reformulation of the age-old theory-practice problem. Acquiring a stock of exemplars, exemplary problem solutions, is acquiring the ability to *see* the theory *in* the practice—to see the problems at the end of the chapter in the terms provided by the theory of the chapter. The task for the theory of education is thus not to provide a list of explicit rules for applying theory to practice, but rather to develop ways of transforming practice so that it is properly describable in the theoretical terms. In just that sense, for example, homework can be seen as giving repeated examples of the similarity relations we, as teachers, want the students to pick up; homework forces the students to deal with the examples in the theoretical terms. Recall the tower argument. What is needed there is a training in perception, not a bunch of rules of application.

Models, or exemplary problem solutions, are, therefore, essential elements in an account of the growth of scientific knowledge. They provide a promising alternative to the discredited notion of direct observation as providing the way of attaching theory to the world. Interestingly, this role of models, involving as it does the idea of being trained and educated into scientific practice, was largely obscured by the received view's insistence on static relations of justification and confirmation. It is only when we bring into focus process considerations, as we are forced to do in considering educational matters, that the role of models becomes increasingly clear.

The educational implication is profound. We can no longer simply assume that our students can all observe the same facts, and that all we need to do is teach the theories which render those facts understandable. The exemplars the student naively brings to a study of motion, say, may not be the exemplars that physicists use in their study of motion. Educators will have to pay a great deal more attention to perceptual learning than has been the case up to now (Petrie, 1974b). Quite literally, student and teacher may look at the same thing and see different things. If this possibility is not recognized and guarded against, obvious misunderstandings and failures of the learning process will result.

The point to emphasize is that a system of representation must be assumed upon which thought can operate in order for us to be able to understand thought at all (Fodor, 1975). We must take into account the twin influences on perception of the causal impact of the physical world and theories we bring to the task of interpreting the causal impact of the world. And, as I have argued, those theories are in turn bound up with our human purposes and activities. We do not perceive the physical light waves impinging on our retinas, or the elastic deformations of our bottoms when in contact with chairs, or the oscillations of sound waves when we hear. Yet those things are, to the best of our knowledge, the sorts of ways the external world does affect us. What we do perceive are objects, events, and relations. Thus, quite clearly, we somehow *represent* the actual physical causes in terms of the psychological systems we bring to bear on these causal influences. The same is true of our behavior. We do not in our representation of action rearrange clouds of atoms; we move a chair. Our thought operates on the system which represents our activity as "moving a chair" rather than on the system which represents what we believe to be the direct physical inputs and outputs. In sum, thought is a computational process of some sort requiring a medium in which to perform its computations, namely, a representational system.

With the breakdown of both the analytic-synthetic and the theoretical-observational term distinctions, and the failure of programs to elucidate the notion of direct observation, it follows that representational systems will be all that we have to go on for purposes of enquiry and the acquisition of knowledge. There may be only one reality, but it does not seem that people must construct only one representation of it, and the choices among the representations people do create must be made without comparing these schemes with unrepresented reality, or reality "itself." Like the participants in the *Meno* dilemma, we too have to account for our concepts, fully recognizing the different schemes of representation which may be operative among different people at different times. Furthermore, it will be the schemes of representation themselves, or at least significant chunks of them, that will have to be accounted for, justified, modified, and justified again, rather than any atomic, separable parts of these schemes.

4. Epistemology Naturalized (Quine, 1969a)

What the foregoing discussion shows is that contemporary problems of conceptual change and the growth of scientific theories can be viewed as attempts to solve the *Meno* dilemma. The problems encountered by an empiricist philosophy of science are just those that I have shown bedevil all old-knowledge approaches to the *Meno*. The received view seems unable to account for the source and acquisition of our concepts and for the diversity and change we do find in our concepts. Either the diversity seems unmotivated, as in the case of theories wholly superseding other theories, or else, if continuity is taken into account by means of simple theory extension, the historical record seems misrepresented.

Additionally, however, the above considerations have brought out two new points relevant to the *Meno* dilemma. In the first place, it seems that conceptual change will have to be understood in a more holistic way than has been realized. The breakdown of the analytic-synthetic and the observational-theoretical term distinctions, the essential role of models and schemes of representation, the connection of theory to the world via human activity, all point to the necessity for taking the epistemologically significant unit to be much larger than atomic concepts or even atomic sentences. Something the size of a Wittgensteinian language game or a Kuhnian paradigm or a conceptual scheme seems to be the proper unit. We are going to have to account for and justify *systems* of behavior and belief and *systematic* changes as well as changes in isolated beliefs and actions.

The other point arising from a consideration of current philosophy of science relevant to the *Meno* dilemma is a methodological one. The working hypothesis I have used so far has been that by distinguishing enquiry into facts from enquiry into concepts we could localize the *Meno* dilemma in the latter area. That distinction formed the basis for separating the work of philosophy from the work of the empirical sciences. Thus, although there might be psychological issues concerning the acquisition of concepts and educational issues concerning how best to organize schooling to teach concepts, still the major task with regard to conceptual knowledge was taken to be philosophical. This was because an enquiry into concepts was seen as an enquiry into meaning, and meaning is that area marked off by the category of the analytic. How the world sorted itself into our concepts was a question for the empirical sciences; how those concepts were structured was a question for philosophy; and the methods of the two were not to be confused.

But the breakdown of the analytic-synthetic distinction reexposes empirical knowledge to the horns of the *Meno* dilemma. Now with a clear methodological conscience we can utilize the resources of science to help understand the nature of enquiry and the acquisition of knowledge. As Quine (1969a), pp. 75–76 puts it:

> If the epistemologist's goal is validation of the grounds of empirical science, he defeats his purpose by using psychology or other empirical science in the validation. However, such scruples against circularity have little point once we have stopped dreaming of deducing science from observations. If we are out simply to understand the link between observation and science, we are well advised to use any available information, including that provided by the very science whose link with observation we are seeking to understand.

And it is, of course, the failure of the received view in the philosophy of science that has made us give up the dream of deducing science from observations or otherwise tightly linking them together.

With the aid of the empirical sciences, however, we may be able to make a new attack on some of the old *Meno* problems. We can, for example, now give a relativistic definition of observation sentence. Quine's (p. 86–87) will do as an example.

> An observation sentence is one on which all speakers of the language give the same verdict when given the same concurrent stimulation.

Without undertaking a careful appraisal of the definition, we note that it is relative to speakers of a language, and we are now allowed to make the determination of who speaks a given language on empirical sociological or anthropological grounds, without fear of begging any important questions. Likewise, what will count as concurrent stimulation may be derived from physiology, or psychology, or even linguistics without raising the specter of circularity. At this point we are not trying to understand how enquiry in general is possible. We are, to be sure, still concerned with the normative adequacy or rationality of the enquiry, but not in a way which can be methodologically distinguished from that same concern shown by the empirical sciences themselves in their day-to-day operation. The sphere of rationality can no longer be reserved exclusively for philosophy without taking account of the claims of the particular sciences to be pursuing rationality as well. Lacking the general account of the grounds of knowledge promised by the received view, the sciences must be allowed to provide limited grounds of rationality and justification within themselves as practiced (Petrie, 1971b).

So a relativized specification of observation terms and sentences can be provided. Given an existential commitment to a particular paradigm or language game, we can empirically determine what the basic elements in that game are by determining what the agreements in judgments are among those who play that language game. Recall that when we considered the empiricist approach of constructing abstract concepts out of concrete particulars, we could not account for the abstract concept of similarity on empiricist grounds. There seemed to be no way to circumvent the primacy of the abstract. On the current view this similarity notion is easily handled. It arises from the similarity judgments people make who have been taught a language game. These judgments are not simply conventional but depend on the exemplary problem solutions around which the language game or paradigm is built. The Gestaltist point is vindicated. The language game embodies the appropriate notions of similarity in terms of which the basic elements of the language game are to be identified. Learning the language game enables new generations to make these same similarity judgments.

This emphasis on learning basic similarity judgments does not, however, justify the "nurture" side of the nature-nurture controversy. Nothing in what I have said would rule out innate or common language games people might play. Given the kinds of organisms we are and having undergone the evolutionary history we have, all of us now possess the capacity to make a certain range of similarity judgments. These similarity judgments could constitute what we might call innate language games. The innate linguistic universals sometimes spoken of by transformational linguistics would probably be of this kind. Let us suppose that people innately use subject-predicate language; then the activities and similarity judgments connected with such language use would form the basis for the general structure of language acquisition.

To continue the example of language learning, although people may as a result of evolution innately possess certain kinds of abstract linguistic universals which enable them to acquire language, still the particular language they acquire seems to depend on the natural language community into which they are born. The similarity judgments at this level thus seem to be due to a common environment and are learned pretty much whether we like it or not. The kinds of activities in which the young in a particular language community engage guarantee that they will be trained into the common language community.

In addition to innate and common language games, we might distinguish another level, which might be called "schooled"; here I mean those language games intentionally taught whether in formal schools or not. An example would be learning to read. The similarity judgments necessary to acquire some language or other seem innate; which particular spoken language is acquired depends on a common environment, but probably not much on intentional tuition; however, acquiring the reading language game does seem to require teaching of some sort.

This view of the "innateness" of some similarity judgments human beings make accords well with the close relationship Quine (1969b) has argued exists between the notions of similarity and natural kind. As he shows, the two notions are interdefinable, and so we can easily see how, given the pervasive and fundamental similarity judgments to be found in common and innate language games, people could easily have felt that they had discovered natural kinds which reflected the basic structure of the world independent of thought. Natural kinds, however, must include the contribution of human thought.

I intend no hard and fast distinction among innate, common, and schooled language games. No doubt they shade off into one another, and how any given language game is classified is probably relative to time, place, and background knowledge. Nevertheless, the rough categorization is useful for understanding how something like the goal of deducing science from observation or at least translating science into observation statements could have seemed at all plausible. It is probably the case that there really are an incredibly large number of innate and common language games that people, being the kinds of organisms that we are and living in the kinds of roughly similar ecologies that we do, all play. Schooled language games probably vary a good deal more according to particular social and individual purposes. We can, I think, understand proponents of the received view if we suppose them struck by the fundamental and pervasive nature of innate and common language games. The ways of behaving and the basic elements associated with the ways of behaving in such language games would appear to provide the kind of absolute justification of knowledge which they were seeking. They probably also noted the schooled language games and their relatively greater diversity and dependence on individual and social purpose and, accordingly, discounted the basic elements to be found there as not capable of supporting knowledge, but only value preferences.

Yet in order to provide the kind of justification which was required, one that could stand against any kind of skepticism, the received view imputed too fundamental a nature to the basic elements found in common and innate language games. The elements were seen as independent of the language games, as reflecting reality itself, as providing the ground-level access to reality about which there could be no question. But as I have argued, and as the criticisms of the received view seem to have shown, even the basic elements of innate and common language games depend on the purposes and activities of people who play them in a given kind of world. However, even such basic purposes and such basic structural ways of representing the world can change, and so we must give up the goal of understanding justification in general in favor of the goal of understanding the more specific kinds of justification to be found in our actual ways of knowing.

A naturalized epistemology does not try to suspend the results of the particular sciences until a general theory of justification is available. On the contrary, such an epistmology makes full use of the justificatory practices and results of the particular sciences in its account of knowledge and coming to know. In this sense such an epistemology is particularly relevant to the educational enterprise where philosophy, psychology, political science, history, sociology, and anthropology, to name but a few of the relevant sciences, must all be brought to bear in order to illuminate the complex issues at stake.

The *Meno* dilemma poses the fundamental question for educational epistemology, namely, How is learning possible? A naturalized epistemology provides the structural framework for answering that question.

But the connection between a naturalized epistemology and education is even closer than I have just indicated. Once the old-knowledge approach of attempting to ground most knowledge with a class of indubitable basic knowledge is given up, the most promising alternative is one that uses the process of learning as the fundamental concept of epistemology. If education is a process of bringing students to behave as we do rather than merely a part of applied epistemology, ways of knowing are understandable as the result of education. The processes of learning the standard examples and the ways of behaving in any field are the processes that bring our theories and representational schemes into contact with the world. Education grounds epistemology.

The same kind of dialectic is often found in educational debates. In the educational realm the argument is one of maintaining standards versus student choice. On the one hand, we have those who insist that if what is taught in our schools is to have any kind of justification at all, it must be firmly grounded in the best that is known. And since the best that is known is codified in the disciplines, our curriculum must teach the disciplines and demand that the standards of the disciplines be upheld. On the other hand, we have those who decry the dehumanizing influence of such schooling and the irrelevance of the disciplines for many students, especially those who do not themselves become disciplinarians. So it is argued that the student's interests must be made the basis of the curriculum and allowed to guide the choices as to what disciplines, if any, should be studied.

"But we teach subjects," it is claimed. We cannot simply teach. There must be a content to what is taught. What is the subject matter of education? We admit that teachers must know perhaps a little child psychology to help them motivate their students, but their central concern must be their subject—mathematics, or physics, or English, or history. If teachers know and love their subject, why, then even the motivational tricks are probably dispensable. One cannot get and hold a job if one cannot read, write, and do arithmetic. One would be less than a complete citizen without some appreciation of literature and history. All of these things have right ways and wrong ways of going about them, and it is the function of the schools to make sure the students get them right. To allow the students to define the curriculum would at least risk mindless anarchy if not ensure it.

"We teach children," so the reply comes. Every child is an individual human being with very different wants, needs, capacities, fears, and desires. Students deserve to be treated as individuals and not as inputs to an educational factory called a school. If a particular course of study seems good or bad to a child, who are we to impose our wills upon that child? The schools must educate, not indoctrinate, and to do that the choice of what is to be learned must be freely the students'. Most will need to learn to read, but it does not follow that we should utilize *our* idea of materials in order to teach them. What is the good of knowing the set theory foundations of mathematics for a clerk who will add and subtract on a cash register at work and on a ten dollar calculator at home? Education must be meaningful for the student.

Even if we get the protagonists to agree to the fairly obvious compromise that, really, we teach subjects to children, the debate does not end. As in the *Meno* dilemma, each side will try to assimilate the strengths of the other position to its own, or will try to avoid dealing with them.

Thus the partisans of standards may grant that attention must be paid to the pedagogical tasks involved with the forms of knowledge. They may admit that we have to know about individual children, their interests and background knowledge, in order to pursue the goal of imparting the forms of knowledge. But they will maintain that it is the forms of knowledge which in the end constitute rational mind, and that any attempts to substitute an individual's idiosyncratic beliefs about knowledge for the publicly tested forms of knowledge must be steadfastly resisted. Such a move would be to give in to subjectivism.

On the other side, proponents of child-centered education may admit that content must be taught, but they will reject any idea that the content must be logically connected to the structures of knowledge as represented in the disciplines. They point, for example, to the obvious absurdity of teaching science to liberal arts students as if they wanted to take a doctoral degree in that area. People can and do think critically, for example, without knowing formal logic. And that is so even if formal logic embodies the "structure" of critical thinking. Once again, there may be one underlying reality, but there are numerous ways of representing that reality, and they are subject to the pressures of different purposes and goals. The individual student's mode of representing reality is what education must be concerned with if it is to avoid the immoral indoctrination of free and autonomous human beings.

The dialectic seems clear. It is carried on in almost the same language as the one in the philosophy of science. Those who plump for standards have the insight that the world cannot be anything we wish it to be. Those who defend the autonomy of the individual have the insight that our access to reality is indirect and is mediated through schemes of representation which are themselves subject to our purposes.

And as in the philosophy of science, we can move the discussion ahead by first agreeing that the unit of discourse cannot be atomistic in any area of education—instructional objectives, curriculum planning, teaching outcomes, pupil knowledge, or whatever. We must look at physics as a whole, a given curriculum as a whole, a child's cognitive scheme, an institution's special mission, and so on. These larger units will determine what elements are to be considered. In short, world views, language games, paradigms, and conceptual schemes are the basic units of intelligibility and *not* specific behaviors, or facts, or skills. If much of what has been thought reasonable and justifiable is context dependent and relative to, e.g., forms of knowledge, then for educational theory an account in terms of a naturalized epistemology must be given of the source of these forms of knowledge and of reasonable changes in them.

5. A Contemporary Approach to the Meno Dilemma

D. W. Hamlyn (1978) explicitly refers to Plato's *Meno* dilemma as setting the stage for his own discussion of the role of experience in the growth of knowledge and understanding. Hamlyn notes that Plato's solution to the dilemma seems to depend on the a priori nature of the geometrical example used with the slave boy. If a situation is one in which the enquirer simply has to work out the implications of what he or she already knows, then a Platonic solution of drawing out logical consequences is plausible. On the other hand, Hamlyn claims (p. 7):

Where a person has to acquire through experience knowledge of new facts (or facts that are new to him at least) it is not like that at all. He cannot in that case apply the knowledge that he already has by simply working out its implications or consequences; or rather he cannot do this alone.

In such a case, Hamlyn continues:

The experience has to provide him with genuinely new information. But my point is that experience cannot do this unless it is somehow fitted into an already existing web of understanding and knowledge, unless, that is, the experience is significant for the learner.

Thus Hamlyn falls clearly within what I have called old-knowledge approaches. The problem for him is not, strictly speaking, how to make sense of the *Meno* dilemma in the abstract, but rather how to account for the role that experience plays in an old-knowledge approach. At the same time, however, he recognizes many of the problems I claim bedevil old-knowledge approaches and believes his account overcomes these difficulties. It will be worthwhile to see how well he succeeds in this task.

Hamlyn considers the same two classical old-knowledge approaches which I have previously discussed, empiricism and rationalism. The former he calls genesis without structure. This title captures empiricism's tendency to try to account for the growth of knowledge through experience by means of simply adding up the experiences as they occur, spatially and temporally. There is no necessary pattern or structure to the growth. It just goes wherever contingent experience happens to lead. Basically Hamlyn's objection to this approach is the same as mine. Experience is not simply given in some independent atomic form. Rather, experience is always an experience of something as characterized by some concept or other, as *this* kind of thing rather than *that*. Thus Hamlyn adopts the conceptual primacy of the abstract which I have also urged.

In the case of rationalism, or structure without genesis, Hamlyn's objections are again similar to mine. Since experience presupposes some knowledge of the concepts in terms of which the experience is had, the question arises as to how the process ever gets started. Put in another way, if we must already know something in order to learn something new from experience, where does this original knowledge come from? If we cannot answer this question, we are faced with a vicious infinite regress, with each bit of new knowledge presupposing other knowledge, which in its turn presupposes some other knowledge, and so on. The resulting picture would not be an adequate account of the growth of knowledge and understanding. It would be an account of structure without genesis.

At least one form of rationalism, of course, attempts to block the regress by postulating innate knowledge at some point in the process. Hamlyn, however, objects to innate knowledge because it is implausible that experience plays no role in the growth of understanding. Furthermore, rationalism's required direct access to the basic, innate knowledge simply does not occur. Hamlyn argues that knowledge presupposes a concept of truth which in turn can be explicated only with reference to the public social criteria of agreement in judgments among persons. Clearly this social criterion could not be innate knowledge. I shall have more to say about this last argument of Hamlyn's, but for now it is sufficient to note that the general considerations he uses to reject empiricism and rationalism are similar to mine.

Hamlyn next considers and rejects Piaget's account of the growth of knowledge, an account Hamlyn labels genesis with structure. I shall be discussing Piaget later, and my own positive account, although different from Piaget's in crucial respects, may nevertheless be fairly characterized as an account of genesis with structure. I shall, therefore, postpone consideration of Hamlyn's objections to this kind of position until I have developed my own account.

The point which needs to be noted now is that Hamlyn's major objection to Piaget is that the normative epistemological condition seems to be missing. As Hamlyn puts it (p. 59):

Adding structure to genesis ensures that the growth of knowledge and understanding is not simply thought of as contingent on the way in which experience falls, as it is with empiricism. Adding genesis to structure ensures that knowledge and understanding are at least thought of as developing in some sense. The idea of genesis with structure, however, does not explain why it is that what develops in this way without being subject simply to the vagaries of experience is in fact knowledge.

This is, of course, the same challenge I have posed in distinguishing between a descriptive and a normative solution to the *Meno* dilemma. We must give an account not merely of how change in belief is possible, but also of when we are justified in calling the change of belief knowledge.

Hamlyn's answer to the challenge of saying how what develops through experience is knowledge is to bring in the social interaction with other people as a conceptual condition for objective knowledge. His positive account thus emphasizes that objectivity and knowledge are founded in the agreement of human judgments. This is not to say that the agreement is what makes something true or known, but only that the possibility of agreement is necessary. Furthermore, people learn from experience by being "put in the way of" things by adults and by being corrected by those same adults. There is, of course, also a causal perceptual condition that must be satisfied. That is, sense experiences, a causal result of the world's impinging on us, are a condition of our being able to apply our knowledge to particular cases, in short, of our experiencing. A final important feature of Hamlyn's account is that this knowledge we bring to cases can admit of degrees. Indeed, one of the functions of experience is to refine our knowledge of concepts so that we can make better applications to cases (p. 72).

Now as far as this account goes, I have no serious quarrel with it. Indeed, my own account will also make use of many of the same points. The problem, as Hamlyn explicitly notes (chap. 7), is how knowledge starts if innate knowledge is ruled out, but knowledge is nevertheless required to make sense of the notion of experience. Hamlyn's acceptance of this latter condition again shows his position to be an old-knowledge approach to the problem. He takes on the task of showing how knowledge can grow through experience even though knowledge is essential to understanding the possibility of experience.

His major ploy is a distinction between learning and coming to know, simpliciter. The latter may occur as a result of guesses, insight, or inspiration (all left unexplained); whereas learning seems to require that the child be aware of coming to know. Hamlyn goes on to say (p. 92):

Any acquisition of knowledge involves the connecting of items of which I have spoken. In learning, however, the connection is between what one comes to know and what one knows already, so that it is right to say what I said earlier: that learning implies knowledge which is preexistent in time. There are no such necessary implications with coming to know simpliciter, even if coming to know involves connecting things; that is to say that in the case of simple coming to know there are no temporal implications about the connecting.

Thus, coming to know, simpliciter, will be a basic process that will stop a potential infinite regress of *Meno* dilemmas.

Hamlyn's next task is, of course, to try to give an account of how this coming to know, simpliciter, occurs. He takes as an example a child's coming to distinguish X and Y. But all Hamlyn does here is to say that this does sometimes occur and we are sometimes justified in saying that it does occur. Such an account is no account at all and simply redescribes the problem. This would be less damaging if the distinction between learning and coming to know, simpliciter, were more obvious, but, as it is, with no account of insight, guesses, and inspirations, we can justifiably wonder if the distinction is not simply ad hoc to give Hamlyn something to hang onto.

He does, however, try to meet two possible objections to his account of coming to know (pp. 92–93). First, it might be objected that without temporally prior knowledge, the child could not be in the appropriate social position to have knowledge. Second, it might be objected that a child could not distinguish X and Y unless he somehow has the concepts of X and Y. Hamlyn's response to both of these objections is essentially to say that the requisite knowledge of the concepts might develop at the same time as the ability to discriminate and that this development may well be a matter of degree. Thus a full-fledged, temporally prior knowledge of the concepts of X and Y need not be presupposed.

This response is, of course, true enough, but it says nothing about how the ability to discriminate and knowledge of the concepts could develop together. Nor will it do for Hamlyn to push the task of giving such an account onto the psychologist, for without at least a sketch of how this is possible, Hamlyn's philosophical distinction between learning and coming to know looks more and more as if its only justification is that it fills a logical gap in his theory. At a minimum Hamlyn owes us a more complete account of how coming to know, simpliciter, is possible, if this notion is to stop an infinite regress of *Meno* dilemmas.

Two other points must also be raised. Hamlyn objects to the tendency of empiricism and rationalism, also found in Piaget, to pose the problem of knowledge as one in which the individual is conceived of as independent of the natural and social world. He believes that his own approach recognizes the essential contribution made to the growth of knowledge by the fact that a child grows up in a society. For Hamlyn adults are always putting the child in the way of things and correcting the child's mistakes, and this reference to the social plays the essential epistemological role of grounding objectivity for Hamlyn. But it has been the burden of this chapter that no single society can claim to embody *the* canons of objectivity, and Hamlyn is silent on the social differences and the historical changes that have occurred in our conceptions of truth, knowledge, and objectivity. Not only must the individual be conceived of in a society, but a given society must also be conceived of in the history of societies. In short, Hamlyn's approach, as is characteristic of old-knowledge approaches, does not take conceptual change seriously. This was foreshadowed by his dismissimg out of hand the new-knowledge horn of the *Meno* dilemma, and is now evident in the radical incompleteness of his own account.

Second, Hamlyn urges both against competing accounts and in favor of his own account that we must take seriously the possibility of agreement in judgments. Again, I agree but claim that Hamlyn carries the argument no further than a parochial agreement among the members of the society in which the child is brought up. Hamlyn is no help at all when the question is, for example, whether and how we are to educate members of such socially diverse groups as blacks, women, and Hispanics. Nor do I believe that it is open to Hamlyn to claim that his account of the necessity of the social is so general as to comprehend all different societies. As I have argued and will continue to argue, there are no transcendental principles of rationality immune to the possibility of conceptual change. But this means that on *philosophical* grounds Hamlyn's account is radically incomplete. It is not just a case of needing more work from the psychologists to fill in the details. We still need to know how and under what conditions the growth of experience, even when we set it into an ongoing social structure, deserves to be called knowledge.

6. Criteria for a Solution of the Meno Dilemma

Before I begin my own positive account of how the *Meno* dilemma is to be solved, two points need to be made. First, I think criteria of adequacy for a successful solution of the *Meno* dilemma can now be stated. These criteria have emerged from the discussion thus far and seem to be of a fairly general nature. Accordingly, whether or not my own particular solution is adequate, I believe that any alternative account must meet these criteria. Second, some particularly promising approaches and features have already been brought to light in a preliminary way. These, too, are of a fairly general nature, and although I believe they accord with the specific account I shall give, I do not think they are equivalent to that account. Once more these "promising directions" might be divorced from the account I shall give and be fruitfully pursued in different ways if that seems desirable.

The criteria of adequacy for a successful solution to the *Meno* dilemma are the following (I claim neither exhaustiveness nor mutual exclusivity for them):*

1. *Conceptual diversity:* There is a diversity of concepts and conceptual schemes across individuals, societies, and cultures at any one time and within individuals, societies, and cultures across time. In terms of the *Meno* dilemma: we sometimes do learn or enquire into things that are radically new.

2. *Conceptual continuity:* Despite the diversity of concepts noted above, there are also continuities and similarities to be found within individuals, societies, and cultures at a time and across time. How this can be so must also be accounted for. In terms of the *Meno* dilemma: we sometimes do already know things, but nontrivial learning, development, and enquiry is nevertheless possible.

3. *Sources of concepts:* Given the diversity and continuity of concepts, their source becomes an important consideration. In short we must understand the processes of both the original acquisition of concepts and their change. This is obviously true for educational epistemology, but equally true for epistemology in general given the current state of affairs in which logical connections among concepts and between concepts and the world are not sufficient for an account of knowledge. Again concept acquisition and concept change must be understood across individuals, societies, and cultures, diachronically and synchronically, across time and at a time. In terms of the *Meno* dilemma: knowing must be studied as a process.

4. *Reasonableness of processes of acquisition and change:* All the processes of knowledge acquisition and conceptual change must be seen as justifiable in a very broad sense. By this I do *not* mean that the justification must guarantee the truth of the outcome, but only that a comparative notion of "better than" be applicable. This adequacy has three levels of application: (a) adequate for individuals, (b) adequate for institutional and social modes of concept use, i.e., adequate for language games as played, (c) adequate for long-range historical pat-

---

*The first two requirements are adaptions of requirements on conceptual change to be found in Toulmin (1972). I am greatly indebted to Toulmin's work, and the evolutionary account I shall be offering in chapter 6 owes much to him as well as to Donald Campbell. However, I believe the criteria have here been generated straightforwardly out of a consideration of the *Meno* dilemma.

terns of learning and enquiry. In terms of the *Meno* dilemma: our learning must be adequate for human life.

5. *Interaction of world and purpose on representational schemes:* Both the brute fact of the world and the influences of our choices, purposes, and activities on our modes of representation, and, hence, on our modes of learning and knowing must be taken into account. In terms of the *Meno* dilemma: we must slip between the horns.

What sort of promising approaches are there, then, for meeting such criteria of adequacy? The representational schemes into which concepts enter must be justifiable, and, even more importantly, these representational systems are to be changed only for some good, not necessarily conclusive, reason. Historically, representational systems have changed primarily in order to reflect most adequately the truth about the world. Our judgments about truth, i.e., our belief systems or theories, are couched in the concepts found in our representational schemes. For the received view the nature of those representational schemes was taken as relatively unproblematic. It was thought that we simply applied the schemes directly to our experience, with the basic observational data we had about the world as the result. Truth would consist of a correspondence between our beliefs and theories on the one hand and our experience given in the terms provided by our representational schemes on the other.

This neat picture changed drastically, however, under the impact of the arguments against the received view. There is no direct access to the world; our representational schemes themselves are intimately bound up with our beliefs and theories; and the influence of the world is seen to be indirect, affecting the theories and representational schemes as a whole. Still we can, I think, make sense of what my colleague Fred Will once called a philosophical concern for the truth. That is, we can ask how well our cognitive structures as wholes—representational schemes, theories, basic concepts and beliefs, methodologies for inquiry, and so on—allow us to deal with the world. And we can ask how and under what conditions we ought to make adjustments in our cognitive structures—how we can be rational. But rationality will now be broader than truth seeking. Truth seeking is only one among many purposes people have for constructing theories, concepts, and representational schemes. Human purposes now must also be seen as directly relevant to determining truth conditions. As Toulmin (1972, p. x) says: "A man demonstrates his rationality, not by a commitment to fixed ideas, stereotyped procedures, or immutable concepts, but by the manner in which, and the occasions on which, he changes those ideas, procedures and concepts."

There are, it seems, two major kinds of adaptiveness possible—assimilation and accommodation (Piaget, 1968). Briefly, assimilation is changing our experience to fit our conceptual and representational schemes, and accommodation is changing our conceptual and representational schemes to fit our experience. I shall explicate assimilation in the next chapter with the aid of the special science of control system theory and accommodation in the chapter following with the aid of evolutionary theory. I shall also attempt to make intelligible their relations by means of an account of reflective equilibrium, the same reflective equilibrium that I believe Socrates was seeking in the *Meno*. Thus, the promising approaches include the following:

1. The units of cognitive and epistemological significance must be taken as conceptual schemes, or language games, or paradigms, or the like.

2. The world must have an editing effect on our representational and conceptual schemes though we have no direct way of knowing the world.

3. A place must be found for the influence of human activity and purposes in shaping our conceptual schemes even at the level of determining truth conditions.

4. Reasonableness and rationality should be conceived as a general kind of adaptiveness. the adaptiveness must include assimilation, accommodation, and a reflective equilibrium between them.

5 | Assimilation

1. Assimilation and the Old-Knowledge Horn

The program that I sketched at the end of the previous chapter for solving the *Meno* dilemma makes central use of the idea of adaptiveness conceived of as a reflective equilibrium between assimilation and accommodation, thereby slipping between the horns of the dilemma. Assimilation is that portion of a general theory of adaptiveness most closely connected to the old-knowledge horn of the *Meno* dilemma and will be examined in some detail in this chapter with reference to results in control system theory. Recall that the proper epistemological unit is something on the order of conceptual schemes, cognitive structures, Wittgensteinian language games, or Kuhnian paradigms. These entities are what old knowledge consists of, and it is in terms of them that experience is assimilated. When accommodation or the acquisition of radically new knowledge is in question, it will be these holistic sorts of structures which will be considered to change.

A word or two needs to be said here about the concept of "experience." By "experience" I intend the full-blooded concept of perceiving, acting, and thinking about our lives, the sense contained in "His experiences as a nurse were quite interesting," "Experience is the best teacher," and "She is an experienced administrator." I do not refer to what philosophers sometimes call the immediate sensory given. When I say that assimilation is varying our experience to fit our conceptual schemes, I am claiming that in assimilation we are experiencing with or by means of our conceptual schemes. Likewise, when I say that accommodation is varying our conceptual schemes to fit our experience, I am claiming that our modes of experiencing are changing in response to inadequacies in earlier modes of experiencing.

The task for this chapter is to explain how experiencing with our conceptual schemes occurs. I need to account for how stable conceptual structures impose a similarity and continuity on the diversity of sensory stimulation and behavioral activity actually observed. To say no more than that conceptual systems do impose such unity and continuity is to give no explanation at all. There are wildly diverse physical stimulations that count as the same perception, and wildly diverse physical behaviors that count as action, psychologically (Fodor, 1975).

For example, we can perceive an acquaintance full on or from the side or back, in good light or poor, fleetingly or for a period of time, in various stages and kinds of dress, through a camera lens, behind a frosted glass door, in a photograph or painting, and so on. The variety of physical events that is thus subsumed under seeing the acquaintance is probably indefinite. How is such diversity assimilated under a single psychological concept? Or take actions. I can go to my office in an indefinite number of ways. I can walk (even walk backwards, or sideways, or crawl on my hands and knees), ride by bicycle, drive my car, take a bus; go by this route or that, travel fast or slow, stop to do an errand, and so on. Again the physical movements which can constitute my going to my office seem absolutely unlimited. How is such diversity assimilated under a single psychological concept?

There is also the question of how to account for minor variants within a given conceptual scheme. On the received view minor variants are handled by suggesting that we change our beliefs while holding our conceptual structures constant. On the current view, no such distinction can be made; concepts and beliefs change in more integrated ways, and so minor variations of concepts must be accounted for as well. An example is the child who has just learned the concept of "dog" and can distinguish dogs from cats, rabbits, and the like, and is then confronted with Aunt Louise's lovely Staffordshire porcelain dog. The concept of "dog" and associated beliefs will have to shift slightly, but not radically. How does the child assimilate this experience to the concept of "dog"?

Finally, the criterion of reasonableness must be met by an assimilative approach to the old-knowledge horn. That is, assimilation must be displayed as adaptively adequate for individuals. This involves showing how routine human action can be seen as reasonable, at least from the agent's point of view. To put it another way, this is one of the important points at which individual purposes and activities enter into and affect our representational schemes. There are also actions falling under institutionalized or social categories of reasonableness. Going for a walk is an individual activity. Walking in formation with a band in a parade involves social norms of reasonableness. General canons of rationality I leave for consideration in the next chapter.

Three of the criteria of adequacy I listed at the end of the previous chapter are, therefore, relevant to a consideration of assimilation as a way of grasping the old-knowledge horn of the *Meno* dilemma. These are, first, conceptual continuity, or seeing the unity in the diversity of physical stimulation and behavior; second, sources of concepts, or accounting for minor variations in conceptual schemes; and, third, reasonableness, or accounting for human purposes and action as individually and socially adequate. And all this must be done in the context of the interaction of purposes, action, and the indirect causal influence of the world on our representational and conceptual schemes. To put the point somewhat differently, assimilation is the generic concept I shall use for the "fine tuning" of a conceptual apparatus; accommodation is the generic concept I shall use for radical changes in a conceptual apparatus.

2. Rules, Rules, and Rules in Psychology

An interesting thing happens once attention is shifted to conceptual schemes as the focus of epistemological scrutiny. Prior to such a shift the grounding of knowledge was taken to be primarily a matter of finding the right basic particles, whether abstract forms or atomic sense data. After the shift the gounding of knowledge becomes a matter of finding out methods by which knowledge is obtained and organized. The shift is from *what* we know to *how* we know. Accompanying this shift from substance to method is a shift of interest from the nature of basic knowledge to the procedures and methodologies for acquiring it. To put the point in terms of Wittgensteinian language games, if we give up searching for the essence of any given term, we are left with looking at the ways in which it is used. And it takes but a moment's more reflection to note that these uses cannot be arbitrary and random, but rather must be regular and consistent for us to extract anything knowable from a study of meaning as use. And so the stage is set for the emergence of the concepts of "rule" and "rule following" as the central concerns of an epistemology that takes something like a conceptual scheme as the basic unit of concern. It is by reference to the rules of the conceptual scheme or language game that such approaches attempt to account for the reasonableness of experience, perception, belief, and activity in accordance with the scheme.

What I want to do in this section is to sketch three illustrations from contemporary psychology of the ubiquitous use of concepts like rules and norms, whether explicit or not. Rules, rule-following behavior, rule-guided behavior, rule-conforming behavior, rule-governed behavior, the application of rules, obeying a rule, tacit rules, and probably dozens of other variations are ideas central to explaining behavior. If I can give an account of how our ordinary action, thought, and behavior are norm regarding in this sense, I will have shown how assimilation as a part of a general theory of adaptiveness deals with the old-knowledge horn of the *Meno* dilemma. The cases I shall discuss come from psycholinguistics, social psychology, and artificial intelligence.

It should take no great amount of argument to show the central importance of the concept of rules for psycholinguistics. George A.

Miller (1970) wrote a fascinating essay entitled, "Four Philosophical Problems of Psycholinguistics." One of the problems he identified had to do with the nature of rules. There seem to be two main problems for Miller with regard to rules in psycholinguistics. Although loath to give up the theory of habit as a potential explanation for rule-governed behavior, Miller (p. 190) cites cases which "impress one intuitively with the huge gap between the simplest habits and the most complex systems of rules, yet the precise nature of this gap is difficult to characterize." That is, he cannot see how simple models of habit could possibly be deployed to account for complex systems of rule-governed behavior, but he can conceive of no other alternative. Second, Miller cites (p. 191) the familiar assertion by many linguists that "when a person knows a language, in the sense that his own utterances exhibit these observed regularities, there must be some sense in which he knows the rules of the language." The problem, well known, of course, is to say just what that sense is in which the person knows the rules of the language, for it is certainly *not* the case that the person can formulate the rules explicitly. Or, as Chomsky (1969, p. 23) puts it,

> The person who has acquired knowledge of a language has internalized a system of rules that relate sound and meaning in a particular way. The linguist constructing a grammar of a language is in effect proposing a hypothesis concerning this internalized system. The linguist's hypothesis, if presented with sufficient explicitness and precision, will have certain empirical consequences with regard to the form of utterances and their interpretations by the native speaker. Evidently, knowledge of language—the internalized system of rules—is only one of the many factors that determine how an utterance will be used or understood in a particular situation.

Here knowledge of a language is explicitly identified with an internalized system of rules—a philosophical grammar as it later turns out to be. This grammar is not a set of prescriptions about how people ought to speak, but part of an explanatory theory of how they can comprehend a natural language. And such a theory of competence is also an essential part of a larger theory of actual linguistic performance. It is a system of *rules* because, as Chomsky (1959) and others have argued so forcefully, a system of associations is inadequate to account for a native speaker's ability to produce and comprehend novel utterances. Furthermore, the whole notion of a deep grammatical structure as a system of rules which underlies our utterances clearly reflects the requirement of seeing the similarity in all the diverse actual speech acts we produce.

My second illustration comes from social psychology (Goffman, 1971; Lévi-Strauss, 1966; Harré, 1974). In this area the idea of rule-following behavior seems to constitute the very meaning of "the social." A familiar example will help. Writing a check to pay a bill is sometimes cited as a paradigm case in which the rules and institutions surrounding the transaction provide its (social) meaning. In the absence of the rules of banking, the economic norms of buying and selling, the law of contracts, and so on, writing numbers and names on a piece of paper simply does not have the significance of paying a bill. Indeed, even so simple a problem as how marks on a paper can constitute a signature requires a whole host of social rules as an explanatory context. In short, many, if not all, pieces of behavior are constituted as (social) actions in virtue of their conformity to certain social rules. And these rules provide the "appropriate" level of description for what is going on. That is, the description "paying a bill" unifies a whole host of disparate physical actions from signing checks, to making one's "mark," to making impressions with bits of plastic (credit cards), to passing paper and metal between people, and so on.

Beyond such constitutive rules, however, there are also strategic rules and rules of etiquette governing our social transactions. Although it is not always legal, people sometimes write checks "on the float." That is, they write a check in time to meet the deadline for paying a bill knowing that by the time the check clears their account, funds will have been deposited to cover it. This can be a useful strategy for avoiding finance charges. Further examples of etiquette and strategy rules could be given. "Write the stub of the check first." "One ought to begin the written description of the amount (as opposed to the numerical description) at the far left of the appropriate line." And so on.

Such social rules, unlike the linguistic rules involved in learning to speak a first language, are often taught explicitly. However, many are not, and it is not obvious that all need to be. Sometimes people can catch on to such rules. And in any event, it is even less clear that, once learned, these rules need be consciously applied to new situations. How, then, do such rules control and account for social behavior? Could we, perhaps, reduce the rules to some complex "habit theory"? Or is the level of description and explanation provided by social rules sui generis?

The last example of the centrality of the concept of rule comes from work in cognitive psychology, especially work with attempts to simulate human cognitive processes on a computer (Anderson and Bower, 1973). In such cases the rules being followed are the rules embodied in the computer program. To the extent that the program actually simulates human cognitive processes, these program rules are presumed to have their counterparts in the human mind. Once again, the concept of a rule, and following a rule, is crucial. To cite just one example, the input into Anderson and Bower's "human associative memory" (HAM) is in the nature of tree diagrams generated by linguistic or perceptual parsers which follow *rules* for transforming ordinary stimulus elements into the trees.

In the case of computer simulation we speak fairly comfortably about an explicit following of rules. In some sense, the computer applies the rules in the program in the course of its operation—much as the beginning logic student applies the rules of proof in constructing derivations. But even here there is the problem of identifying the "appropriate" situation in which to apply the rule. This problem is masked to a large extent in computer simulations by the fact that the inputs to the program are guaranteed to be perceptually appropriate. The relative simplicity and explicit nature of well-formed formulas are easy to simulate on a computer. Human perceptual systems have a much harder time of it because part of the learning task for humans is to come to recognize when the circumstances are "the same" so that the appropriate rule can be applied (Petrie, 1974a). I have already discussed this problem in the preceding chapter when I urged that cognitive structures are to be attached to the world through exemplars rather than through "applying" theory to practice. As Green (1967, p. 204) puts it, "To learn a principle [rule] is not, therefore, simply to develop a disposition to do the same thing in similar circumstances, but to learn what counts as 'doing the same thing' or what constitutes 'similar circumstances.' " (See also Wittgenstein, 1968). How, for example, do we differentiate a situation which calls for tact from one which calls for forthrightness? Once again, disparate physical situations are unified by an appropriate rule.

3. Rules and Rules in Philosophy

In this section I want to sketch two more examples of the central position of the concept of rules in human thought. The first has to do with accounts of human action. Psychologists, on the whole, view rules as part of a causal-explanatory framework. Many of a behaviorist persuasion would like to reduce rules to habits and colorless movements in response to stimuli. Others who are wary of such a reduction still believe that rules and the apprehension of them play straightforward causal roles in accounts of human behavior. Philosophers, on the other hand, tend to emphasize the justificatory and normative aspects of rules. What impresses philosophers is the fact that rule-following or rule-guided behavior can be assessed as more or less appropriate, more or less reasonable, and so on. Indeed, they are so taken with this aspect that many philosophers argue that an explanation of human action is of a fundamentally different sort from that sought by much of contemporary psychology (Meldon, 1961; Peters, 1960; Ryle, 1949). Such philosophers admit that in cases of breakdowns in normal human action, compulsive activities, and mere reflex behavior, causal explanations of the type sought by psychologists may be appropriate, but not for full-blooded human actions.

Thus Peters (1960, chap. 1) argues that the basic model for understanding ordinary human action is a purposive rule-following one. That is, there are social norms, customs, and rules that constitute the appropriate description of actions falling under these norms. Not only does a reference to norms constitute the appropriate description of some piece of behavior as an action, but that very classification also serves, in the ordinary case, as an explanation of the action. One explains an action by setting it in the context of such normative expectations and rules. No further, causal, explanation is appropriate in such a rule-governed context. "Why did he cross the street?" "To get some tobacco," "To catch his bus," and even "To get to the other side": all explain by putting the action into a purposive rule-following context. The particular parts of the context which are deemed relevant may vary from occasion to occasion, but essentially the action is explained by reference to the norms in their role as standards of assessment, justification, and reasonableness. Explanation of actions is on this view to be given in terms of reasons rather than causes.

Peters admits that causal language is appropriate for compulsion, and also, perhaps, for breakdowns in ordinary routines, but not for reasons. Another kind of explanation which bears at least a family resemblance to the rule-following model of explanation is explanation by reference to motives. Motive explanation, according to Peters, involves three characteristics. First, its propriety is properly assessable by reference to the norms of reason. This is because we ask for motives when the action does not fall under our ordinary norms and expectations, i.e., when there is a question as to its appropriateness. Second, motive explanations are of directed behavior. We assume that a goal or norm is operative; the goal is initially puzzling to us, however, so we ask for the motive and then assess it as worthy or not. Third, motive explanations must give *the* reason for the action. We do not attribute motives to people if we do not believe the motives were really operative. Once again the philosopher's concern with motive explanations is with the underlying rules and norms in their role of providing standards of assessment, and not with the potential causal role of the motive.

All human action that fits into the purposive, rule-following model is, for that very reason, subject at a basic level to assessment as more or less intelligent, more or less suited to the end. At this level, even an animal's behavior can be seen as intelligent or not. It is instructive to note the kind of language typically used to describe the intelligence of human action. Peters (1960, pp. 23, 46), for example, says: "It really was a goal in the sense that our movements flowed towards it in an unimpeded and co-ordinated manner. . . . And anything is called a goal if we can see that behavior *varies* concomitantly with changes in the situation which we call the goal in the conditions necessary to attain it."

Note the ease with which concepts like adaptiveness are used in describing the flowing result of intelligence as it constantly adjusts action to changes in situation and goal. How could causal explanation ever account for such delicate fine tuning of behavior? How could a reference to the norm-regarding nature of rules ever do more than redescribe such delicate adjustments? Once more the reference to a rule and rule following enables us to see diverse patterns of behavior as essentially unified in virtue of their regard for the rule.

Yet the psychologists' concern with the mechanisms of production of intelligent behavior does not seem obviously out of place. Can we really do no better in explaining action than see the purposes and rules it follows? Why can we not ask how those rules operate? Thus the minimally norm-regarding nature of human action situates it neatly on the borderline between obviously empirical explanations in terms of production and effect, and obviously philosophical assessment by norms and reasons. And the concept of "rule" is precisely the crucial bridge idea.

My second example of a philosophical concern for rules involves the "norms of reasons." Peters (1974a, pp. 147–48) says: "Human beliefs and behavior cannot be made intelligible without the basic postulate of the rationality of man. But this, in its turn, can only be made intelligible if we write into rationality the responsiveness to normative demands." That is, above the level of the norm-regarding nature of ordinary human action—its intelligent character, so to speak—is the level of reason and rationality. Norms are necessary to constitute human action as intelligible, goal directed, purposive, and rule following. The norms are implicit in the basic level of description of action as action. But once we know what a person did, and even why it was done, we may still ask if the action was reasonable. And in answering that question, we have recourse to the norms of reason.

What are the norms of reason? Peters (1974a, p. 127) characterizes them in fairly general terms as "the normative demands of consistency, relevance, impartiality, and the search for grounds for belief and decision." These general norms require subsidiary ones such as clarity of expression and honesty in checking assumptions, evidence, and reasoning. Once more we see the philosopher's predominant concern for assessment and justification. But even here, we can make sense of a psychologist's concerns for whether or not and in what way these very high-level norms are ever operative in human behavior. Are people guided by a concern for consistency? Under what conditions? And while it may be the case that the psychologist will be unable even to formulate such questions unless the nature of a concern for consistency is presupposed, it still seems sensible to ask why people ever do have a regard for consistency.

Peters (1974a, p. 143) suggests that we can go no further at this point than ascribing to persons two basic but related dispositions to respond to experience—assimilation and accommodation. We do tend to impose a conceptual scheme on our experience to the extent that we can, and we do modify that conceptual scheme when necessary in the light of recalcitrant experience. These processes embody for Peters the basic norms of assessment.

But there is a crucial ambiguity lurking in such a characterization of the norms of reason as basic and beyond question. Peters may mean that human beings possess what I have called a philosophical concern for truth, a very general concern for how well our cognitive schemes as wholes allow us to deal with the world both in thought and in deed. But as I have developed the idea of a philosophical concern for the truth, it depends upon a naturalized epistemology which gives full rein to the possibility that results in the empirical sciences may supply us with at least part of the response to our concern for truth. This emphasis on a naturalized epistemology was motivated by the failure of the philosophical attempts to provide general, presuppositionless, or self-evident accounts of knowledge, learning, and rationality. We have only the actual historical processes, both empirical and philosophical, of persons dealing with the world via the representational schemes constructed in response to human purpose and the editing effects of the world. If this is the sense in which Peters views assimilation and accommodation as basic to the development of reason, then I have no quarrel, but likewise there seems to be every reason to supplement Peters's story with a naturalistic account of how these processes arose, under what conditions they change, and how we shift between assimilation and accommodation.

But Peters objects to such a naturalistic account of the norms of reason, and on precisely the grounds that such an account cannot properly make intelligible the rules and rule following which are centrally involved. For this reason, it does not seem that Peters intends his norms of reason to be construed as another way of talking about what I have called the philosophical concern for the truth. Rather, he must be interpreted as attempting to provide a general account of rationality after all—an account that is prior to and presupposed by the special sciences. In short, Peters is attempting to grasp the old-knowledge horn of the *Meno* dilemma, not by identifying basic elements we already know, but in a neo-Kantian way by attempting to find *methodological* norms and procedures, the norms of reason, that will guarantee the objectivity and rationality of the representational schemes and cognitive structures we develop.

In any event, the centrality of the concepts of rules and norm-regarding behavior is apparent even at the level of norms of reason. And at this level too there is the critical tension between, on the one hand, the concern for the causal or "operative" role of rules as they figure in explanations of human behavior, and, on the other hand, the concern for the assessment or "normative" role of rules as they figure in justifications of human behavior. Once more we can see the unifying effect that a reference to rules has in classifying otherwise very diverse phenomena of testing, asserting, questioning, denying, inferring, and the like as part of the development of reason—or, as I would put it, our adaptive dealing with the world. From the implicit rules of transformational linguistics, to the constitutive rules of socially defined action, to the explicit rules of computer simulation of thought, to the purposive rule-following model of human action, clear up to the guiding norms of reason, the concept of a rule, in both operative and assessment modes, is crucial.

4. A rule is a rule is a rule is a. . .

One of the common distinctions often drawn between different kinds of rules is that between descriptive and prescriptive rules—between rules which describe or explain linguistic or social behavior as it is empically observed, and rules which prescribe correct grammar or social behavior. In one sense, the descriptive-prescriptive distinction is similar to the operative-assessment concerns which I have been using to distinguish psychologists' and philosophers' concerns with rules. And, of course, in that sense the distinction is a perfectly valid one. Psychology is, and ought to be, concerned with the descriptive sense, and philosophers with the prescriptive sense, of rules. At the same time, however, I believe that this distinction has also been one of the most pernicious influences hindering a proper recognition of the unique function of descriptive rules as part of an explanatory model. The problem is that once the prescriptive variety of rules has been noted, it becomes nearly impossible to see that descriptive rules still have a fundamental norm-regarding feature. If rules are normative, it is mistakenly thought they must be prescriptive. Once the norm-regarding nature of descriptive rules is overlooked, the temptation for psychologists to assimilate descriptive rules to empirical generalizations, and to habits in particular, becomes virtually irresistible; and since prescriptions belong in the realm of assessment, philosophy fastens on prescriptive rules, and the temptation to deny a causal explanatory role to rules also becomes irresistible.

Let me illustrate in my examples the operation of this essential norm-regarding feature of descriptive rules. Within a theory of linguistic competence, we do not count a nongrammatical or anomalous piece of verbal behavior—such as "the is of when"—as contrary to some psychological generalization as to what linguistic strings will or will not occur, but, rather, depending on how far the behavior strays from the norm, we may not even count it as a piece of language. The example above does not meet the minimal conditions for being a meaningful utterance, and thus the rules of language *legislate* what counts as *appropriate* linguistic behavior. This legislation is not on the level of linguistic etiquette or even linguistic strategy—that kind of legislation might be construed as a prescriptive rule. Rather the legislation is on the *constitutive* level of what counts as meaningful discourse. These rules are what enable us to decide whether very different physical phenomena such as sound waves, marks on paper, and typing are or are not linguistic behavior.

With respect to social systems what constitutes writing a check is defined by reference to the rules, the norms, for classifying any piece of behavior as that of writing a check. Once again at the descriptive level, behavior must be *appropriate* in order to be judged as the writing of a check, and once more, some deviations are allowed, but when they become too large, the deviation is "ruled" out.

Even in the case of the computer simulation the rules of the program, as opposed to the physics of the hardware, are norm regarding in the sense I am discussing. The input to the linguistic parser must be judged to be signal as opposed to noise, to be a linguistic string as opposed to something else. As I have mentioned, this requirement is not always obvious since computer programs generally ignore the perception problem by designing the inputs to be automatically perceptually significant. Yet significant they must be.

Philosophers recognize the essentially norm-regarding nature of descriptive rules in that such norms are precisely what is stressed in, for example, the purposive rule-following model of human action. Yet, they are seduced in the opposite direction into trying to assimilate the norms to contexts of assessment. However, it is on the constitutive level of description that the norm-regarding character of human action must be emphasized and not (necessarily) on the prescriptive level. Norms at the descriptive level provide us with conceptual tools for classifying very diverse physical behavior as the same. The question is, how is that possible?

Once the sense in which even descriptive rules are norm regarding in being constitutive of certain kinds of meaningful behavior is recognized, an explicit-implicit distinction between kinds of rules is often invoked. That is, there is the temptation to reserve the notion of a rule for those cases in which the rules are explicitly formulated. Typical models here include the constitutive rules of chess and the explicit rules of logical deduction. The movement of a chess piece that does not accord explicitly with the rules fails to count as a move in chess. A step in a proof that is not in accordance with the rules is not a part of the proof. There is, of course, a border area of wrong or illegal moves, but these shade off into not being moves at all.

Much educational practice seems to subscribe implicitly to the view that for activity to be rule governed, the rules must be explicit. It then becomes natural to insist that if certain actions are constituted by explicit rules and we want people to engage in that kind of behavior, we must teach them the explicit rules. But it is surely a mistake to suppose that this is what we must do. People reasoned correctly and evaluated their reasoning long before Aristotle began to make the rules of logic explicit, and even now that such rules have been made explicit, it is not at all clear that a course in formal logic will help us reason any better. It is a prejudice to suppose that we must consciously apply explicit rules in order to reason correctly. Not even logicians do that. The point is that perfectly proper judgments of good and bad reasoning are often made without appeal to explicit rules.

But at the same time normative judgments are unintelligible without *presupposing* rules or principles. A piece of reasoning is good or bad *because* it does or does not come up to the standard, the criterion, of good reasoning. We must somehow know what we are doing. But in such cases where the norm is implicit and not even consciously held, what is the criterion for the operation of rules? We must look at the attitude taken toward the behavior manifested in situations that would be violations of the supposedly implicit norm. For rules to be operating in such situations such behavior must in some way be judged as "incorrect"—as violations of the norm. The idea of correcting the behavior in the direction of the norm must be applicable even in cases of implicit norms.

It might, nevertheless, be objected that rules are rigid, formal, explicit, and consciously followed, and that norm-regarding behavior which is not of this nature must be called something else. It may be that in ordinary use the term "rule" does have such a narrow range of application. However, I am trying to call attention to some crucial and important similarities between a narrow notion of rule-governed behavior and a broader notion of norm-regarding behavior. These similarities are, I believe, so important that the narrow notion of rule-governed behavior deserves to be broadened to encompass all cases of norm-regarding behavior (Polanyi, 1966; Haynes, 1977).

In a slightly different manner, Max Black (1967) demonstrates a continuum of uses of the concept of rule. At one end is what he calls *rule-invoking* behavior, which is characterized by a fairly explicit attention to explicit rules, e.g., filling out an income tax return or following a recipe. Next, *rule-accepting* behavior occurs when the agent is not explicitly applying a rule, but would immediately accept an adequate formulation if one were offered, e.g., the experienced cook who makes a hollandaise sauce without consulting the recipe. Then, there are cases of *rule-guided* behavior in which the routines involved in the rule, even in the rule-accepting sense, merge into a new unitary perception of the situation. Good examples here are seeing where the knight can move in chess instead of working it out, and, even more impressively, seeing that one is, for example, "strong in the center." This kind of behavior is essential for becoming really expert in a field. Finally there is *rule-covered* behavior in which a rule may be formulatable by some appropriately placed outsider, but does not in any obvious sense have to be accepted or invoked or even guide one's behavior as those terms have already been defined. The example Black uses here is of the complex rules of physics which describe how we keep our balance on a bicycle.

The order of pedagogy, however, need not follow the order of how explicitly rules are held. Black suggests that often we must train or even condition people into much rule-covered behavior, e.g., learning to ride a bicycle, or forming a purl stitch in knitting. Then we might put such basic skills to use in more complex rule-invoking activities. As the student gets better he or she internalizes such routines into rule-accepting behavior and ultimately may become expert in seeing the situation whole—rule-guided behavior.

Black makes a sharp distinction between rule-covered behavior and the other kinds of rule-governed behavior on the basis of the possibility of providing a linguistic formulation of the rules in all but the rule-covered case. This formulation is primarily to enable Black to speak of all but rule-covered behavior as more or less adequate, more or less reasonable. Thus he reflects the philosopher's pull to assessment in all but rule-covered behavior. Rule-covered behavior, on the other hand, is held by Black to be primarily of psychological interest. Yet even in the rule-covered case Black is constrained to use the notion of rule to gather together and make intelligible the diverse physical behaviors that fall under even so simple a description as riding a bicycle. Furthermore, we can assess skill in riding a bicycle without knowing the underlying principles of physics. Our ordinary perception of these complicated physical activities is called, simply, "riding a bicycle." It is because the notion of a rule enables us to group together such diverse physical activities that I am urging an expansion of the concept of rule into the broader area of norm-regarding behavior.

Let me offer one last indirect argument for a broadened conception of rules. Explicit rules can be and sometimes are changed. Why? Consider the arguments for a proposed rule change in chess. They would appeal to the general purposes of games like chess and the extent to which the proposed change might help or hinder such purposes. We would also cite the consequences for playing the game and the revisions that would be entailed. I have been told, for example, that at one point in the history of chess the queen's versatility of movement was increased precisely because the game had become too routinized—much like a complicated tic-tac-toe. In short, one argues over the appropriateness of such changes. Appropriate to what? The implicit standards, purposes, goals, norms we ordinarily do not consciously hold, but which are to be found in the historical practice of games like chess. So judgments as to the appropriateness of changing explicit rules are made by reference to implicit historical norms of practice, and as such are a species of norm-regarding behavior.

Norm-regarding behavior in this broadened sense involves judgments—judgments that *this* behavior is appropriate or falls under the norm. And in such judgment it seems possible to distinguish such norm-regarding behavior from mere habit, even if the behavior does not consciously follow the norm. The concert pianist knows when a wrong note has been hit even though no conscious episode of the form, "Now that note was appropriate to the score and I missed," occurs. The pianist just plays, concentrating on technique and especially interpretation. In the case of mere habits, on the other hand, we do not judge the appropriateness of behavior, but rather the same circumstances simply call forth the same behavior. There is no obvious way in which there can be mistakes in habitual behavior. We can acquire bad habits, or unintended habits, but the notion of there being a mistake in the operation of the habits seems queer. Habits are what they are.

It is perhaps misleading to speak of "judgments" of appropriateness in norm-regarding behavior; for such language is heavily biased toward conscious activity and the judgments need not be conscious at all. Furthermore, the language of judgment seems to suggest the "application" of rules to situations independently recognized. I have already argued that we do not apply theory to practice, but that we rather structure experience in terms of theory. Thus a more adequate formulation would be in terms of seeing the situation as one in which the given norm-regarding behavior is appropriate. I recognize this as a situation in which the writing of a check is called for. In short, I experience or perceive the situation in the descriptive terms provided by the norm or rule, and it is because of my perception of the situation as appropriate to the given norm that I behave as I do (Fodor, 1975, p. 74).

But there is another crucial feature of norm-regarding behavior which must be noted here. Although my perception of a situation as appropriate for behavior of a certain variety is in some sense operative in producing that behavior, nevertheless, the behavior need not always completely live up to the norm. I may misspeak. I may enter inconsistent amounts on my check. The pianist may strike the wrong note. My proof strategy may fail. My behavior may not live up to the norm, but unless the behavior is grossly inadequate, it may still be appropriately described and thought of as norm-regarding. Conversely, there are actions which bring about certain unintended states. In such cases the state is not necessarily to be regarded as being the goal referred to by the norm implicated in the given action. A teacher may unintentionally cause his or her pupils to become indoctrinated, and yet it might be false to say that the teacher actually indoctrinated the students. In other cases we might want to hold the teacher responsible for the indoctrination whether intended or not. How can we tell such cases apart?

The test for whether the behavior was aimed at the actually occurring state, and, hence, properly characterizable by it, would be whether impediments and disturbances to reaching the state are treated as mistakes. If they are, then what the person is doing is properly describable in terms of the end state as a goal. If disturbances to the course of action leading to the supposed goal are not resisted, then what the person is doing is not properly described by the goal, even though that state may in fact be reached.

Such a situation almost never happens when we are speaking of purely descriptive generalizations that lack the norm-regarding feature. For example, it would certainly be possible that there has never been and never will be a completely error-free performance of some complex piece of music. If that is so, and we tried as good empiricists simply to describe all the performances as they actually occurred, we would at best get some rather strange-looking statistical approximation to the actual score. Yet clearly such a generalization does not capture what any performer was doing. The performer was playing the piece, even if there were mistakes. The statistical generalization level of description is simply all wrong. The performer was engaged in norm-regarding behavior even though the norm was not perfectly fulfilled. I was writing a check even though I made a mistake. Another way of looking at the distinction I am attempting to draw here is that what eventuates as a result of our doings is not always what we are properly described as doing.

To summarize: although falling short of an analysis of "rule," the following, not necessarily independent, conditions seem to be criteria of a rule:

1. *The normative condition:* Although rules can be divided into prescriptive and descriptive, descriptive rules presuppose norms just as do prescriptive rules. Behavior in accordance with descriptive rules is norm-regarding; it requires seeing the appropriateness of the norm in diverse situations.

2. *The self-correcting condition:* Norm-regarding behavior can be in accordance with implicit or unconscious rules, if we stand ready to correct deviations from the norm and recognize our mistakes.

3. *The perceptual-causal condition:* In norm-regarding behavior it is *because* we perceive (judge) a situation as structured or constituted by the operative rule that we behave as we do. Again, the rule need not be consciously invoked.

4. *The nonsuccess condition:* We can properly be said to be following a rule without succeeding in attaining the norm implicit in the rule.

5. . . . But a Rule Isn't a Generalization

Egon Brunswik (1952) provides an illuminating lens model of stimulus-response generalizations (see figure 3). The "stimulus" object represented by one distal focus can affect the sensors of the organism on different occasions by very different physical means, represented by the bundle of "rays" leading to the "lens" or organism. Likewise the organism's behavior can achieve the same response—the other distal focus—by quite different specific behaviors. Another way of expressing the insights in Brunswik's lens model is in terms of the classical psychological problem of the definition of the stimulus and the response (Campbell, 1966).

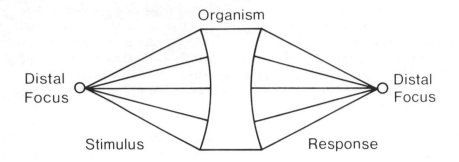

Figure 3. The Lens Model of Stimulus-Response Generalizations. Adapted from Egon Brunswik, *The Conceptual Framework of Psychology* (University of Chicago Press, 1952)

This picture neatly describes the situation in most stimulus-response theorizing. But the lens metaphor misleadingly suggests to many psychologists that with enough work the generalization underlying the connection of the distal stimulus to the distal response can be found, much as the laws of light explain the focusing properties of lenses. I do not believe that a rule can be reduced to a descriptive causal or statistical generalization, nor will habits account for norm-regarding behavior. As I have been pointing out at some length, the situation in the case of action is that the rays in the stimulus (or response) bundle are wildly different in any physical sense. Even a rat can press a lever with any number of different muscle arrangements, e.g., by sitting on it or dropping an object on it. Thus the power of the organism to "focus" its detailed specific behavior onto an action which turns out to be the same action each time or to focus its detailed stimulation onto the same stimulus is the power of *judging* or *perceiving* the action and the situation to be appropriate to the norm involved. The focussing metaphor must be explicated in terms of the appeal to norms defining very different detailed stimulations or responses as "the same." On the level of generalization, we could determine the minimum force needed to trip a lever, and, quite independently of any normative judgments, the lever will be tripped by that force. On the other hand, it is only by reference to the norm of what counts as lever tripping that we could judge that the event described as my asking a research assistant to trip the lever could count as lever tripping.

Considerations such as these lead to an examination of the perceptual-causal condition of rules. In rule-following behavior it is not just that the norm determines or constitutes what will count as the same stimulus or behavior, but also that in some sense it is *because* of the perception of the situation as appropriate to the norm that we do what we do. In some sense the judgment or perception of the situation as appropriate to the norm causes or at least is operative in producing the action. In commonsense terminology the organism behaves as it does in order to reach a goal, which is defined by the norm. But, of course, this introduces teleology into rule-following behavior with a vengeance, and modern psychology has spent a good portion of its short history trying to do away with teleology.

One of the main reasons for objecting to teleolgy has been that psychologists committed to straight-line causal models have been at a loss, conceptually, to explain how a nonexistent goal can cause present behavior directed toward that goal. Causation appears not to work that way, and in the absence of an alternative model the most rational course for psychology has seemed to be to deny the efficacy of goals. An alternative for the more cognitively oriented psychologists has been to move to explanatory models consisting of a presently occurring desire for the goal along with beliefs about means to attain it. Such presently occurring beliefs and desires could, conceptually, serve as causes. The difficulty with this move is that an indefinite number of beliefs and desires are needed to account for all of the nuances of behavior and adaptive changes of behavior that occur in different situations leading to the same goal. In terms of Brunswik's lens model in figure 3, the "rays" are indefinite in number, and are rays of the *same* bundle solely in virtue of their leading to the same goal. The goal in mind determines what "rays" could possibly be a part of the bundle, and that still seems to be the wrong direction of influence for a causal generalization account. Norm-regarding behavior, on the other hand, seems to be determined by judgments as to the appropriateness of the given situation to the norm or goal.

The self-correcting criterion of rule-following behavior also seems at odds with a habit or generalization account. Habits seem to be relatively narrow-tracked dispositions and are often contrasted with the adaptive nature of principled or rule-following behavior (at least in the broadened sense of norm-regarding that I am here urging). If our behavior is under the influence of habit, then we engage in it whether appropriate or not; whereas, the self-correcting nature of rule-following behavior implies a sensitivity and responsiveness to changing situations. To cite a shopworn example, a parrot may acquire the habit of saying hello in response to a certain stimulation, but there seems a world of difference between the parrot's automatic mechanical response and that of a person who understands the norms of greeting and says hello in response to those norms. It may be that very complex habits or generalizations might be discovered that could account for the apparently indefinite plasticity and adaptiveness of norm-regarding behavior; however, it is clear that no examples of such theories currently exist.

There is, however, a deeper reason why no account of self-correcting behavior in terms of causal generalizations is likely to be successful. Self-correcting behavior presupposes a standard or norm of correctness. But, as already noted in discussing the perceptual-causal condition, the perception or judgment of the situation as appropriate for the operation of the norm is causally efficacious in producing the "correcting" behavior. The purpose of the correcting behavior in turn is to correct the deviation from the norm. The norm operates in its own realization in the situation. Ordinary causal generalizations do *not* operate in their own production or realization. In a sense, this is the same point often made by philosopers to the effect that conceiving of human actions in terms of a purposive rule-following model constitutes explaining them by bringing to light how the action fits into the patterns specified by the rule. Thus the action of crossing the street to get some tobacco realizes the norm or goal of getting tobacco. The norm operates in its own realization. Philosophers go on from this insight, illegitimately I shall later argue, to urge that because of this logical connection between norm and the the action it rationalizes, we cannot give any further psychological explanation of the action. In any event, the situations described in straightforward causal generalizations have no such role in their own production.

Finally, consider the nonsuccess condition. Norm-regarding behavior is still classifiable as such even if the norm is not attained. There is a serious conceptual problem here for those who would reduce norm-regarding behavior to generalizations. For when situations do not correspond to hypothesized generalizations, that counts as evidence against the generalization. Of course, a few anomalies can be tolerated, but not too many. On the other hand, behavior that is norm-regarding can fail to create the norm and not count at all against describing the behavior in terms of the norm. Indeed the norm may never be reached, and the norm-regarding description would still not be refuted. Recall the complex piece of music. There are some limits here. The behavior usually and over a period of time has to come close to the norm, and it must always be corrective in the direction of the norm, to be described as norm regarding, but it need not get there. With generalizations such a situation would necessarily count against the truth of the generalization. It is unclear how generalization theories would handle this difficulty.

Finally, I shall offer a formal argument to refute the possibility that an analysis of norm-regarding behavior could be given by a straight-line causal generalization account in terms of necessary and sufficient conditions (see Ryan, 1970). One form of the basic locution used in the purposive rule-following model is "X in order to Y." I crossed the road in order to get some tobacco. X refers to an action and Y to the goal which explains the action. Note here that in a sense "crossing the road" is not a fully specific description of the action on the rule-following model of action. We do not immediately see the point of the action, and to specify it fully we need to set it into the context of the norms or goals that rationalize it; hence the "in order to get some tobacco." Once fleshed out in this way the action is ipso facto explained on the rule-following model. Once we appreciate that the complete description of the action would be something like "getting some tobacco," we will on the rule-following account have explained the action by referring to its point or goal. Those who favor a causal generalization approach to explanation would insist on the finer analysis of "crossing the street in order to get some tobacco," X in order to Y. For that reason I shall use that locution although on the rule-following model the "proper" description of the action would unify the two "parts."

Presumably, to fit the generalization model of explanation X would have to be either a necessary or a sufficient condition of Y or both. But in fact it is neither.

X cannot be a sufficient condition for Y because of the self-correcting condition on norm-regarding behavior. Alterations in behavior X are used to correct deviations from Y and maintain behavior which constitutes achieving the goal. Thus I may stop crossing the street momentarily if a car is approaching in order better to get to the other side. If X were a sufficient condition of Y, however, changes in X ought to produce corresponding changes in Y; my stopping ought to change my goal, but it does not. Second, the nonsuccess condition shows that the goal may not actually be reached by a given action. Recall the mistake in playing the piece on the piano. The behavior of hitting the wrong note, X, need not count against playing the piece, Y. But it would have to if X were a sufficient condition of Y. Third, X's being a sufficient condition of Y reverses the ordinary meaning of "X in order to Y." In accordance with the perceptual-causal condition, we commonly take Y to explain X.

Nor can X be a necessary condition of Y in "X in order to Y." First, since Y need not actually be reached, it is hard to see what explanatory work it could be doing with respect to X. Second, if X is a necessary condition for Y, Y is a sufficient condition for X. Yet the goal, Y, may be reached fortuitously. But if Y is a sufficient condition for X, then the action, X, would be required. The self-correcting condition on rules insists that we merely stand ready to initiate behavior to reach the goal *Y*.

6. Control Systems

If causal generalizations give little promise of explaining norm-regarding or rule-following behavior, what account can we give? I believe the special science of control system theory, properly understood, provides a promising conceptual model for understanding and giving a unifying perspective to the wide range of examples of norm-regarding behavior I have mentioned. For a detailed description of control systems in psychological theorizing, I refer the reader to a seminal work by William T. Powers, *Behavior: The Control of Perception* (1973a). Here I will use a more generalized diagram and explanation by Powers (1973b) of the basic control system unit of behavioral organization in an attempt to show that the basic concepts provide a method for attacking the problems of the explanation of norm-regarding behavior (see figure 4). My procedure is somewhere between explication and

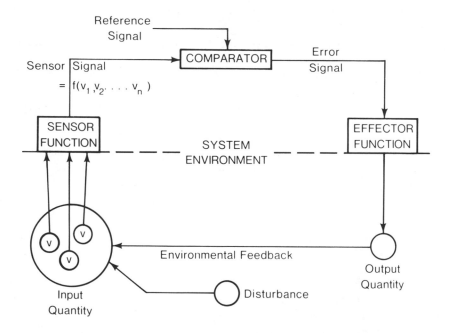

Figure 4. The Basic Control System Unit of Behavioral Organization. Redrawn from W. T. Powers, "Feedback: Beyond Behaviorism," *Science* 179 (26 January 1973): 351–56, Figure 1. Copyright 1973 by the American Association for the Advancement of Science

methodological proposal. I am in essence saying that this model conceptually meets the criteria I have developed for norm-regarding behavior, and gives promise of new and more powerful understanding.

Powers (1973b, p. 352) describes his model as follows:

> The *Sensor function* creates an ongoing relationship between some set of environmental physical variables (*v*'s) and a *Sensor signal* inside the system, an internal analog of some external state of affairs. The sensor signal is compared with (subtracted from, in the simplest case) a *Reference signal* of unspecified origin. The discrepancy in the form of an *Error signal* activates the *Effector function* (for example, a muscle, limb, or subsystem) which in turn produces observable effects in the environment, the *Output quantity.* This quantity is a "response" measure. The environment provides a feedback link from the output quantity to the *Input quantity,* the set of "*v*'s" monitored by the sensor function. The input quantity is also subject, in general, to effects independent of the system's outputs; these are shown as a *Disturbance,* also linked to the input quantity by environmental properties. The disturbance corresponds to "stimulus." The system, above the dashed line, is organized normally so as to maintain the sensor signal at all times nearly equal to the reference signal, even a changing reference signal. In doing so it produces whatever output is required to prevent disturbances from affecting the sensor signal materially. Thus the output quantity becomes primarily a function of the disturbance, while the sensor signal and input quantity become primarily a function of the reference signal originated inside the system. For all systems organized in this way, the "response" to a "stimulus" can be predicted if the stabilized state of the input quantity is known; the stimulus-response law is then a function of environmental properties and scarcely at all of system properties.

Despite the fact that Powers uses stimulus-response language, it should be clear even from his description that these are stimuli and responses of a very peculiar nature. The "stimulus" or disturbance is only part of what has traditionally been taken to be the stimulus in classical psychology. The other part is supplied by the effects of the organism behaving. Indeed, this is one of the central features of a feedback system—it reacts to its own effects. In fact its effects are "designed" in part to keep the input quantity as close to the reference level as possible. Variability of detailed output is unified by the requirement to keep the input close to the reference level. I will elaborate on this point below, but for now the important thing is to note that this is no ordinary S-R mechanism. Indeed, the explanatory force, as I shall show, goes through the input side of the loop, *not* the output side. Paradoxical as it sounds, what feedback systems do is control perceptions—not behavior.

It is important to note here that any organism is probably a mass of control systems, organized in complex trees and hierarchies. Indeed the reference signals for many lower-order systems will be the outputs of higher-order systems. Thus, for example, if I am pointing at an accelerating object with my finger, a very simple action, the output of the control system which is the basis of that action will have to serve as reference level for at least two other control systems. These would be the system controlling the angular displacement of my arm and the system controlling the rate of change of angular displacement of my arm. My purpose is not the important psychological one of beginning to map these control systems or even the theoretical purpose undertaken by Powers of giving enough detail to make the theory psychologically plausible. Rather my purpose is conceptual. The basic control system unit of behavior enables us to solve the conceptual problems that we have encountered in accounting for norm-regarding behavior. Thus, for the purposes of this book a control system should usually be thought of as the basis for an ordinary action, with the output of the system schematically representing a host of other control systems which form the basis of those things that have to get done in order for the original action—e.g., pointing—to occur.

Investigations into "black box" control systems to find out empirically what quantity is being controlled are clearly possible. The internal structure postulated by the model does have empirical implications which can be used to investigate the structure. Of course, the connection of control systems with the world is nothing like the naively direct one enjoined by a behaviorist methodolgy which defines all internal structural concepts operationally. Negative feedback neither relies on mystical purposes nor is unconnected with the world. It satisfies the requirement for having testable consequences without putting those consequences into the operational definition straightjacket. That is, from the psychologist's point of view, the control system model can be elaborated into an empirical theory, whereas the talk about the operation of purposes and goals often seems simply to redescribe the phenomena to be explained.

The way in which the control system model can be tested is in principle very simple. If we suspect a negative feedback system is in operation, we then hypothesize a controlled quantity for the system. Note that this "discovery" step depends on intuition and professional hunches no more than does the comparable step of suggesting fruitful empirical operations for the behaviorist. In any event, once a controlled quantity is hypothesized, the experimental procedure is this: introduce a disturbance near the sensor (it has to be the right order of magnitude so it neither escapes detection nor overwhelms the system) and see if the output opposes the disturbance. If it does, that quantity probably is being controlled. Further, different kinds of disturbances can be tried in order to rule out merely adventitious opposition to the disturbance. If there is no opposition to the disturbance, the hypothesized quantity is probably not under control. Utilizing the model we can even predict appropriate magnitudes.

Finally, note that the line of control of a feedback system runs through the perceptual or input side of the model. There are no reference signals delicately controlling the detailed outputs. Indeed the reference signal can stay the same and the detailed outputs can vary considerably precisely to counteract the effects of disturbances on the controlled quantity. Feedback controls *sensed* quantities, *not* outputs. It affects outputs to be sure, but it does not control them. The error signal causes the outputs but it does not adjust them except in the gross manner of "more error-more output." "Control" is a technical term which refers to the operation of the feedback system in maintaining the sensed signal near the reference signal no matter what the disturbance within the range of possible control. The perceived quantity will be brought to match the reference signal by means of a wide range of outputs.

There is, of course, much more to be said in explanation of the model. For one thing the characterization I have sketched above is highly abstract. Powers's very readable and exciting book gives many commonsense examples and fills in some of the psychological, neurological, and theoretical evidence for the model. Furthermore, there are a host of questions and problems that I have not touched. Some of these remain for investigation, but many of them are treated by Powers (1973a). Let me mention just a few. Where does the reference signal come from for any given system? How many hierarchies are there? How many individual systems? What is the nature of the sensor function, the effector function, the comparator function in any given system? Can systems be changed? How? How does a system come to be organized in the first place? What about memory, imagination, choice, consciousness, justification? Can systems conflict? What happens when they do? And so on.

These issues will all need to be treated in a more complete development of the control system model. For my purposes I will show that the abstract model just described meets perfectly the four conditions of rule-following or norm-regarding behavior elucidated above and gives some interesting insights into the examples of norm-regarding behavior with which I began this chapter. Control system theory thus promises a real alternative to habit or generalization accounts of rule-following behavior while at the same time preserving the philosopher's insights concerning rule-governed behavior.

7. A Rule by the Name of a Control System Actually Smells Sweeter

Clearly, the normative condition on rules and rule-following behavior is satisfied by the control system model. The reference signal is just the component to serve as a norm or goal or purpose. The system acts to change the environment so that the sensor or perceptual signal matches the reference signal. "I need to write a check to pay my monthly utility bill," says the reference signal. The system outputs operate with materials in the environment, paper and pens, until the sensor signals indicate a check has been written. (Actually about five or six levels of Powers's hierarchy of control systems would be involved in this action, but that complication can be ignored for present purposes.) The behavior controls the perception to make it match the reference signal.

Moreover, the self-correcting condition of rule-following behavior is obviously met by the model. Since control systems maintain the sensed environment in the condition specified by the reference signal, they counteract any external disturbance that would tend to deflect the controlled quantity from its reference level. "Writing a check" could be disturbed by any number of things which, if they registered as sensor signals, would create an error when compared with the reference signal and lead to corrective behavior. Such disturbances could be at any number of different levels. I might transpose some figures, misspell the name of the payee, remember I have insufficient funds in the bank, run out of ink, and so on. In each case, if sensed, such disturbances would lead to typically rulelike or norm-regarding self-corrective behavior.

Along similar lines, the nonsuccess condition is easily accounted for by the control system model. Occasionally disturbances may occur that overwhelm the system's effective range of control. If the system tends, nevertheless, to counteract such disturbances, the proper level of description of what is happening is still that given by the control system model. The musician who makes an error usually notices it and tries to correct it next time. Even if an error-free performance is never achieved, the musician is still properly described as "playing the piece." Or again, I may not have enough money to deposit to cover the check I want to write. If I try to borrow it or earn more, then I am clearly still behaving within the norms of checkwriting, even if I never actually write that particular check.

The most interesting thing, however, about the control system model is the way in which it satisfies the perceptual-causal condition. In the first place, the error signal, the difference between the reference signal and the sensor signal, is what drives the output. Thus the desired pattern, the reference signal, is operative in its own production in the situation as actually sensed. The system operates to reduce error—the difference between the desired pattern and the sensed pattern. Here is a physically realizable model that captures the essence of rule following in which the rule *as* a rule operates in producing rule-conforming behavior. For on the view that what is happening in a control system is that perceptions are being brought in line with goals, the "dimensions" of the goal treated as reference signal and the actual situation treated as sensor signal must be the same so that they can be compared. Yet it is the difference between desired and actual perception that operates through the effector function and through the natural laws of the environment to change the actual situation so that it is closer to the goal. If I want to get some tobacco and the movement of my legs across the street causes the perception of my getting closer to the tobacco, then I will just keep going. By recognizing that control systems control inputs, not outputs, we can at long last give a plausible account of directed behavior and how a rule or goal can operate in its own production.

But there is another important feature of the control system model related to the perceptual-causal condition. The line of control runs through the perceptual side of the model. The model does not delicately apply its outputs to indefinitely varying situations carefully changing the output or behavior to match the situation. Instead it controls its inputs or perceptions. It operates on the environment, changing the environment until a sensor signal is produced that matches as closely as possible the reference level. This feature accounts for the adaptability of rule-following behavior—as opposed to the straight-line operation of causal models. When an error is sensed, the system operates in *any* environment within the effective range of control using any means at its disposal to remove the disturbance and bring the perceptual signal in line with the reference signal. The error signal causes the effector function to operate, but it does not "control" it except perhaps in the sense of causing it to do "more" of whatever it does if the error is large and "less" if the error is small. The system is "blind" as to the nature of the effector function and "sees" through the sensor function only the changed situation which results from the operation of the effector function. And, indeed, that fits well with our ordinary notions. We are not *aware* of delicately controlling our muscles as we walk over uneven pavement. We are aware only that we are making whatever allowances have to be made.

Recall the classical behaviorist objection to purposes, goals, or rules as explanations of human behavior. A purpose or rule not yet in existence seemed unable to cause behavior leading to it. Recall also the classical move to meet the objection. The goal exists in present intentions and can be causal. It is a disposition to act. This reply is fine as far as it goes, but as has been argued repeatedly, it does not go far enough. The initial situation must still be perceived *in terms of* the intention or goal. Is the situation appropriate for the operation of the rule? The goal or role conceived as intention must still operate "backwards," in the sense that it at least partially structures the organism's perception of the existing situation. On a generalization view, there would be no way of knowing in detail what features of a novel situation would need changing to lead to the desired goal. But as soon as the model provides for the control of perceptions rather than behavior, the necessity for detailed knowledge of how to change a current situation into a desired one disappears. The system just acts, and, if at all adapted to the general environmental conditions in which it finds itself, will produce situations which give rise to perceptions closer to the goal or reference signal.

Nor, as I shall now argue, am I giving a trivial dispositional analysis. Often when a behavioral analysis of norm-regarding behavior is seen to be inadequate, there is a shift to a dispositional account. A goal is taken to be a disposition to behave in whatever ways are appropriate to reach the goal. Now either this account simply renames the problem of accounting for adaptive behavior and is hence trivial; or it faces the "overabundance" problem. For example, Peters's purposive rule-following model of human action appears to be a dispositional account that simply redescribes the action without really explaining it. If, however, we interpret Peters's account causally, we think of the disposition as being set off by varying occurrent beliefs and desires. These beliefs and desires will have to be minutely tailored to differences in the situation calling for just the right variations in the exercise of the disposition. Clearly we are conscious of no such meticulous control of outputs, but even if we waive the consciousness point, the situation remains intolerable. Since there are an indefinite number of potential variations, we would have to have an overabundance of unconscious occurrent desires and beliefs—far more than we could possibly admit. A dispositional account cannot cope with the overabundance problem, and yet the control system model with its control of perceptions, not outputs, solves the overabundance problem at a stroke.

One more feature needs to be noted concerning the control of perceptions. The line of control runs through the input side, but presumably ordinary causal mechanisms operate around the feedback loop in the opposite direction. Thus, as noted above in connection with Peters's account of the purposive rule-following model of human action, causal accounts are appropriate not for normal actions, but for breakdowns in normal action. And that is exactly right in terms of the control system model. When a control system is operating normally, what it is doing is bringing about a match between reference signal and perceived situation. The rule, *as* a rule, is operating in its own production. But when such a system breaks down, an analysis of the causal systems in the loop is often required. Again the control system model matches perfectly with the requirement derived from the philosophical analysis.

Furthermore, the model is not just a jargonistic redescription of commonsense notions or of other psychological theory. For it solves problems and promises insights which the psychologists' and philosophers' accounts did not. Returning to the example of psycholinguistics, we can now see in some detail why the transformationalists' critique of behaviorist language learning and use is so powerful. The transformationalists urge that an associationist account could not possibly explain the production and comprehension of an indefinite number of novel utterances, and they offer an account in terms of transformational rules instead. But adaptive rule-governed utterances in novel situations are formally identical with the infinite number of ways an output can remove a disturbance from a control system. If a certain deep structure is to be realized, the system will operate in (almost) any linguistic environment until it perceives that deep structure realized in the concrete situation. Neither behaviorism, nor causal generalizations, nor dispositional analyses seem capable of accounting for the adaptive novelty we actually find. Yet the control system model of behavior with its feature of the control of perceptions shows how we would expect such adaptive novelty as a matter of course.

D. W. Hamlyn (1978) is a good example of a philosopher who objects to the idea that learning rules is an appropriate or informative way of expressing what is going on when one learns a language. Hamlyn's objections are fairly straightforward. First, he construes learning rules as akin to learning explicitly formulated recipes. On this construal, it is obviously a mistake to suppose that a child learning a language is learning anything remotely resembling a recipe for forming past tenses, for example. Adult grammarians are hard put to formulate such explicit grammatical rules. It is absurd to suppose that every child who learns the language is doing so.

Second, Hamlyn objects to Chomsky's model of the child as a miniature scientist propounding hypotheses and testing these against the available linguistic data. One of Hamlyn's major concerns, which I share, is that too often we conceive of children as small adults without taking account of the possibility that children's ways of thinking, learning, and understanding may be quite different from those of adults. If "testing hypotheses" means consciously entertaining the hypotheses, designing experiments, and testing results, then the child conceived of as little scientist is indeed absurd.

Finally, Hamlyn argues that even if we could somehow construe the learning of rules as less than the conscious following of a recipe, we must also specify some independent access to the data. This is necessary so that our testing of the rules can get off the ground. In short, experience as the ground of the correct application of the rules must somehow be consulted. All of these objections seem to me to be well taken, given the model of learning rules that Hamlyn seems to presuppose. If rules must be as explicitly learned and followed as he assumes, then indeed the model is unlikely to be of much help.

At the same time, however, Hamlyn's own account plainly needs something very similar to the learning of rules. In criticizing extreme empiricist accounts of learning, Hamlyn (pp. 26–27) contrasts learning how and, hence, knowing how to do something with merely being able to do it. Knowing how for him involves a knowledge of principles, which, of course, does not imply that the principles can be formulated or stated. At the same time, however, Hamlyn explicitly rejects the idea that a knowledge of principles could be explicated by a causal theory of frequency of occurrence of particular instances or any such behaviorist ploy. Knowledge of principles looks much like knowledge of rules, albeit not a conscious, explicit knowledge of the rules.

In his account of perception Hamlyn (p. 72) is clear that "perceiving something involves applying knowledge to particular cases." Thus experience consists both of the causal conditions provided by sense perception and the application of knowledge and understanding to the particular case. The knowledge and understanding are of the concepts appropriate to the situation at hand. Thus, even perceptual experience for Hamlyn cannot be accounted for solely with causal language.

But for Hamlyn (p. 57), "having the concept of X involves a knowledge of the principles of classification that apply to xs." Thus, it is clear that it is crucial for Hamlyn's views of the growth of knowledge and understanding that we are able to make sense of a knowledge of principles, where principles seem to be essentially implicit rules.

One final example will show the importance of a knowledge of principles for Hamlyn. His account of how children do come to learn depends heavily on the possibility that they can be corrected by adults who share the form of life that gives point to the epistemological notions of truth, knowledge, understanding, and the like. In short, the notion of a correction does not presuppose something merely different from what has gone before, but rather different in the "right" way. As Hamlyn says (pp. 84–85):

> It would seem that a necessary condition of anything's being said to have knowledge (and perception too, since perception presupposes knowledge in at least the form of concepts) is that it is possible for it to stand in relations to us in the way that I have indicated. We cannot fully understand the possibility of such knowledge unless we see those who have knowledge in the framework of such relations (relations which, as I have argued, cannot be merely cognitive). What emerges from all this is the connection between such concepts as those of knowledge, truth, learning, the possibility of correction, common interests or wants, and thus the possibilty of standing in relation to other beings in ways which are at least akin to human relations.

What follows from all of this is that we cannot live with a knowledge of explicit rules as an account of knowledge, or without an account of norm-regarding behavior.

The account I have offered of norm-regarding behavior meets just the conditions that it must meet. It does not treat the language learner as a little scientist because the control system theory does not require consciousness of the rules or principles that are being followed. It does provide another access to the data other than the hypotheses or principles, namely, action.

Finally, the notion of correction is central to the control system account as well as to Hamlyn's. The difference is that correction in control system theory is not located solely in the social group doing the correcting, although it is located there as well. Recall that one of my earlier criticisms of Hamlyn was that in reacting against the view of the child set over against society, he adopted the view of a particular society set over against other historical and contemporary societies. By expanding the notion of correction beyond that obtaining within a given society, my account shows both how correction is necessary for understanding the growth of knowledge and how it can accommodate changes and differences in the specific notions of correction held by different societies at different times.

With respect to the social psychology example, the control system model shows how social rules of meaningfulness can constitute certain situations. The social rules serve as reference signals, and we learn them as well as ways of transforming physical situations into sensor signals that represent these social norms. Again, because the line of control goes through the perceptual side of the model, situations are "sensed as" being of certain kinds. This situation is a check-writing one, and it is perceived and treated as such. Control systems can, with appropriate input and output functions, control such nontangible items as social meanings. Social meanings are not at all mysterious with the control system model. The whole question of the "reduction" of the social to some more tangible ontology is avoided. Some very nonconcrete items can serve as controlled quantities.

As a number of workers (e.g., Rummelhart and Ortony, 1977) in artificial intelligence have begun to realize, the perceptual component of human intelligence is the one that has been most neglected in work to date. Computer simulation has been most successful in those areas in which the perceptual component is highly explicit, even though the problems of concern are highly abstract. Proving logic theorems is an excellent example. The explicit rules of well-formedness and legitimate inference leave little room for perceptual ambiguity by either person or machine. The perceptual component is there; it is just nonproblematic in much current work. What the control system model does is to point to the structural features which must be simulated if computer programs are to advance beyond theorem-proving capabilities. Perceptual components must be built, and they must be built not only with atomistic, bottom-up features analyzers, but also with top-down Gestaltist control systems. For the control system model exhibits on its face the Gestaltist insight that the whole determines the significance of its parts, and even what will count as parts.

It is also easy to see that the control system model does not simply redescribe the purposive rule-following model of human action in jargonistic terms. In discussing the rule-following model Peters (1960, pp. 8–9) draws a distinction between a person's reasons for acting and the reasons the person acts. For example, I might give my reason for crossing the street as wanting to see what is in a shop window; whereas, *the* reason may be that I want to avoid a group of young rowdies on my side of the street. Most often a person's reasons are *the* reasons for action. The distinction, between "a reason" and "the reason," although Peters claims it is noncausal, must surely be drawn on something like causal grounds. Peters himself says *the* reasons are the "operative" ones and fall under lawlike generalizations. Such a characterization clearly uses causal language no matter how much Peters denies it. And, of course, if we are to draw the distinction between two reasons, each of which could rationalize an action, and say one was *the* reason, the difference seems prima facie a causal one (see Davidson, 1963).

Despite such overpowering considerations for including a causal role for rules in explaining human action, Peters and most philosophers are adamant in resisting such pressures. It is important to note that *the* reason for an action is, for Peters, still of the same logical kind as a person's reason. And this is so, whether or not it is a reason of which the person is fully conscious. It is still a reason and not some compulsion which forces or drives me to act. How can the distinction between my reason and *the* reason for my action be drawn?

On the control system account, *the* reason will be the (usually highest-level) controlled quantity that is operative. Often that will be the same as the person's reason, but it need not be. A different controlled quantity might in principle have been operative, and the agent perhaps gave a lower-level or different-level reason as his or her reason. On the control system theory we have an empirical test for any hypothesized controlled quantity. Introduce a disturbance and see if it is counteracted. If the shop has no tobacco, do I go on down the road to get some or am I satisfied having gotten to the other side of the street from the rowdies? Nothing stops there being several reasons for an action; and in principle they can all be empirically tested. Moreover, the control system model honors the insight of the purposive rule-following model that a causal explanation becomes appropriate only if there is a breakdown of normal routine. Thus the control system model adds to the rule-following model both an empirical content to the distinction between a person's reason and *the* reason for an action and a procedure for testing the empirical distinction.

I have been arguing that the norms governing human action in its ordinary aspects can be accounted for with the control system model, but there remains the realm of "pure" assessment. What of the norms of reason as an example of rule following? Is a given intelligent piece of behavior reasonable and rational? Would it be rational to change some of the basic norms of ordinary human action? Although I suspect that a careful deployment of control system theory could partially sort out these questions and give answers to some parts of them, there will remain, I think, a core that cannot be accounted for by control system theory. Control system theory looks most promising in providing an account of the minor variations in the operation of existing conceptual schemes. The problem raised by the norms of reason is that of potentially *changing* existing conceptual and representational schemes, so I will postpone a consideration of the account of major variations until the next chapter, on accommodation.

One last task remains in my defense of control system theory as providing a potentially helpful model which goes farther than current psychological or philosophical theories in accounting for minor adaptiveness in representational schemes. I have already indicated how it copes with the weaknesses of earlier theories; let me now briefly indicate how it meets some of the standard objections from those quarters. In the first place, there is the point just noted that somehow if an action is intelligent, i.e., suited to its goal and flowingly adaptive, it cannot be causal, for causes operate in a straightforward way. We can now see that if this objection means that causal accounts of intelligent action are inappropriate, it is well taken. Control system theory does not account for outputs; it gives an account of the control of perceptions. If, however, the objection is taken to mean that causal processes are not operative in the production of human action, that goals, reasons, desires, beliefs, and so on, cannot play causal roles, then the objection is false. The control system model of human action provides a physically realizable system within the purview of causal processes, but its account is irreducible to causal terms, precisely because what a control system does lies in the opposite direction from what causal processes do in the feedback loop.

The second objection to giving a merely psychologically descriptive account of learning and action is one that I myself posed in the first chapter. *Learning* is inextricably bound up with standards of correctness, with getting things right, with norms. If psychologists want to investigate mere processes of change of cognitive variables without regard to the normative feature, then they owe us an argument to show that what they are doing has anything whatsoever to do with our ordinary concerns with learning and action. Does the control system model fall prey to a similar sort of objection? Clearly not. The idea of correcting disturbances builds in from the outset the notion of a norm or standard that defines "disurbances" and what a "correction" would look like. The objection to merely descriptive psychology fails to get started when applied to control system theory.

Why do most philosophers insist that goals and purposes cannot causally explain actions despite the embarrassment of being thereby unable to account for the distinction between a person's reasons for an action and *the* reasons for the action? Essentially the argument goes something as follows: There is said to be an analytic or logical or conceptual connection between a reason, goal, or motive, and the action it is ordinarily taken to explain. On the purposive rule-following model this is acceptable, since citing the reason, purpose, or goal with which an action was performed explains the action by rendering it reasonable, not by putting it in a causal nexus. But if two concepts are analytically connected, they cannot be causally connected, for causes and effects must be independent events and analytic connections between independent events are not possible. Thus, crossing the road to get some

tobacco is actually a fuller description of the specific action to be explained, and the goal—to get some tobacco—is not analytically separable from the particular action it explains.

I could, of course, note that with the breakdown of the analytic-
synthetic distinction, this argument is at least greatly weakened from
the very start. But let me assume that one can draw a relativistic
analytic-synthetic distinction and see if the control system model can
meet this objection. In the first place it needs to be noted that under
the supposition of a relativistic analytic-synthetic distinction, the relativity will be to certain ways of describing the phenomena. This means
that under alternative descriptions statements about the same things
may turn from analytic to synthetic and vice versa. For example, "The
murderer's killing of Smith caused Smith's death" is arguably analytic.
But if "Jones's slitting Smith's throat" is referentially the same event
as "the murderer's killing of Smith," we get by substitution "Jones's
slitting Smith's throat caused Smith's death," and this latter is a full-
fledged causal claim. It might be argued that causal contexts are
opaque, and I cannot simply substitute referentially identical expressions and hope to preserve truth value. If that is the claim, then my
point is granted that we cannot rule out causal connections by noting
that two events are analytically connected. For on this defense what
counts as causally connected is not a matter simply of reference but
of the linguistic context in which causal assertions are made. Either
way, the objection that reasons or goals cannot be causes of actions
because they are analytically connected to action fails.

In the control system model the description of the reference signal
is given in "goal" language; but for the reference signal to be comparable to the sensor signal so that they can be compared to produce the
error signal which drives the system, the sensor signal must have the
same "dimensions" as the reference signal. In short, it must be describable in "goal" language as well, and will have, under that description, an analytic connection with the goal. Thus, the situation as
sensed before, during, and after any errors have been corrected will
have a "goal" description. Very often the action performed in any situation is identified with the outputs of the system. Typically we have
available some fairly general descriptions of outputs, such as crossing
the street, which are compatible with a whole host of goals. But in the
control system model, since the outputs are specifically designed to
counteract any disturbances of the controlled quantity, the sensor signal has the same dimensions as the controlled quantity or goal, and
it follows that the output can also be described in terms of the goal.
Thus, the specific output description of "crossing the street to get some
tobacco" is in terms of the goal and rationalizes the action under the

purposive rule-following model. But as I have already shown, the goal is operative in its own production, and it is, therefore, apparent how there can be an analytic connection between goal and action (under certain descriptions) and the goal still figure in causal processes bringing about the action.

Let me try to get at this point in another way. A typical answer to the question "What is he doing?" is "Crossing the street." If the questioner continues to ask "Why?" the answer comes, "To get some tobacco." It appears, prima facie, that we have two entities here, an action and an intention, and it seems perfectly reasonable to ask for their relation. Any number of accounts of the relation have been proposed, means-end, causal, and so on. The insight of the rule-following model is that in an important sense we do not have two separable entities here, at least insofar as we are concerned with what the agent is doing, as opposed to what the agent is causing to happen. For example, the agent is causing the soles of the agent's shoes to wear down, but ordinarily that is not an action the agent is performing (although with a suitable story, it could be). The insight of the rule-following model is to the effect that qua agent's action, the proper description of the action must involve the point or purpose. Thus, crossing the street as a means of getting tobacco seems to drive too large a wedge between purpose and action. An analytic connection between purpose and action then appears essential, and it looks as if ordinary psychological concerns with the production of the action are ruled out of court.

The control system model, however, allows us to ask questions about psychological mechanisms while honoring the insight concerning the close interconnections between purpose and action. The purpose is operative in its own production in the action on the control system model. But, further, we have an empirical test for whether what the agent is doing is "crossing the street" or "getting tobacco." Introduce a disturbance and see if it is counteracted. For example, we could have a friend give the person some tobacco and see if our pedestrian continues to cross the street. If not, then "crossing the street" is probably not what the person was doing. The control system model provides a general model of human action and a general empirical procedure for determining what a person is doing. Insofar as knowing what a person is doing constitutes an explanation of the action, as it often does, control system theory also provides a model for the explanation of human action. The control system model thus reconciles the philosopher's concern with reasonableness with the psychologist's concern with effective processes, and constitutes an improvement on both.

The control system account also vindicates my decision at the beginning of the chapter to treat experience in its ordinary full-blooded way. The basic control system model involves a perceptual component, a purpose component, and an activity component, and it shows in some detail how these things are related. An experience is not just passive reception, it involves changing perceptions through purposeful activity. Experience is not just blind activity either; rather it is guided by perception, purpose, and the difference between the two. Experiencing X means that a control system with X as a controlled quantity is in operation.

8. Control System Theory and Education

Thus far, my discussion has been at a very abstract level, and, at best, I have settled an esoteric dispute between philosophers and psychologists concerning the nature of human action and its explanation. What possible difference could that make to education?

Perhaps the most obvious area of potential impact is in the whole stimulus-response-oriented realm of educational psychology. It is ironic that in one of the few cases in the history of human thought when science listened seriously to philosophy about scientific method, behaviorism was the result. For a case can be made that the main methodological features of behaviorism were drawn directly from a positivistic philosophy which, it was thought, represented "real" science. And yet positivism in philosophy is all but dead, killed partly by the very fact that it did *not* accurately represent science, but rather tried to reconstruct it. In psychology proper, various cognitive modes of theorizing are already fully acceptable as alternatives to behaviorism, but, in at least some of the policy applications of educational psychology, we have such outrages as behavioral objectives and management by objectives.

However, I do not wish to undertake any detailed polemic against behaviorist psychology beyond the foregoing discussion of models of action and action explanation. Rather, I want to focus on just one area that would look very different if the control system model were adopted. I refer to the area of instructional objectives, learning goals, and the means for assessing them. According to conventional wisdom we need to specify our instructional objectives not in terms of processes the students undergo, but rather in terms of learning competencies we wish them to have. After all, it is the competencies that we wish to achieve, and unless we focus on these competencies we may undertake processes which really do not contribute to the goals. Furthermore, if we state our instructional objectives in terms of learning outcomes, we will be able to design tests for assessing how well we have reached the instructional objectives. Indeed, most partisans of this approach go further and insist that the learning goals be directly defined in terms of the tests used to measure them. Such "operational definitions" are supposed to be very scientific. What strict operational definitions really do, however, is to commit the logical blunder of confusing a measurement with what it is measuring (Petrie, 1975a).

I will concentrate here, however, on those who already appreciate the distinction between learning and the measurement of learning. What happens is that learning is usually conceived of as learning to *do* certain things, perhaps answer questions of a certain kind, perhaps perform physical actions, perhaps engage in critical thinking. Thus an account of human action and a model for the explanation of action are needed to make sense of the learning. However, under the impact of extant measurement methodology we ordinarily pick one fairly stereotypical response, or at most a few, that would demonstrate the action or skill that is supposed to have been learned. Speed tests in typing corrected by a formula for errors are a good example of a standard measurement of a good typist. Now, there is nothing intrinsically wrong with such a procedure as long as we keep the measurement of the skill conceptually distinct from the skill. There is also nothing wrong with relying, at least to some extent, on such simplified measures when we are fairly clear that the measures do encompass the major part of the simple skill in question, as perhaps speed tests do in typing.

Problems arise, however, when policymakers tend to forget the distinction between skill and measurement and make decisions solely on the basis of the measurement. We are all too familiar with phenomena like teaching to the test, making budgetary decisions on number of students per square lecture hour, and so on. Once the confusion between measurement and skill is allowed to creep in, it is almost inevitable that teachers will aim their teaching at the test rather than at the skill. In control system terms, a very different quantity comes to be controlled. Teachers start to resist disturbances to their perception of progress toward the students' getting good test results rather than toward the students' acquiring the skill. The two obviously are not equivalent, even on operationalist grounds, since they involve different behaviors by the teachers.

The students likewise suffer by the confusion. What the clever of them learn is not the ostensible skills being taught, but how to get good grades and outsmart the teacher. Again we are familiar with students who become "test wise," who write what the teacher and the tests demand, who speak grammatically, and whose heads are empty. Once more there has been a shift in the controlled quantity. The reference signal for the students becomes expressing themselves well and getting good grades rather than mastering the material. It is the former controlled quantities to which students resist disturbances. Yet even the students inchoately recognize the confusion when they protest that grades often get in the way of learning.

Yet even this would not be *so* bad if most learning were as simple and narrow as learning to type. If we did then confuse skill with measurement and the measurement illegitimately became the reference signal for both teacher and student, at least doing well on the measurement would overlap with a large portion of skill. The problem arises when the learning skills become more complex and outstrip our capacity to devise output measures which tap most or even many of the indefinite variations necessary to exercise the skill adaptively. Consider skills like appreciating music, writing a poem, doing physics, engaging in critical thinking, and so on. Instead of admitting the inadequacy of our measurement tools, far too many educators simply insist that the measurement really defines the skill after all.

How would control system theory help? The problem with the above approach is that the measurements get defined in stereotyped *output* terms. What is going on, I have argued, is that the system is controlling *inputs*. No serious problems result if the output description is easily translated to the input description or largely overlaps it in ways I have already illustrated. But confusion sets in when what is being done (by teacher or student) is actually thought to be described in the output terminology. Remember, what control systems do is control inputs, not outputs. If we confuse the measurement description of outputs with the input description of what the system is doing, then either the controlled quantity will have subtly shifted and we will really be teaching, and children learning, how to get good grades instead of the intended skills, or even the students will perceive the inadequacy of our procedures for what we claim to be testing.

Control system theory dictates a whole new approach to testing for learning. Instead of devising standardized, narrow, output descriptions of what students should be able to do, we must think of a variety of things that would count as a disturbance to perceptual inputs. If the student really has learned what we intend, the student will tend to counteract the disturbance to inputs. This is implicitly just what is done on the level, say, of a doctoral oral. The amount of varied disturbances that can be generated in such a setting far exceeds what we might do with a standardized test. Questions can be asked that disentangle various competing hypotheses as to what the student knows, and then these leads can be followed up. The possibility of individually varying disturbances also explains why interviews of job applicants often provide more information than even the most complete written personnel form.

Notice, too, that it will do no good to say that we must simply make our measurements more complex and capable of tapping a wider range of outputs. For as long as the test is conceived of as measuring outputs in output language, it cannot possibly be measuring what the system is really doing, namely, controlling inputs. Or else, the testing procedures themselves run the risk of causing us to change and distort what we are really doing; for example, getting good grades on the test. The inadequacy of proliferating the measurement of outputs is due not just to complexity, but to a logical constraint on how we can find out what a student knows. What the system is doing is controlling inputs, not outputs, and within its effective range there are an indefinite number of ways the outputs can vary to correct for disturbances. Intelligent action is adaptive. So what I am urging is an entire conceptual change, a shift in perspective, on the part of educational testers from measuring outcomes to checking for corrections to disturbances of inputs. Put in another way, I believe we need to pay more attention to phenomena of perceptual learning and, to repeat an old theme, how experience comes to be structured in terms of our theories (Petrie, 1974b).

Although the conceptual shift I am urging would obviously have a profound influence on education, I do not mean to imply that we should throw out all our standardized tests and start from scratch. As with most conceptual changes we need to keep most of what we have but learn to see it in new ways, and that in turn will change the peripheries and lines of extension. This particular change seems all to the good. The shift from a focus on outcomes to a focus on correcting disturbances in inputs is a shift toward a more individualized view of learning and teaching. We will now have to justify standardization rather than the individual's creative correcting of disturbances. We will have to justify standardization on the grounds that routine correction of disturbances does indeed tap the potential range of correcting behavior. What a salutary shift! (See also Petrie, 1979).

The point can be approached in another way. Contemporary test theory approaches testing with the model of statistical sampling theory. This approach is fine as long as we are clear as to just what it is that the tests are sampling. However, recent work shows that test theorists are extremely unclear about this (Tomko, 1980). They have a general notion of a domain or repertory of potential responses to test items which the subject may exhibit. The test then, somehow, samples from these responses. In just what sense "potential" responses can belong to this domain is quite a problem for psychologists who deny mental capacities, but I will waive that problem. Control system theory can contribute here, however, in emphasizing that it is the student's perceptions of the situation rather than the outputs with which we must be concerned. The question for control theory is not "Does the student select the right answer from a preexisting repertory?" but rather "Does the student adaptively remove disturbances?"

Of even more importance, however, is the implication of control theory for another feature of test theory. There is a growing realization among testers (Cornfield and Tukey, 1956; Cronbach, et al., 1972) that the statistical inferences sanctioned by sampling theory are insufficient by themselves to reach conclusions concerning what a student knows or can do. We need, in addition, to infer substantively from the description of what is sampled to people's abilities and knowledge. It is not, of course, that we do not make this inference; the problem is rather that we make the leap from test score to capacity mindlessly and unconsciously. However, the reality of the inference is brought home to us in those cases where we intuitively know that the test has not measured the capacity. This failure of inference can occur for two reasons. On the one hand, we all know of "test-anxious" pupils who, nevertheless, really know the material. On the other hand, it is now believed, at least by some (Slack and Porter, 1980), that good test scores may be due to coaching, rather than real knowledge of the material.

The point is that control system theory provides an empirical model for making this second inference from score to capacity. The inference will not be deductive or even statistical, but it will show how, in principle, to test for whether or not the capacity presumed to be responsible for the test scores is really present or not. With regard to the test-anxious student, control system theory reminds us to look at a wide range of adaptive responses. If the student cannot correct disturbances as represented by standardized tests, can he or she correct other disturbances? With regard to coaching for the test, control system theory calls our attention to the way in which a test answer really is a correction to a disturbance of the hypothesized capacity (represented by the control system). Does a given question really test the desired knowledge, or is it rather something which can be solved in a mechanical way because it comes in a certain standard form? Does the student know the material, or is the student merely "test-wise"? Those are two different hypothesized controlled quantities and can be tested for by introducing quite different disturbances. This intuitive distinction between real knowledge and being test-wise is very difficult to maintain when one concentrates simply on outputs. Then the test is merely a sample of outputs. By shifting to the control of inputs, however, we can test for which disturbances are controlled, and how this occurs.

Let me show by an example what shifting our attention to inputs means. Intuitively we know that a good teacher should sometimes praise a pupil and sometimes correct the pupil's mistake. Yet if these two teacher behaviors are tested in standard ways, they almost invariably cancel each other out. If directly observable measures such as praising and blaming are used to define an inferential measure of good teaching, then it is likely that the inferential measure would prove to be ineffective. The praise and blame simply cancel each other out when subjected to standard statistical treatments. This sort of result typically leads psychologists to be suspicious of inferential measures and to concentrate on behavioral outcomes. It is believed that the characteristics of the situations in which the teacher should praise and those in which the teacher should correct the student should be specified behaviorally. The problem here is that such specification is not possible except on the level of "those situations which call for praise *in order to* teach effectively." The control system notion creeps in.

If we approach the situation from the standpoint of control system theory in the first place, no such difficulties arise. What good teachers try to do is to control their perceptions of good teaching. If they sense an error, they act to remove the error, and sometimes "contrary" outputs can both be instances of good teaching. Sometimes praise and warmth are needed; sometimes correction and holding to standards. "Praise" and "blame" are simply not appropriate independent variables to assess good teaching. We need to concentrate rather on teachers' perceptions of what children need.

A second educational example comes from the history of education. In *Class, Bureaucracy, and Schools,* Michael Katz (1971) argues that educational structures mediate between ideology and the results of schooling. Furthermore, this mediation is an absolutely essential one in the sense that on Katz's view the goals of schooling could not be changed without changing the structures. Thus, in a sense, he is claiming that the function of the educational bureaucracy is to promote class bias and racism, where "function" here is a term often used by sociologists to indicate some stronger kind of relationship than mere consequence.

Of course, Katz needs the stronger relation to make his case. If the class bias and racism are merely consequences of the system, no matter how unwanted, it remains conceptually possible to intervene in the ordinary operations of the system to block these consequences. It would then be theoretically possible to change the consequences without changing the system. And, indeed, just this kind of criticism is typically leveled against radical critics such as Katz, who believe we must change the system. On the other hand, if racism is a *function* of the system, then perhaps Katz can maintain his stronger thesis.

However, sociological methodologists have typically been unable to explicate the notion of the "function of a system" in any way that avoids reduction to a straight-line causal analysis. Thus, although anthropologists may claim that a rite of passage performs a certain function in a society, it is not clear what more this means than that the puberty rite has the purported function as a consequence. Similarly, we can grant the evidence Katz cites as to racism in American education but claim this is nothing more than an undesirable consequence, to be eliminated by intervention in the straight-line causal sequence that gives rise to the racism.

Control system theory, however, provides the conceptual apparatus to find a way out of this impasse. If functional explanation is to be anything more than straight-line causal explanation, then it must be interpreted in the social sphere analogously to action explanation in the psychological sphere. There must be a reference level for a controlled quantity, and the system must be organized so that its operation will tend to counteract perceived disturbances to the controlled quantity.

Katz believes that a function of schooling is to promote the social status quo, and, hence, to limit social mobility. To prove this he needs to find cases in which it looks as if the schools are trying to promote social mobility and then check to see if the school system reacts to counter this disturbance. Thus, the inability of society to absorb over-educated young people, and the recent arguments that not everyone needs to go to college, would seem to be evidence in favor of Katz's hypothesis, as would the renewed attacks on the native intelligence of blacks just at a time when they are beginning to gain access to "establishment" higher education. On the other hand, the single most potent source of criticism of society continues to be the universities. It is still the case that nowhere else can a radical get as influential a hearing. Such facts argue against Katz's hypothesis.

Of course, my purpose here is not to judge the truth or falsity of Katz's thesis, but only to point out the kind of argument he needs if he is ever to convince the liberal establishment of the thoroughness of his critique. He must not merely build up evidence of class bias as a *consequence* of schooling, no matter how widespread. Rather, he must look at those crucial cases where there would appear to be a disturbance in the hypothesized controlled quantity and see if the system acts to counteract that disturbance.

Finally, let me briefly sketch a problem in ethics and education to illustrate the versatility and scope of the control system analysis. The problem is that of indoctrination. It is agreed on all sides that education ought not to be indoctrination, and yet a persistent criticism is that formal education—schooling—does indoctrinate. Once more, I am not here concerned with the merits of the arguments, but rather with illustrating a point upon which control system theory can shed some light.

One of the main issues in the dispute is over the nature of indoctrination. Does it require intent? It has been argued (Rosemont, 1972) that analyses of the concept of indoctrination are beside the point if the teacher's activities, intended or not, end up with the student's being indoctrinated. This is a position similar to that taken by the partisans of concentrating on learning outcomes rather than instructional processes. What in fact do our educational institutions produce, and is that a good thing?

There are at least two points that might be raised from the perspective of control system theory. In the first place, we can ask whether or not the indoctrination that is supposed to result from schooling is a mere consequence or a function of schooling. If it is a mere consequence, then we conceivably could block the causal sequences that produce indoctrination without essentially changing the system. This might, for example, be what we should do to eliminate sexism in schools. Raise the consciousness of teachers, eliminate sexist readers, and so on. On the other hand, if indoctrination is a *function* of the school system, then no such measures will suffice, for the system will counteract such disturbances and find new ways to indoctrinate. Thus, as in the Katz example, we see the type of argument needed to show that indoctrination is a function of schooling. Not only must it be shown to result from schooling, but it must be shown to persist in the face of "disturbances."

However, the second point has to do with the ethical question of the extent to which we may properly hold teachers responsible for indoctrination. This point is crucial if it turns out that a given case of indoctrination was at most a mere consequence of schooling and not a function of it. In such a situation, teachers should be vitally concerned as to whether or not they were at fault. The situation is tremendously complex (see Snook, 1970, 1972). Sometimes responsibility follows only if we determine that the teachers did intend to indoctrinate. In other cases—e.g., if they should have known better—we want to hold teachers responsible even if they did not intend to indoctrinate. We can also construct cases in which the teacher did intend to do X, did not realize X was indoctrinating, but should have realized it, and so on. My point is that judgments of what the teacher was doing figure centrally in all these ascriptions of responsibility.

Intentional action, conscious or not, is either action done with a certain intention or a necessary part of such an action. The control system analysis of an action done with a certain intention is straight-forward. The intention is the highest-order reference signal operative, and I have already indicated how to test for that—introduce a disturbance and see if it is counteracted. But we are also acting intentionally if our subactions are parts of an action done with a certain intention. Thus, intentional acts are subparts of actions done with an intention. They are control systems lower down in the hierarchy in which the action done with an intention is the highest unit. And the test for whether a certain action is intentional is the same—introduce a disturbance and see if it is counteracted. A necessary condition for holding a teacher responsible for indoctrinating would be whether the behavior which resulted in indoctrination was intentional under some description or other, and that is something for which we can test. Once more control system theory provides a deeper insight into how to approach a significant educational problem.

6 | Accommodation

1. Accommodation and the New-Knowledge Horn

I have urged that a general concept of adaptiveness is needed as a replacement for the discredited attempts to grasp either the new-knowledge or the old-knowledge horn of the *Meno* dilemma. It would emphasize the processes of acquiring knowledge rather than the static analysis of structures of knowledge. As such, adaptiveness promises the possibility of slipping between the horns of the *Meno* dilemma, and with its emphasis on the processes of conceptual change seems peculiarly appropriate to an *educational* epistemology.

That part of adaptiveness in which conceptual schemes do not change radically, but are merely elaborated and modified in minor ways, I have called assimilation. The key concept in understanding assimilation is that of the broadened notion of norm-regarding behavior. That is, the reasonableness and adequacy of our conceptual schemes are to be understood by noting that these schemes involve an implicit appeal to norms or rules. The rules that constitute any given scheme unify otherwise very disparate physical stimulation and physical behavior as being situations of the same kind. These rules also provide the standards of intelligence and reasonableness—they allow us to assess our perceptions, behavior, and beliefs. The move has been from a concern with finding ultimate grounds of knowledge and enquiry to the process notion that our enquiry will be rational if it is carried on in terms of our conceptual schemes which are in turn constituted by rules and norms of procedure and assessment.

In the preceding chapter I explained the processes of norm-regarding behavior or assimilation to rules in terms of the control system model of action. However, the causal and assessment functions of rules have been thought by many to be incompatible. Psychologists tend to emphasize the causal nature of an appeal to rules, and, as a result, run the risk of failing to be concerned with learning and knowledge. A behaviorism that supposedly concentrates only on processes is the all-too-frequent result. On the other hand, philosophers, impressed by the role of rules in assessment and rationality, tend to draw a sharp distinction between the normative function of rules and the explanatory concerns of psychologists. This approach emphasizes our concerns with learning and knowledge all right, but at the apparent cost of cutting off these concerns from the psychologists' investigations into how we come to have beliefs at all. An arid, nonhelpful intellectualism is often the result. Thus, neither the philosophers' nor the psychologists' approach to rules fits the criteria for an account of assimilation.

However the criteria of continuity, diversity, and reasonableness can be met by the control system model of assimilation of experience, where experience is understood in a full-blooded way as involving the interactions of perception, purpose, and activity. Since what are controlled are perceptions, very different physical events can be seen as falling under the same norm, meeting the criterion of continuity. Since we are freed from the bogus demand to account for indefinitely varying outputs, we can see how a control system can plausibly operate in a variety of perceptual environments (within the given effective range of control) to produce flowing, adaptive, intelligent behavior, thus meeting the diversity condition. And, finally, reasonableness *within* a given conceptual structure has been accounted for as well. For if the norms of reason are not themselves under question, then they can be conceived of as higher-order reference signals which condition the lower-order systems by providing reference signals for them. Intelligent behavior is thus explicated by the basic control system unit of organization itself, and reasonableness is accounted for by higher-order control systems governing the various kinds of intelligent behavior we might employ.

But assimilation remains only one part of the strategy of meeting the *Meno* dilemma by an appeal to adaptiveness. Even if I was wholly successful in the preceding chapter, I will at best have pointed to some new directions in understanding how our experience is to be understood, categorized, and processed in terms of existing, relatively stable conceptual schemes. Since the nature of such schemes seems changeable and not discoverable a priori, the other part of any account of adaptiveness involves asking the question of the source, adequacy, and reasonableness of radical changes in these conceptual schemes. How, and under what conditions, do those schemes themselves change in response to both the editing efforts of an independent reality and our human purposes? To put the contrast another way, I have argued that rules provide the explication of how conceptual schemes change experience. But since there is no absolutist source of those schemes, the other part of the question of adaptiveness is whether it can explicate the source, adequacy, and reasonableness of changes in the rules which constitute the conceptual schemes.

In short, I must now give an account of accommodation, of how we change our conceptual schemes to fit our experience. And, ultimately, I must account for the connections and discontinuities between assimilation and accommodation. It is only in this way that adaptiveness as the way of meeting the *Meno* dilemma can be shown to be appropriate. As my analysis of assimilation gives us a more adequate understanding of the old-knowledge horn of the *Meno* dilemma, so now my account of accommodation will provide a more adequate understanding of the new-knowledge horn. Finally the continuities and connections between assimilation and accommodation will provide the account of reflective equilibrium which, I believe, will ultimately allow us to slip between the horns of the *Meno* dilemma.

The first step in any account of accommodation must be to acknowledge the existence of alternative conceptual schemes. Different ways of conceiving of and thinking about the world seem to have existed at different times in the history of scientific thought, and these ways seem sufficiently unlike each other to warrant being called different conceptual schemes. In addition, there are the social-anthropological findings that draw our attention to the different ways in which different cultures view the world. Educationally, this diversity currently manifests itself in a mistrust of the homogenizing, "melting pot" function of education and a call for an emphasis on "pluralism." At the same time, the growing influence of developmental theories such as Piaget's in psychology attests to the possibility of a succession of conceptual schemes within the space of the cognitive development of a single individual. So there is no question but that we do sometimes enquire into and learn things that are radically new, i.e., that do not fit into our current conceptual schemes. Any account that admits the existence of different conceptual schemes will meet the criterion of conceptual diversity.

There is, however, a philosophical objection to such an admission of conceptual diversity (see, for example, Davidson, 1973–74). The objection is this: Even to assert that there can be radically diverse conceptual schemes is to involve ourselves in either an outright falsehood or an incomprehensible claim. On the supposition of radically diverse conceptual schemes, the criteria of reasonableness, even of intelligibility, are relative to a conceptual scheme. We must understand the claim that there are diverse conceptual schemes *within* another conceptual scheme. Thus, *that* conceptual scheme, the one used for understanding the diversity, has encompassed the diversity after all and shown it not to be a radical diversity. On the other hand, if the claim that there are diverse conceptual schemes is supposed to transcend conceptual schemes, then it is incomprehensible, since the criterion of intelligibility is relative to a conceptual scheme. (Although it is not a part of the objection proper, it is this kind of move that, I think, lies behind many philosophers' reluctance to give up attempts to grasp the old-knowledge horn of the *Meno* dilemma. Impressed by this objection, they feel that the conceptual scheme that enables them to make sense of the claim of conceptual diversity must, after all, contain sufficient old knowledge to enable them to understand the possibility of new knowledge.) What am I to make of such an objection?

The answer to this kind of argument is to admit its premise but to deny that anything disastrous follows. In other words, I admit that the way in which I, or anyone else, understand alternative conceptual schemes is indeed in terms of that person's own conceptual scheme, and in that sense the diversity is not, within the conceptual scheme, a radical one. Put in yet another way, I cannot conceive of radically different conceptual schemes, for if I could, they would not be radically different. And yet, I *can* push against the limits of my own conceptual scheme in various ways. Good science fiction writers do it all the time.

We can also see in the historical record evidence of some fairly impressive and far-reaching conceptual shifts. I have illustrated several "midsize" changes in chapter 4 already—combustion, the rotation of the earth, and Newton's laws. Other examples could be given of "larger" changes, the Copernican Revolution, the recognition of gases as "substances," the relativity of space-time, and so on. It may well be admitted that from our current standpoint such differences are comprehended within our own (unitary?) conceptual scheme, but surely that is a contingent historical achievement of ours. Even though we must interpret both pre- and post-Copernican thought from *our* standpoint, the historical evidence is simply overwhelming that the conceptual schemes of pre-Copernicans were much different from those of post-Copernicans. The burden of the first part of this book has been to show that there is no absolutistic framework from which to judge conceptual changes, i.e., no old-knowledge approaches succeed. We have every reason to suppose, historically, that our own current conceptions will likewise change in similar radical ways, even though future historians in their turn would presumably comprehend the changes from their own conceptual schemes. The point is that from the fact that our only access to conceptual diversity is through our own conceptual schemes, it does not follow that such diversity is not, after all, a centrally important fact for epistemology.

In a sense, it seems to me that proponents of the objection are simply calling attention in a somewhat perverse way to the second criteria of adequacy that an account of accommodation must meet—namely, conceptual continuity. That is, despite historical diversity and the possibility of future conceptual change, we do have to give some account of the continuity of the changes in conceptual schemes.

But how can we speak of the "reasonableness" of changes in conceptual schemes? Is not the idea of reasonableness tied up with a conceptual scheme and hence inapplicable to changes of conceptual schemes? In particular, are not the norms of reason—those very general, very pervasive rules of consistency, relevance, impartiality, and the search for grounds for belief and decision—constitutive of all conceptual schemes?

I am willing to grant that our current (ordinary language) account of justification and giving reasons involves an appeal to the basic rules and procedures embodied in what might be called the norms of reason. It also seems to follow from that account that any question of whether those most basic rules and procedures are themselves reasonable, rational, and justifiable would itself presuppose some yet higher order set of norms and rules in terms of which we could answer the question. Now either this higher-order set is somehow self-evident, or we are involved in an infinite regress. I have already argued that such norms and rules are not self-evident, at least not in any helpful way. Does that mean we must be involved in a regress? Not really, if we recognize precisely what the history of the attempts to demonstrate the self-evidence of the norms of reason teaches us—namely, that there is at least some diversity and change involved. If that is so, then why not consider changing our concept of justification and rationality to include not only assimilative processes of giving reasons in terms of our existing conceptual schemes, but also the historical processes which have led to changes in these conceptual schemes? Those processes will then provide the basis for an account, not merely descriptive, of the development of rationality. It will be not merely descriptive because it will lay bare how the changes were adaptive. In short, this whole book can be taken as an extended argument to the effect that we ought to change our concept of justification and rationality to include the substantive historical processes that have led to changes in human thought, both in general and in terms of the special sciences. I am arguing for a conceptual change, a change that will join much more closely an account of the justification of belief with a historical account of our belief in justification.

Basically this change has two elements. One of the elements of the change has permeated much of the earlier discussion in this book. Our current concept of rationality seems to locate rationality primarily in static analyses of scientific theories or conceptual schemes. It is the structures of those theories and schemes that are supposed to provide the basis of rationality. I have argued that this concept should be broadened to take account of the purposes and activities of scientists. In short, I have urged a shift away from a concern with the analysis of scientific knowledge structures to a concern with the processes of scientific theorizing. The philosophical concern for truth is, I believe, better interpreted as adapting to the world than as understanding the world.

The other part of the proposed change in the concept of rationality that I am suggesting is that we take seriously the historical growth of knowledge. What this means is that an irreducible part of judging any proposed knowledge variant rational is the retroactive considerations we bring to bear on the variant. That is, we shall not always be able to settle from our present vantage point the rationality of a proposed variant. As I shall argue below, the way in which we retroactively determine the rationality of knowledge variants is through a broad evolutionary notion of variation and selective retention.

The educational significance of this second proposed change in the concept of rationality is profound. We must distinguish the reasonableness in current ways of looking at things from the rationality of changes in conceptual schemes, the latter to be seen, in part, retroactively. Thus, if students' current conceptual schemes are reasonable, we may be able to justify to the student the rationality of changing those schemes only after the schemes have been changed. A proper appreciation of the twin notions of current reasonableness and retroactive rationality is crucial for educational theory.

2. Anomalies and New Knowledge

Recall that under the control system model of assimilation, what the system does is to counteract disturbances to the controlled quantity. To the extent that the perceived situation deviates from the norm being controlled, the system acts, in its normal range of control, to remove this disturbance. There is undoubtedly a complex hierarchy or heterarchy of control systems operating in ordinary circumstances, but the idea of the normal or typical range of control is an important one. What happens when a disturbance overwhelms the normal range of control, and does so in a way so persistent that ordinary correcting mechanisms do not work? In short, what happens when our conceptual schemes are no longer adequate to assimilate experience and we must rather accommodate our conceptual schemes to our experience?

From the point of view of a control system an error is an error, but upon analysis the error can be seen to come from either of two very different places. Recall that an error is the difference between the reference signal, i.e., the controlling norm, and the sensor signal, i.e., the sensed situation. Thus an error could be due either to the fact that the actual situation differs from the guiding norm or to the fact that the guiding norm is "asking too much." And indeed we are familiar with both kinds of errors in ordinary situations. I may lose my job because the external economic situation causes a retrenchment in universities. If we assume I have a norm of "adequate income" guiding my activity, then the sensed error of "inadequate income" will be due to the fact that I do not have a job. On the other hand, my expectations of an adequate income may be so high that not even the highest academic salary would meet my expectations. The result would be the same—an error of "inadequate income"—which my ordinary ways of behaving are insufficient to overcome.

Now the notion of an error, or a problem, or an anomaly is a recurring one in analyses of enquiry and thought. It is particularly familiar to educators, appearing as it does in Dewey's (1938) celebrated analysis of a complete act of thought. For Dewey, an error is a sensed difficulty which sets thought off on the round of problem solving, and my analysis, with its abstract concept of error, is certainly compatible with Dewey's approach. Ordinarily problems are solved and errors removed by the persistent application of larger and more involved sections of our existing conceptual schemes. I try to find another job, for example, or I quit academics and enter a more lucrative field, or I lower my income expectations, and so on. What I am concerned with, however, are those occasions on which a persistent application of our existing conceptual schemes proves inadequate, and we are forced to change them.

Let me illustrate this point with two examples, one from the philosophy of science and another from contemporary politics. Thomas Kuhn's (1970b) account of the growth of scientific knowledge is somewhat similar to my account of adaptiveness. Just as I use the terms assimilation and accommodation, so Kuhn divides the processes of science into two phases, normal science and extraordinary or revolutionary science. Normal science is analogous to assimilation in that during such periods the scientific community is in possession of (and is even possessed by) a paradigm of what scientific enquiry should look like. This pradigm is a complicated matter consisting of exemplary problem solutions, common theories, shared formulas, agreed-upon definitions of key terms, common methodological principles, similar training, and so on. In essence it defines what will count as an appropriate problem for the science, how that problem should be solved, and what will count as a solution. Thus normal scientific activity is very much like what I have described as assimilation. The various problems, puzzles, and new applications of the science constitute the disturbances to the paradigm, and, by the usual workings of the paradigm, these disturbances are assimilated to the theory and thus removed.

However, on occasion these disturbances and puzzles resist the ordinary efforts at solution. They seem important in that they ought to be solvable within the paradigm, i.e., they cannot be ignored. These puzzles call for the attention and effort of the most eminent practitioners of the science. Sometimes the puzzles yield to such further concentrated effort, and sometimes they do not. When the puzzles persist and cannot be assimilated to the existing paradigm, Kuhn calls them anomalies, and a crisis stage is entered wherein the very foundations of the science come into question. We enter the arena of extraordinary science. If there is no reasonable alternative to the existing paradigm, the anomalies are stored, but not forgotten, and the field is not characterized by steady advance. If there is an alternative paradigm that can account for the anomalies in some way, sometimes by actually showing them not to be a problem, there is a battle and often a change of paradigms. This change of paradigms is analogous to what I have been calling accommodation. The conceptual scheme is changed because of the persistent "error" or anomaly.

Consider next the gradual changes that overtook the consciousness of many Americans as the Watergate affair eventually led to the resignation of Nixon as president. As various problems occurred—e.g., the blank eighteen-minute section on the tape—various efforts were made to assimilate such problems to the existing ideological frameworks. For example, the media was out to "get" Nixon, the erasure was accidental, transcripts of the tapes would be provided, and so on. Then further strain was put on our ordinary conceptual schemes; the transcripts had deletions, there were contradictions, and so on. The problems became anomalies, and in the end only a radical change in ideological and conceptual scheme could accommodate the anomalies. A man elected president of the United States by a landslide majority had participated in a cover-up of criminal activities. This was a difficult change for many people to undergo, and the fact that it has still not occurred for large numbers of people illustrates another feature of the interplay between assimilation and accommodation. If one is assiduous in processing experience with the use of existing conceptual schemes, the errors can often be reduced. This, of course, happens only at a cost—the cost of holding some rather strange and what we might call fanatical views, or alternatively of so insulating oneself that error-causing experience can be largely avoided.

What both these examples show is a continuum of changes between the simple assimilative operation of routine control systems and the radical changes of concept that sometimes characterize scientific revolutions. The attempts to assimilate before an accommodation occurs will be seen as "ad hoc" or "inappropriate" only ex post facto, from the point of view of an achieved accommodation. This is because the anomaly, qua anomaly, is defined in terms of the prior conceptual scheme. An accommodative solution, qua solution, will be seen as such only from the point of view of the successful change. An anomaly from the point of view of the successful accommodation will often have changed its character, sometimes not even appearing as a puzzle for the new conceptual scheme. The important point for now, however, is that the kind and range of changes in conceptual schemes forms a continuum, and it thus is not helpful to try to specify in advance just what will change.

It is important to note here that the persistent error that becomes an anomaly forcing an accommodation is not arbitrary, even though it depends upon the cognitive structure of the person for whom it is an error. This is clear when the error is due primarily to the sensor signal. No matter how much we may want to see a given situation as structured by a certain norm, the actual environmental laws that mediate the outputs of the control system in correcting the sensed error may simply not allow such a correction to be made. At the same time, the widespread phenomenon of people's continuing to see what they want to see shows that the brute facts of the world force changes in our conceptual schemes only with great difficulty. The control system model gives a picture of both how we can perceive what we want to perceive for a long time, and how we may not be able to do so forever. But even in the case in which the anomaly is primarily due to the reference signal, the situation is not arbitrary. For the reference signals of any reasonably experienced human being are the product of heredity and a long history of experience with the social and physical world. Thus, even though the anomaly is a "sensed" anomaly in that it is the difference between a sensory representation and a norm as represented in a given individual's cognitive structure, the error is not merely subjective.

The task then is to specify a mechanism for the generation of variants in conceptual schemes. These may be individual concepts, groups of concepts, relations between them, ways of applying the concepts, and so on—all the kinds of conceptual change I have already illustrated. The variants must be reasonable, in terms of both initial plausibility and ultimate acceptability. There is an important discontinuity between the problem's being seen as an anomaly from the initial conceptual scheme and its being seen as "solved" from the second conceptual scheme. Despite this difference a sense of continuity must be demonstrated between the two conceptual schemes.

3. The Variation and Selective Retention Model

Once we have given up trying to grasp the old-knowledge or the new-knowledge horn of the *Meno* dilemma and recognized the complementary strengths and weaknesses of these approaches, an evolutionary account of accommodation becomes the most natural alternative. If we look at biology where an evolutionary account has had some success, the analogies with the conditions set by the *Meno* dilemma are suggestive. The problems faced in trying to understand the origin and growth of biological species are similar to those faced in looking at the origin and growth of knowledge. On the one hand, it was once assumed that biological species are simply given in terms of natural kinds, and the only problem of growth and change was that of how these essentially given species were elaborated and could reproduce. This was the biological analogue of the old-knowledge approach to the *Meno* dilemma. Some basic knowledge was given in one ontological form or another (abstract forms or concrete particulars), and the problem of the growth of knowledge was how these are elaborated. But just as no plausible case could be made for foundational elements of knowledge, neither could a case be made for the ultimate givenness of biological species. The historical facts of conceptual diversity and conceptual change could not be overcome, nor could the historical facts of species diversity and species change.

The new-knowledge alternative in the case of the growth of knowledge emphasized the radical newness of conceptual variants. Similarly in biology there has also been a revolutionary kind of view. It was held that species do change, but almost as if by magic and with no account given of their perpetuation and growth, or why earlier species die out. In the philosophy of science, Kuhn is often accused of propounding such a revolutionary account of paradigm change (Toulmin, 1972, pp. 98–117). The problem seems to be that the connections between the earlier and the later paradigms and the reasons for changing from one to the other are left mysterious. Thus the strength of the new-knowledge approach is its recognition of new conceptual variants. Its weakness is its inability to account for the source and reasonableness of these variants. Similarly in biology, once it is admitted that new species emerge and old ones die out, the problem is to account for such changes in an intelligible, nonmysterious way.

The solution to this problem in biology was, of course, the introduction of the variation and selective retention model of explanation. Very crudely, the individuals of a species vary in their manifestation of certain traits. Sometimes novel traits are exhibited. If the ecology is such that these variations provide the individual with a more advantageous breeding position, then the traits will gradually come to spread throughout the species. This is so because the less-favored individuals will reproduce fewer of their kind. Variants are retained through the mechanisms of genetic transmission.

I do not mean to imply that there are not still problems and controversies within biology concerning evolution; they abound. But what does seem clear is that the variation and selective retention model of explanation seems to have been accepted and the controversies range *within* that basic framework. The situation within biology concerning the variation and selective retention model is thus quite different from that obtaining in, say, psychology, where I urged the adoption of the control system model as opposed to the stimulus-response causal generalization model. The type of argument appropriate for choosing a basic model for organizing a given field is quite different from the disputes that arise within the field once the model has been adopted. In Kuhn's terms, the arguments over a basic model are more characteristic of extraordinary science, while arguments within the framework of a model are more characteristic of normal science.

What is important to point out here is that the variation and selective retention model of change in populations is quite general. The biological instantiation of this model is only one form it may take, and it does not follow that an explanatory evolutionary model must involve biological evolution in particular. Of course, sometimes a more general evolutionary account is asserted in which the emergence of certain social characteristics is due to biological evolution (Wilson, 1975). Such a claim is a substantive one, however, and would need to be argued on its merits in individual cases. Nothing in the "logic" of a variation and selective retention account of changes in populations requires a biological basis. Although Donald Campbell (1974), one of the evolutionary epistemologists I shall be citing, does believe in a "reduction" to biological evolution, another, Stephen Toulmin (1972), is at least noncommital. For the purposes of this book I shall defend only the weaker view that a variation and selective retention model is appropriate for understanding conceptual change without any necessary reduction to biological evolution.

Thus, in order to apply the model, I need to specify the population upon which it works and characterize the variation, selection, and retention mechanisms for conceptual change. In the preceding chapter I showed how the control system model seems to meet the general intellectual demands imposed on an adequate account of assimilation. I argued that an elaboration of it would prove fruitful. Similarly, in this chapter I will show how the variation and selective retention model shows promise of meeting the general intellectual demands imposed on an adequate account of accommodation. And since adequate accounts of assimilation and accommodation are what will give substance to the concept of adaptiveness, if I succeed, I will have solved the *Meno* dilemma.

Unfortunately, a precise specification of the population with which I am dealing would require an account of just what a concept is, and I have already foresworn that task. Furthermore, I have urged that conceptual change ranges from simple extensions and changes of modes of observation to shifts of direction in our basic categories such as substance and cause. This diversity renders it extremely unlikely that I could give a general account of the population with which I am dealing. Nevertheless, the possible objection that such vagueness renders my account inapplicable is not well founded. For in specific cases I can say what is undergoing a change. Recall my examples of conceptual change. In the first case it was the fairly localized concept of combustion that was changing. This was primarily a change of meaning. In the example of the tower it was the perspective from which to view the falling object that was undergoing a change. In the case of the change from impetus to Newton's laws, a whole theory, including its associated methods of measurement and observation, was changing. Since it seems that in specific cases of conceptual change a fairly clear specification of what is changing can be given, the lack of a general account of the populations upon which variation and selective retention work is not a crucial defect.

Another way of approaching the problem of specifying the population of conceptual change is provided by Campbell (1974). He lists a nested hierarchy of selection and retention processes, and thus implicitly specifies a range of populations in which they operate. The list begins with nonmnemonic problem solving. This level is simply that of locomotor activity of the organism itself to move to either a nourishing or nonnoxious environment. Second is the level of *vicarious* locomotion devices. Examples are the blind man's cane, radar, and sight. Then come habits and instincts that can vary. Here Campbell makes the interesting point that if a learned habit is advantageous in a stable enough environment, then any mechanism that would bring the habit into play faster would automatically be advantageous. Without invoking the inheritance of acquired characteristics, he can say that organisms who *learned* the habit or parts of it faster or more certainly than other organisms would have an adaptive advantage. And so with a stable enough environment over a long enough period of time, learned habits comprise an ecological niche that can select instinct components. "Innate" capacities turn out to be simply a form of species learning.

Visually supported thought is next mentioned by Campbell, and he cites the example of the visual thought trials made by Kohler's apes in solving various fairly complex problems. Mnemonically supported thought follows. At this level not only do we have vicarious search procedures, such as sight, but we have vicarious representations of the ecology in memory. Note the increase of abstraction and complexity of what is being varied as we move up Campbell's levels. A general specification of the populations that vary seems implausible, but at each level their nature is fairly clear. The next level Campbell calls socially vicarious exploration: observational learning and imitation. Here we get the crucially important feature of intersubjectivity and the "public" nature of knowledge so often remarked by philosophers (e.g., Hamlyn, 1971). The eighth level is that of language, and it is here that the kinds of conceptual change that are most often fastened on by commentators seem to occur.

The next level for Campbell is cultural cumulation where what is involved are fairly complete and complex social and cultural forms, such as a monetary economy. The tenth and last level is that of science. Here is the level of change that concerns Kuhn and Popper, for example. What emerges from even a brief consideration of such a collection of levels of selection processes is the ubiquitous nature of the variation and selective retention model and the concomitant impossibility of giving a general account of the populations on which the model works. At the same time the levels themselves begin to point the direction for specifying the requisite populations in specific cases of change.

The discussion of the wide range of populations that might be appropriate for a variation and selective retention model leads to a consideration of the wide range of ecologies of these populations. Most obviously, of course, there is the brute physical world itself. Vision is a successful vicarious locomotion system because of the very significant, but contingent, overlap between visual opacity and locomotor impenetrability. Yet the match is not perfect. We completely lose our bearings when we try to see in dense fog, and people unsuspectingly still run into glass doors. So the world not only partially accounts for the system we do have, but also poses problems for human inventiveness. Given the complex organisms we are, the effects of the world as an ecological system on us are almost always indirect. Most of what we deal with are our *representations* of the world. From our systems of perceptual representations of sight, sound, touch, taste, and smell, to our complex scientific theories of atomic physics, what we actually deal with are exceedingly complex systems of representations. Indeed this follows from the earlier considerations regarding the theory-ladenness of observations. We have no experience, qua experience, that is not informed by our conceptual structures.

Among the significant portions of the ecologies in which we find ourselves are the systems of social representations. Not only must we deal with other persons as objects in our scheme of physical representations, but they also form significant parts of the social world. From the earliest contacts of warmth and nourishment to the social processes of education to the intimate relations of lovers, the fact that there are other organisms with which we must deal forms a major portion of the ecology against which our variations must be tested. Given an economy of moderately scarce resources, it seems that social organization would prove to be a highly adaptive mode of behavior. Thus in the evolutionary perspective, we can view the major human institutions as relatively adaptive (so far) embodiments of some very basic human needs and purposes. Legal and political systems embody modes of adjudicating conflicting claims over scarce resources. Economic systems assign relative values to the goods needed for life. Science embodies the general need to know what the world, physical and social, is like if we are to carry out virtually any of our purposes. Morality is concerned with the need for judging among competing purposes and values. And so on. The point is that although clearly fallible and contingent, the modes of justification embodied in these social institutions provide ecological niches into which any proposed variant must prima facie fit.

4. Variation

I turn now to a consideration of variation mechanisms. The source of conceptual variants does not seem to be a particular problem once we presuppose an active, seeking organism, as is done, for example, by psychologists as diverse as Skinner, Piaget, and Chomsky. Human drives and purposes can, in general, be satisfied only through activity, and I have already indicated the intimate connection among purpose, activity, and perception in discussing the control system model. What needs further elaboration, however, is why the variants that tend to be proposed have an initial plausibility. This, of course, does not mean that every conceptual variant will, in the event, prove out to be acceptable, but only that they almost always seem to be in the right "ball park."

This problem of the initial plausibility of conceptual variants is rendered particularly pressing for me since I am urging that a variation and selective retention model is an appropriate one to account for conceptual variation. Such a model is often identified as a *random* variation and selective retention model, or even a trial and error model, where the trials seem wholly independent and at least arational. Once such an identification is made, it becomes extremely difficult to see how the apparently insightful nature of most variants could possibly be accounted for. The evidence, it is argued, clearly shows that we simply do not introduce conceptual variants in a trial and error way; rather they almost always have some initial plausibility. In addition, there does not seem to be time enough to test out all of the possible trials, even if it was admitted that they could be generated. A well-known objection is that it would take an impossibly long time for a monkey at a typewriter to produce a Shakespearean play if the keys were randomly struck. The variation and selective retention model looks incoherent on its face.

The problem here is allowing ourselves to be trapped by misleading pictures of "random" variation and "trial and error." Campbell (1974, pp. 421–22) meets this problem head on by insisting that at the very least the variation must be conceived of as a *blind* one where "blind" has a very specific technical meaning. "Blind" for Campbell connotes (1) that the variation is independent of the specific environmental circumstances at the time of the emission of the variant; (2) that the trials are not individually correlated with the solution; and (3) that any variation subsequent to an incorrect trial does not need to be a correction of the previous trial. A trial is appropriately described as a "correction," only after there has been a truly blind search at a higher level which in turn constitutes the "wisdom" seen in the subsequent "more nearly correct" variation. For example, in Kepler's search for the correct description of the orbit of Mars, first he tried a circle and then an oval; the next variation had to fall between the previous two because at a higher level he knew that the orbit could not be so discontinuous as to jump in and out of the smooth curve joining his observed points. Thus the "correction" depended on already-achieved knowledge about the generally smooth curves describing the orbits of stars, and knowledge of such continuity was the earlier achievement of blind variation. Another example of a blind variation for Campbell is the sweep of a radar. The sweep, although systematic and rational, meets Campbell's criteria for blindness noted above. The variation is independent of the environment; the sweep is uncorrelated with any objects it might encounter; and there are no "corrections" to previous trials.

Campbell's reason for insisting on blindness in his description of the variation and selective retention process is closely correlated with the *Meno* dilemma. He says (1974, p. 422): "The point is also analytic. In going beyond what is known, one cannot but go blindly. If one can go wisely, this indicates already achieved wisdom of some general sort." In short, Campbell is saying that if truly new knowledge is to be obtained, we will recognize it as such only after it has been selected for. We recognize new knowledge only ex post facto after selection mechanisms have operated. Campbell's insistence that the ultimate justification of a knowledge variant can be made only ex post facto after the selection mechanisms have had a chance to operate is a sound one; I made the same point at the beginning of this chapter in urging an extension of our concept of rationality to include retroactive justification. Nevertheless, the point does not seem to me to have any particular bearing on the *inital plausibility* of the variant, which is the present concern.

Campbell is, however, eager to grant that the variants are insightful and do show an initial plausibility. How does he account for this in a way compatible with his emphasis on the blindness of the variations? He offers three general points concerning the initial plausibility of variants. First, there is the already-achieved wisdom which limits the range of trials. This was illustrated above in the Kepler example. It is not the case that just anything can be varied. We do *not* start at ground zero varying the atomic parts of our conceptual schemes; there are no "atomic" parts to vary anyway, but even if there were, what we vary contains a great deal of wisdom already selected for. The second consideration is the obverse of the first point. If the situation is novel, the already-achieved wisdom may be wholly inappropriate; that is, there may be a maladaptive limitation on what can be varied. In either case, however, the knowledge variants do contain some amount of "initial" plausibility (which, of course, does not guarantee their ultimate acceptability). The third of Campbell's considerations will be taken up in the next section because it introduces the notion of vicarious selection.

These kinds of considerations show what is wrong with the "monkey at the typewriter" objection to variation and selective retention. We almost never start our variations at the level of individual letters. In order to get a proper analogy, we would have to equip the monkey with a more complex typewriter. It would have to include whole Elizabethan sentences and thoughts. It would have to include Elizabethan beliefs about human action patterns and their causes, Elizabethan morality and science, and linguistic patterns for expressing these. It would probably even have to include an account of the sorts of experiences which shaped Shakespeare's belief structure as a particular example of an Elizabethan. Then, perhaps, we might allow the monkey to play with such a typewriter and produce variants, but the impossibility of obtaining a Shakespearean play is no longer so obvious. What is varied really does encapsulate a great deal of already-achieved knowledge.

Variation and selection hierarchies are connected to my assimilation and accommodation model in two ways. In the first place, higher-order selectors might be operating in the selection of lower-order variants. Even if the higher-order selection mechanism is only heuristic, i.e., the variants it tries are not guaranteed to be correct, the plausibility of these variants derives from the fact that they are selected by a system that has, in its turn, already been selected by prior considerations. Thus, this is essentially an old-knowledge approach, and, as such, provides no particular problem in accounting for the initial plausibility of the variants. They are plausible because they have been selected on the basis of already-existent heuristic knowledge, however short such knowledge may fall of guaranteeing truth. The heuristics built into computer problem-solving programs are of this nature. Thus a heuristic strategy in a chess-playing program will generate "insightful" moves precisely because it represents already-achieved knowledge of the generally best moves in the given situations. This "top down" selection process can be represented conceptually in terms of the control system model as a type of assimilation. The output of heuristics serves to set variant lower-order control systems in operation. These lower-order systems represent certain moves or sequences of moves. Thus the plausibility is that derived from falling under a higher-order norm—the heuristic—and has been examined in the last chapter.

On the other hand, there is the case in which the higher-order selection systems, e.g., the heuristics themselves, are being varied. If we assume there are no "meta"-heuristics guiding this variation, it is still true that the heuristics will be limited by the existing lower-order systems. For it is only if variations of the heuristics are compatible with the lower-order systems that they will have any effect. Thus even in the case of a "blind" variation of heuristics there will appear to be an initial plausibility. An example of this has already been mentioned in connection with the ecology that a set of learned habits provides for the selection of higher-order instincts. The instinct is selected for because it provides a faster,. more certain way of acquiring the habit. So in accommodation, too, the existence of lower-order systems representing old knowledge will give an initial plausibility to the variants which are actually radically new. For these variants will utilize the existing, "relatively wise" lower-order systems both as components and as selective systems of the variation.

The fact that the new-knowledge variants in part already represent knowledge of some sort gives us a clue as to how we might mitigate even further the harshness of Campbell's "blind" variation. Recall that cases of new-knowledge variation (as opposed to the operation of existing higher-order control systems) occur only where there is an anomaly. An anomaly is not merely a disturbance, but a disturbance that has resisted the efforts of existing control systems and theories to remove it. It thus poses a special intellectual problem for our adaptive processes to solve. The anomaly is defined in terms of our existing conceptual schemes or control systems. Thus its initial significance is constituted by our current ways of looking at things. And in turn this means that putative solutions of the anomaly will also depend for their general characterization on the norms of reason as embodied in our current conceptual schemes and paradigms. Thus, the variants we initially try are bound to seem initially plausible, and this for two reasons. First they will be variants of components that represent already-achieved wisdom as noted above, but, second, they will be variants seen as reasonable for removing an anomaly—and an anomaly is defined as such in terms of existing notions of reasonableness. In short the variants are focused not on a new way of looking at the world in general (although that might be the end result), but rather on specific problems that by definition are calling out for reasonable solution (Blachowicz, 1977a; Haynes, 1976). *All* the data must in principle be accounted for by the new variant, but, in terms of the genesis of the variant, *part* of the data, namely, the anomaly, is much more relevant than the rest.

Whether or not focusing variants because they are responses to an anomaly contradicts Campbell's notion of blind variation, I am simply unsure. Such focusing still seems to be independent of detailed environmental conditions, and the trials seem individually uncorrelated with the ultimate solution. However, it may be that such focusing does constitute a "correction" of a previous trial and hence goes against Campbell's "noncorrection" criterion for "blindness." But even this is not obvious, for the standpoint from which a variation is judged as a "correction" also needs to be taken into account. If the standpoint is the currently accepted conceptual scheme, rather than the ultimately accepted one, then the variants are aimed at, and may well profit from, earlier mistakes in attempting to correct an anomaly (defined in currently accepted terms). In thus changing the variants we can be said to be correcting the trials and even making use of the direction of error, for the notions of "error" and "correction" are still defined from our currently accepted standpoint. Campbell's noncorrection criterion, however, insists only that the trial not be a correction from the standpoint of the ultimately accepted solution.

However, once we can take a historical point of view and see both the original conceptual scheme and what it ultimately becomes, then what counts as a solution in the later scheme may be quite differently defined from what would have counted as a solution in the earlier conceptual scheme. Indeed sometimes the "anomaly" from the earlier point of view simply is "solved" by dropping out of consideration. After the Michelson-Morley experiment, there was no more aether. Motion in a straight line was "unnatural" and problematic to Aristotle; falling to earth was problematic to Newton. If I am right in my reinterpretation of testing for learning, the problem of specifying learning outcomes will be changed to that of seeing if disturbances are counteracted. Campbell points out that from the point of view of the later solution, early variants are often not reasonable and do not correct the errors precisely because they make use of what seems a reasonable variant from the earlier conceptual scheme. If the ultimate solution turns out to be a revision of some of those earlier conceptions of reasonableness or ways of looking at the world, then any variant that depends on those to-be-changed beliefs and methods, will, ipso facto, not represent a correction from the resulting point of view. In the sense, then, that the early variants need not be corrections from the later point of view, we could perhaps retain even Campbell's third characteristic of the blindness of variations, while admitting a focussing effect of the anomalies on the variants, thus rendering them more insightful and initially plausible. Of course, from the historical perspective of the completed accommodative change, we will often be able to pick out points in the process when variants look like corrections from both the earlier and the later perspectives.

The point I have been trying to make here is that there are a number of resources that can be exploited to show that the variations in a variation and selective retention model can be insightful and exhibit an initial plausibility. The model is not just "trial and error." The variations are of items which already embody achieved knowledge, and they are focused by being responses to anomalies. The view I have been trying to counteract is that which tends to view an evolutionary process from too distant a perspective causing it to look like a very implausible revolutionary process. At any point in the evolutionary process, we do not start at ground zero. We start with a great deal of presumptively achieved knowledge and vary it in response to specific problem demands formulated in terms not of ultimate adequacy but of our current situation.

5. Selection

Let me now turn to the schematic characterization of selection mechanisms. The essential task here is to show how selection mechanisms can provide an account of the ultimate reasonableness of the variants. Remember that this account is an attempt to make intelligible the historical processes involved not only in the justification of belief, but also in the belief in justification. Thus I am explicitly wedding a causal account of how our rational enterprises have arisen with an account of how changes in them viewed as a result of variation and selective retention would be reasonable. I am making no attempt to give a general account of rationality but am rather examining the account of rationality provided by a variation and selective retention model. In this regard the selection mechanisms are of crucial importance.

In the previous section I urged that variation involves not merely random "atomic" trials, but rather very complex focused processes. Analogously, selection may involve the life or death of whole organisms in the biological instantiation of the variation and selective retention model, but not necessarily in its application to conceptual change. This point was already hinted at when I discussed the enormous range and diversity of ecologies that need to be considered in thinking about evolutionary epistemology. Not only is there the influence of the physical world, but there are also the numerous representational systems we have constructed of the world. Indeed these are so ubiquitous that our access to the world seems always to be mediated by representational systems. Even our descriptions of the direct lethal impact of the world on organisms are given in terms of the ways we represent the world. Furthermore, among the representational systems we have, the ones in which we find social reality are of paramount importance for our ordinary notions of reasonableness and objectivity. As I argued in chapter 4, it is the social language games and paradigms into which we are trained that give sense to our ordinary judgments of reasonableness and objectivity. It is social agreement that provides the possibility for assimilation in large numbers of cases.

The point is that all of the selection mechanisms for what we ordinarily call knowledge are *vicarious* selection mechanisms—vicarious in that they *represent* the world and that representation cannot be thought of as "picturing" reality. We have no direct access to the world against which to check our observational representations, and this means that our observational representations may be imperfect and occasionally in error. There are numerous examples of these generally adaptive but occasionally errorful observational systems. Sweet taste is used as a generally correct representation of nourishingness, but nonnutritive saccharin could lead to starvation and possibly even cancer. What this means in the abstract is that reasonableness is no guarantee of truth.

How does this work in the case of the vicarious representation of nourishingness by sweetness? We can easily see how such a vicarious system could have arisen in the first place. Given the large overlap of nourishingness and sweetness, the substitution of the immediate judgment of sweetness for the direct trial of all kinds of foods would have an adaptive advantage. It would be a reasonable system to have from the evolutionary standpoint. At the same time, the representational system, qua system, contains its own built-in norms of "how it works." Thus, from the point of view of the system itself the criterion of reasonableness in eating is that food be sweet. From within that system alone it does not appear reasonable to question the identification of sweetness with nourishingness, and so in some cases, e.g., saccharin, the reasonable will fail. Only if the failure becomes widespread is the system likely to become "anomalous" in terms of the other existing systems, and whether or not the sweetness-equals-nourishingness system will change depends upon judging it from this larger framework. We see how an evolutionary-pragmatic theory of observational systems of representation can develop in a rational, albeit fallible, way. If the observational systems "do the job" they are supposed to do for the other systems, then they will be acceptable. Remember that "doing the job" involves both the pragmatic considerations of how the system works in assimilating inputs and the evolutionary considerations that render the system intelligible in the first place.

There is a distinction between structural and ecological vicarious selective systems that will allow me to discuss accommodative selection in yet another way. Roughly, structural selective systems select variants on the basis of whether they are a variant of a certain kind, thus reflecting the already-accumulated wisdom that variants of the given kind are generally adaptive. To be a mutant gene a variant must first be a gene. To be an alternative theory a structure must first be a theory. The role of ecological selection systems is to select from among the variants those that have already passed the structural selection test. Structural systems account for, e.g., the continuing interest in a demarcation criterion for science. If we can on structural grounds decide that a given schema, e.g., astrology, is not scientific, we need not expend any resources in exposing it to the ecological selection systems, which in the case of science is often a costly process.

It should be noted, however, that, as Campbell (1974, p. 421) puts it, "What are criteria at one level are but 'trials' of the criteria of the next higher, more fundamental, more encompassing, less frequently invoked level." What this seems to mean is that the structural criteria for a variant's being a variant of the given kind are themselves variants in terms of some higher-order structural criteria (Petrie, 1971a). Thus even at the level of the scientific enterprise, the criteria for what constitutes science as a truth-seeking enterprise can be viewed as a trial, apparently quite adaptive, to be sure, of higher-order criteria of, say, fulfilling human purposes. If we could reach our goals by merely wishing, then we would not have need of the enormously costly processes of science to tell us what is possible and what is not.

The point is even more obvious at more intermediate levels. For example, replicability is a criterion for good experiments. That is, the ability of results to be intersubjectively verified in a public social consensus is a criterion of anything's being a "scientific result." At the same time intersubjective replicability can be seen as a trial with respect to higher-order demands for objectivity. Plato's appeal to an intuition of the Forms would be another trial competing with intersubjective verifiability as a way of reaching objectivity. Again the importance of the public, social nature of objectivity as we currently understand it is apparent.

Thus, once more we see the familiar picture of variants in the first instance being judged by structural criteria. If the variants pass the structural test, vicarious ecological systems—especially observational systems of representation—come into play to select among initially plausible alternatives. The procedure thus far fits mainly the account of assimilation given in the previous chapter. If we look at variants in structural criteria from the point of view of a higher-order set of criteria, an account in terms of assimilation to the higher-order set of concepts is still possible. Of course, lower-order variants may constitute accommodative changes from the point of view of the overall conceptual scheme. No intellectual problem occurs, however, as long as there are higher-order structural criteria selecting the variants. The puzzle occurs when we are looking for selective criteria for variants in the higest-order structural criteria.

What selective systems are available for variants in the highest-order constitutive rules or concepts of any given rational enterprise? Consider the nature of the anomalies which provide the context for a variation in the highest-order criteria of a given rational enterprise. If the basic rules of methodology and procedure of the enterprise are in doubt, but its place in our overall human activity is not in question, then the lower-order systems of the enterprise can still provide an ecology for selection of higher-order principles of procedure.

This is the sort of case that characterized physics when relativity theory was introduced. It may also characterize it today as physicists debate whether the search for ever smaller and more transitory "fundamental particles" is really providing an explanation of physical reality or not. In the social realm ideological debates over liberal capitalism versus Marxism or socialism constitute another example. An example in education is the controversy over whether schooling is a form of social control or a mode of individual realization. In all of these cases the great body of lower-order generalizations, phenomena, procedural principles, and so on will have to be dealt with in one way or another by any successful variant, and hence these systems provide a selective ecology for the variants. In short, the question becomes whether the anomalies are handled, even if handling them amounts to dissolving them. The anomalies may be dissolved and other data may even look quite different after such a hypothesized fundamental conceptual change, but those elements are a part of the selective system for the variant. It is not that the earlier and the later conceptual schemes must account for the same data, but rather that the earlier conceptual scheme with its way of looking at the data evolves into the later conceptual scheme with its way of looking at the data. The first conceptual scheme has, by hypothesis, anomalies; the second does not. The theoretical and observational representational schemes have been brought into an equilibrium that honors the evolutionary achievements of the earlier schemes. It honors these because if it did not, new anomalies would arise requiring further adjustments.

There is another way in which we can conceive of existing systems operating as selection systems on variations of rules and criteria that have no higher-order criteria defining the activity. Human rational enterprises form more or less isolable sets of conceptual schemes— politics, religion, morality, science, and so on. In addition to lower-order systems selecting higher-order variants within such sets, there are also situations in which the systems from one set can serve as selection criteria for proposed changes in another set. Thus, for example, current pressures for a more careerist education can be interpreted as selective pressures on the very concept of education. These pressures do not come from within education itself so much as from an external social system concerned about the role and place of education in the social fabric. It is irrelevant in response to such external pressures to point out what a marvelous classics department a university may have; that can be granted. The question from outside the university is not whether it is a good classics department but what the classics department is good for.

It might be objected that what I have done is to sneak back in a higher-order selection system that I had hypothesized away. If general social concerns can act as selection systems on variations in the concept of education, such concerns are more comprehensive and of a higher order than the educational concerns. Not at all, for conversely, educational concerns could act as selection systems on social conceptions. In other words the anomalies may be conceived of as arising primarily from inadequacies in our social conceptions rather than from inadequacies in our conception of education. Again what will remove the anomalies is a reflective equilibrium among proposed variants and the remaining conceptual and observational systems.

Just one more example. It has often seemed that truth and the pursuit of truth are absolute values and ones that are not properly subjected to selection pressures from any other area of human activity. I do not wish to deny that the reflective equilibrium reached may in each case uphold the value of the pursuit of truth, but I do want to deny that we can be assured of that result a priori. In other words I claim that it does make sense to question the concept of the pursuit of truth from the perspective of other rational enterprises. The example I wish to cite here is the very real concern over recombinant DNA research. Not only are the areas in which we choose to seek understanding subject to selection by other human purposes than the pursuit of truth, but also the very nature of that understanding depends at least in part on these broader purposes (Petrie, 1977).

My view of adaptiveness as a reflective equilibrium is neither a pragmatic nor a coherence theory of truth. It is not a pragmatic theory of truth for it does not identify what is the case with our ability to deal with the world, even though it admits that our ability to deal with the world is our only clue as to what the world is like. Nor is it a coherence theory of truth for it does not identify truth with the simple consistency of representational schemes. Rather I draw a distinction between observational or lower-level representational systems and theoretical or higher-level representational systems and admit that the observational representational systems do provide a selection system for the theoretical representational systems. And this is so despite the fact that the observational representation systems are themselves fallible and changeable. They are pragmatic, evolutionary systems determined by the operation of a variation and selective retention model which insists on a conceptual distinction between the system and its "fit" with reality.

What this essentially amounts to is noting that representational systems that do not "picture" reality in any straightforward way, may, nevertheless, serve as vicarious selection systems of conceptual variants. And this can occur in a rational, albeit fallible, way. In other words, we can allow *both* that observation is by means of representational systems and, hence, theory-laden and unstable, *and* that we can distinguish observational representation systems from other systems and use the observational systems as general selection systems for conceptual and theoretical variants. This is so because an evolutionary view of observational systems gives reason to suppose that the stabilities of the world around which such observational systems are organized are stable for a whole host of basic activities that human beings pursue. Thus even though observational systems associated with different paradigms and language games may describe these stabilities in different ways, the contours of these varying descriptions largely coincide as we act in the world, and so the observational representational systems possess a relative stability and "robustness" across paradigms and conceptual schemes (Wimsatt, 1974; Campbell, 1958, Campbell and Fiske, 1959). By "a node of stability in the world," I shall mean the fact that a control system can be focused on the node and control for it, and a node will be "robust" if it can support numerous different control systems.

6. Retention

The notion of robust nodes of stability provides me with the means of exploiting Feyerabend's idea of a pragmatic theory of observation (see chap. 3, sec. 2, above) as a way of accounting for the continuity of observation through conceptual change. Under the supposition of the theory-ladenness of observation, the problem of continuity is how relatively stable observational systems are retained despite changes that occur in them as a result of coming to be associated with different theories. There seem to be two requirements that would render these phenomena intelligible, and both of these presuppositions seem perfectly plausible. The presuppositions are, first, that there are fairly robust nodes of stability in the world and, second, that any representational system we have for a node of stability interacts with the world and other representational systems, providing the basis for similarity judgments about the node.

Consider first the requirement of relatively robust nodes of stability in the world. Recall that a robust node of stability is one such that the contours of a number of control systems, i.e., representational systems, focused on the node will coincide. For the sake of definiteness consider the node under consideration to be that underlying a physical object. Control system theory requires a certain stability of perceptually controlled quantities in order to counteract minor disturbances to the quantity. Thus, we can identify the same physical object in different lighting conditions because of the stability the object possesses of always reflecting light, even if the colors change. Likewise with respect to shape. The actual geometric appearance of the object on our retinas can vary considerably depending on our perspective, but because the changes in geometric progression are unified by a stable single shape, it is conceivable that a control system could remove disturbances in projected images by moving around and seeing just those shapes that ought to be seen from the various perspectives. Control systems can account for minor variations against the background supposition of basic stabilities.

The requirement of the robustness of the nodes of stability in the world can be seen even more clearly from the perspective of the variation and selective retention model. The spatial continuity contours of physical objects coincide with the light-reflecting contours and their touch-resistant contours. This means that in varying the lighting conditions, we may vary the color of light reflected by a physical object quite dramatically. However, the light reflects from the same object as is represented in the modalities of spatially continuous shape and touch resistance. We therefore experience a physical object that, although differently observable in the color observation system than in the spatial observation system, responds in similar ways to our activities directed toward it. Thus our color observation representation system can come to include a compensation for lighting conditions and still be of the "same" object.

This account also applies to the philosophical puzzle of how the concept of color could ever be learned without learning the concept of the particular color the object is, and vice versa. Color depends on the reflectance of light in a stable way; particular colors depend on the particular light waves reflected from the surface. The contours of "color-reflecting" and "red-reflecting" are, therefore, for a great number of purposes, identical; but not for all purposes. It is conceivable that someone might in learning colors believe that "color" meant merely "red color" (or vice versa). That would be one possible variant of a control system we might try out. Until we met either in the natural or the social ecology a case where such an identification was inappropriate, we might go happily along for some time not distinguishing the two. But there are a huge number of instances in the world where the two modes of representation are not equivalent for purposes of acting in the world. "Bring the colored block," where there is no red block but there is a blue one, will bring a correction from a parent if we fail to act. Yet because "color" and "red" both match exactly the same stable contours, there is a sense in which we learn the two together.

Note, too, how the robustness of physical objects helps account for the question of whether physical objects are "really" hard and impenetrable as represented in common sense or clouds of atomic particles as represented in physical theory. The contours given by common sense happen to coincide with the contours given by physical theory. The resistance to touch coincides with the relative denseness of the atomic particles in a table compared with the molecules of air at the surface of the table. Thus the "same" physical object can be represented in quite different ways, and quite different control systems applied to it.

Note, too, that it is only a relative stability of the world that is required—relative to our sensory control systems. Impenetrability to touch can be controlled for despite a fairly significant decay of the atomic boundary of a table. We are the same people despite the fact that the molecules in our body change completely every seven years or so. Why? Because the control systems with which we judge sameness of persons do not control for atomic-level sameness.

Thus the supposition that at least some of the nodes of stability in the world are robust is all that we need to make sense of the possibility that observational representational schemes can both change with changing theories and yet provide a way of testing theoretical representational schemes against observational ones by means of reflective equilibrium. Robustness means that the contours that we run into by means of a variety of ways of acting in the world turn out roughly to coincide, and, indeed, this general supposition seems to be well borne out by our ordinary experience.*

However, the supposition of robust nodes of stability in the environment would be insufficient to account for the formation and change of observational systems without the second supposition of modes of interaction with these nodes that provide selection of variant representational schemes. In other words, the nodes do not automatically impress themselves on a passive receiving subject. Thus the second presupposition is that of an active organism pursuing its purposes in the world and trying out various control systems on the world as variant representational systems. I have already discussed how such variants can be initially plausible and how the different kinds of selection systems operate on the variants. Here I want to concentrate on the retention of the variants that are selected. Some of the variant control systems will be genetic and will be retained or propagated by genetic means. However, a large number of the ways of dealing with the world will be retained by social means, and these are of crucial importance to education. These retention mechanisms range from a baby's learning the concept of, say, "ball" to a graduate student's learning the concept of, say, "complementarity."

Basically, for social retention mechanisms to work, different organisms capable of interacting with the "same" (in the sense outlined above) environment must be supposed. We need not assume that the organisms have the same detailed purposes or ways of representing the environment, for whether they do or not can be discovered through

---

*Although I cannot pursue it here, the "structural core" view of physical theories being developed by Sneed (1971) and Stegmuller (1976) seems very similar to my more informal notions of robust nodes of stability.

their interaction. The variation and selective retention model contains a strong tendency for evolutionary achievements at whatever level to focus on the knowable, i.e., the robust nodes of stability of the world. Variants of control systems that focus on less robust, or less stable, nodes tend to get weeded out. Furthermore, the robust nodes of stability are reasonably well represented by now in the existing social schemes. Thus, the problem becomes one of how to initiate new members into these socially sanctioned representational schemes. Education is the retention mechanism for a great number of rational enterprises.

What typically happens is this: The student is put in an environment in which the physical and social ecological stabilities exist. Through various mechanisms already described in general and to be illustrated in more detail later, the student tries out a variant control system. The control system will typically have an initial plausibility and will match at least some of the contours of the stability being learned. Disturbances are then introduced, sometimes naturally, sometimes intentionally by the other social actors, e.g., teachers and parents. The teachers already know from their own case what a correction to the disturbance would look like, or, more precisely, they would recognize a correction if they saw it, even if they could not specify it in advance. If the student fails to correct the disturbance, they point this out in one way or another. If the student does something that the teachers do not recognize as being a correction, they might try to diagnose with what control system, if any, the student is operating and try to move the student from there to where the teacher wants the student to be. As Wittgenstein (1958, part II) puts it, at this level we *train* the student to behave as we do, by constantly checking to see if the student counteracts disturbances as we would.

The great advantage of social retention mechanisms is that they present the student not only with the physical ecology, but also with the ecology of other organisms with already-existent representational systems putatively about the "same" things. There are thus more chances that control system variants on the part of the students that are close to the ones being taught, but not quite the same, can be weeded out. Thus the ability to distinguish "color" from the specific colors is enhanced by the many social ways such a distinction is utilized, e.g., red traffic lights, blue balls, and so on. We could get along for some time with similar not-quite-right control systems if we relied solely on the direct effects of the environment to weed out mistakes.

A child is in a social context from the moment of birth and is constantly having his or her purposes and actions aided and frustrated, praised and corrected. Thus the selection mechanisms embodied in the social milieu are constantly in operation on the child's variations. And these social mechanisms embody, on an evolutionary account, virtually all of the wisdom of past ages, having survived selection processes in their turn. The correcting activities of parents and other people, other children as well as adults, ensure that the child learns to take things as we do, to make the same similarity judgments as we do, and to perceive the things we do long before the child learns *any* language, let alone the languages used by philosophers, psychologists, linguists, and educators for describing what has been learned. What we learn is often not identical to the descriptions we give of that learning. Once again, learning is the grounding of epistemology, for learning is the main retention mechanism for perpetuating selected knowledge variants.

Recall the rough distinction I introduced in chapter 4 among innate, common, and schooled language games. On the variation and selective retention model, innate language games turn out to be very general ones, selected and retained on biological grounds. The species, through evolution, has come to be able to speak a language. Common language games are the games we learn to play almost necessarily by being thrust into the social situations in which we are brought up. We will typically learn to speak a particular language on growing up with people using that language. This is the area in which an emphasis on the social selection mechanisms is particularly appropriate—somewhere between biological evolution and intentional tuition. Finally, schooled language games are those, like learning to read, that seem to require intentional teaching efforts rather than merely a haphazard interaction with the social milieu.

In the case of scientists on the frontiers of knowledge, there is a sense in which only the environment can weed out mistaken conceptual variants, for there is no teacher deliberately testing the variants. However, even there, the social system is crucial. For if scientists focus on a node of stability, they can tell by means of interactions with the node and with each other whether they are focusing on the same one or not. Again the method is disturbance and correction. Kuhn (1970b) reports the historical fact that new conceptual variants often cluster around a given laboratory or a new measuring or experimental device, or a new technique of analysis. Such exemplary problem solutions are grounded by robust stable nodes, the interaction of the organism with the node, and the interactions among the varying modes of representation within the social milieu. Social interaction provides the guarantee, although it is not infallible, that all the concerned parties are focusing on the same thing, whatever that thing is. Notice that such reliability is no guarantee of ultimate adaptiveness. Scientists once reliably focused on a phenomenon they called phlogiston, but that focus was not adaptive in the larger ecological scheme. That larger judgment is made in the process of bringing the observational and theoretical representational schemes into a reflective equilibrium.

Let me conclude this section with a brief consideration of a typical problem in learning to count. At one point in learning the one-to-one correspondence that we believe constitutes the essence of counting, children can count up to about twenty, in the sense not only of repeating the numerals, but also of being able to count that many objects. But they cannot "go on" and continue the mapping process, even though they may have memorized the higher numbers. The problem is to get the student to "go on" as we do. Notice that although *we* can characterize the "going on" in a fairly abstract way as acquiring the recursive successor relationship of counting, that kind of description is surely not how the student eventually learns to count. It is these kinds of examples that lead Kuhn to conclude that what is learned in the analogous scientific case is not a "rule of application," but rather the ability to make similarity judgments.

What is necessary here is that the student learn to extend the one-to-one mapping process which has already been acquired for small groups of things to large numbers of objects. However, this must be done under descriptions that are relevant to the student's view of the matter. What the socialization process can do in the first instance is to make sure that the student does go on as we do. Later we might also teach the student to formulate what is being done as we formulate it—i.e., as forming a one-to-one mapping. At this basic level, however, it is the example we set, the activities we perform ("This makes twenty-one marbles, twenty-two, . . . ," as we move the marbles with the student from pile to pile), and the corrections we make to the student's performance that are of crucial importance.

Because of the underlying robust nodes of stability that ensure that countable objects do not suddenly split or coalesce, we can be fairly certain that the student has got it when his or her activity is as ours is. However, there is no guarantee that at, say, a thousand, the mapping does not take a radically different turn for the student; we simply do not check out how that disturbance would be counteracted.

Counting allows us to deal with the world precisely because certain actions of ours in the world pick out contours of robust nodes of stability that in turn are also made use of and controlled for by higher-order systems of representation formulated in slightly different ways. The explicit rules of arithmetic coincide, at least to some extent, with the actions of counting. The boundaries of the activity of counting coincide with the boundaries of arithmetic rules, although the latter are not constrained by mappings only to physical objects and are hence more abstract. It is in this way that the lower-order "observational" or "data" systems can be both relevant to higher-order theories (they control for the same boundaries) and yet relatively independent of the higher-order theoretical systems of representation (they control for these same boundaries in different ways). Thus, the neglected problem of perceptual learning is thrown into a new relief (Petrie, 1974b). The social retention system of education is thus crucial to the variation and selective retention model. The vicarious selection systems contained in our social system constitute the rationality of our ordinary conceptual schemes and provide the best checks we have for changing our schemes. In their turn these systems are justified by the evolutionary view of human enquiry sketched earlier in this chapter.

7. Reflective Equilibrium

The variation and selective retention model applies self-reflexively to the account of enquiry, learning, and the growth of knowledge I am offering in this book. The variation I am suggesting is that the question of rationality should be how well our schemes of representation allow us to deal with the world, where the special sciences are seen as partial answers to how well we deal with the world. The selection mechanisms are the criteria of reasonableness to be found in all the areas of human enterprise—science, religion, morality, politics, and so on—and not merely those explicated by philosophy. On the evolutionary account these criteria embody ways of representing fairly robust nodes of stability in the world, and the question of the justifiability of any proposed variant is settled by how well it fosters a reflective equilibrium among our representational schemes and our activities in the world.

The notion of reflective equilibrium is what accounts for how any radically new conceptual scheme can be better than the current one with which it is in competition. Typically, variants do not arise unless there are anomalies within current schemes, and anomalies are those problems which by definition the current scheme is incapable of handling. If a proposed variant can give us a reflective equilibrium among observational and theoretical schemes of representation and our actions in the world, it will have removed the anomalies and at least given promise that no new ones will immediately arise. The variant must lead to an equilibrium because equilibrium implies that the boundaries picked out by the observational and theoretical systems roughly coincide with each other and with our actions in the world. If the boundaries did not coincide, we would be unable to deal with our total ecology which includes, e.g., our representational systems. The equilibrium must be reflective because by now in our evolutionary development, we have evolved social systems for judging adequacy and not merely falling into it. In short, we do have an evolutionarily grounded belief in justification, which means that part of the selection mechanisms will involve subjecting conceptual variants to the standards of reasonableness and justification we currently have.

Reflective equilibrium does not guarantee truth, although it does encapsulate the search for truth as a goal. That any variant is capable of being seen as an attempt at truth is one of the selection mechanisms the variant must pass through. It thus remains logically possible that a given reflective equilibrium is not, in the end, adaptive. Since no other method does guarantee truth, the fallible character of reflective equilibrium is no objection to it. Furthermore, it must be remembered that the probability that any given reflective equilibrium would be totally inadequate for dealing with the world is low. After all, the equilibrium is of subsystems which themselves have been evolutionarily selected and judged reasonable by criteria of adequacy which have in their turn been subject to an evolutionary selection. We may change the description of the boundaries of our ecology, but it is highly unlikely that we have missed the boundaries entirely with our previous attempts. It is in this way that we can account for the insights of both old-knowledge and new-knowledge attempts to solve the *Meno* dilemma while at the same time counteracting their individual weaknesses. Reflective equilibrium allows for truly new knowledge which is validated by old knowledge and our activity in the world. Furthermore, the new knowledge may end up changing that old knowledge. We *can* slip between the horns.

Granted, then, that reflective equilibrium is not arbitrary or unconnected with the world on an evolutionary account, there still seems to be a problem. For the equilibrium can be reached, it would seem, by any number of ways. Someone might assimilate beyond what would be appropriate or accommodate much too easily. Recall that I have myself raised this problem in the example of the millions of people who still refuse to accommodate the fact that former president Nixon obstructed justice. Can they be rationally criticized for their persistent attempts to assimilate their experience to a concept of an honest president? Can it be determined in general when to assimilate and when to accommodate since either process can reach a reflective equilibrium (Petrie, 1976a, Phillips, 1976)?

The philosophical answer to the question is fairly straightforward. Yes, we can often, although not always, say when to accommodate and when to assimilate by an appeal to the reflective equilibrium that is judged best by reference to the critical judgment of mankind at large as opposed to the reflective equilibrium which might be reached by, say, an individual Nixon supporter. That is, we must distinguish between an individual or idiosyncratic reflective equilibrium and that of the judgment of the collective human understanding. Nor is the collective human understanding to be determined simply by majority vote. It is rather the collective understanding reached by the best and most reasonable means we have currently available and endorsed by the authoritative reference groups in each area. Nor is the appeal to the "best" resources currently available question-begging, for as I argued in chapter 4 we must give up the search for a general account of rationality and accept instead, in the spirit of an epistemology naturalized, the partial accounts of rationality offered by the special sciences and areas of human enquiry. Furthermore, we *can* identify the best opinions in those areas without circularity by, say, sociological means. The experts thus identified may, of course, be wrong, but an appeal to the experts does not by any means make truth depend on the experts. On the variation and selective retention account it is the experts in any field who would be expected best to deploy the variation, selection, and retention mechanisms of the field, and these mechanisms can be reasonably expected to have some fairly stable contact with the world. So we do in general have an abstract account of when to assimilate and when to accommodate, and it matches what we actually find in historical practice.

The objection, however, raises an extremely important issue for education. To anticipate just a bit, I shall argue in the next chapter that the *Meno* dilemma and the problems it raises for general human enquiry have analogues in the case of the learning of an individual. If this is so, the educational question becomes when and under what conditions are we justified in forcing individual students to accommodate to our curricula and what account must be given of the relative autonomy of an individual's conceptual scheme. I shall be spending the next chapter pursuing these issues, for I believe that the general account I have been outlining offers the promise of being able to reconcile a respect for the student's interests, autonomy, and personal ways of knowing with the objective ways of knowing sanctioned by society and embodied in standard curricula.

8. Accommodation and Education

For now, however, let me counter several possible educational misinterpretations which might be placed on my account of variation and selective retention.

Notice first that my evolutionary account gives no solace at all to the nativists in the nature-nurture controversy. Indeed, in a sense it

dissolves the controversy, because those human capacities due to nature are seen as a form of species learning and subject just as much
or as little to a variation and selective retention model as are those
capacities due to nurture. The question rather becomes *what* variation,
selection, and retention mechanisms ought we to concentrate on in our
educative efforts, and prima facie we might look at biological, social,
or schooling areas for potential changes. It takes an argument, and
one that is never given, to say why we should not tamper with genetic
material but may, nevertheless, enforce our current social selection
mechanisms of good citizenship. It takes an argument to show why it
is acceptable to teach children to obey the law, but not acceptable to
question the law, and so on. Seeing the whole of the nature-nurture
controversy as concerned with different aspects of the same variation
and selective retention model should help us recast our questions in
new ways and force us to take into account the broader context of
human activity and purpose in deciding what ought to be done.

Another current educational fad that might be thought to find some
support in my account is the emphasis on pluralism. This emphasis is
found in a number of places, from a recognition of different individual
styles of learning, to treating value conflicts as noncognitive by certain
approaches to moral education such as values clarification, to a belief
in local control and local differences in educational policy. In all these
instances we are asked to recognize the existence of a pluralism of
viewpoints. Not very far below the surface is also the implicit and
sometimes explicit suggestion that any one of these alternative approaches is just as good as any other, and this suggestion seems to be
based somewhat vaguely on the ideal of tolerance. Is an emphasis on
pluralism supported by the evolutionary account?

It is certainly true that I have urged the recognition of conceptual
variants and conceptual diversity. So in the sense that a recognition
of pluralism is a needed antidote to a dogmatic absolutism in matters
cultural, intellectual, valuational, political, and educational, my account can be pressed into service. It is also true that a certain limited
support of tolerance can be extracted from the variation and selective
retention account. There is a support for tolerance, in that historically
we never know in advance what variation from accepted conceptual
schemes will prove adaptive in the long run. The support is limited,
however, in that tolerance of radical variants is not justified *tout court,*
but only when existing schemes are unable over a period of time to
solve the puzzles posed of them, i.e., when the puzzles become anomalies. Furthermore, it is extremely important to note that an anomaly
can be identified as such only from the perspective of our current conceptual schemes. There is a valid bias in favor of current ways of doing

things, and only as those prove inadequate is toleration of radical alternatives justifiable. Put in another way, variation mechanisms are always in competition with selective retention mechanisms for available resources. If we presuppose a relatively stable but slowly changing ecology, it follows that if either variation or selection is emphasized at the expense of the other, adaptation will not be the result. An unbridled pluralism is not justified.

Finally, the variation and selective retention model gives no support at all to the view that any approach in a pluralistic context is as good as any other approach. Such a claim may be true in certain areas, e.g., matters of taste in ice cream, but the argument must be made on the merits of the particular case. The variation and selective retention model provides no general support for such a view. Indeed, if anything, it provides a counter to such a view, for although it suggests that variants are needed, it also emphasizes that the variants are to be *selectively* perpetuated and the grounds of selection are not simply individual tastes.

Thus, it may indeed be a good thing to recognize the diversity of ethnic cultures in the United States as a remedy to a too-easy acceptance of the melting pot idea. It may even be the case that on political grounds in a democracy most, if not all, of the diverse cultures should be allowed to coexist and pursue their particular goals. It does *not* follow from this that any culture is as good as any other culture. Likewise with intellectual learning styles. We should recognize the differences if they exist, but it may be that instead of patronizing one or another of them, we ought to counteract the less efficient and less successful learning styles. This point is even clearer in the case of values clarification. By all means, different values and the consequences of acting upon them should be recognized and clarified, but it does not follow that any one set of values is as defensible as any other set. Hitler may well have been perfectly clear as to what he was doing. The point is that none of these "pluralistic" positions which seems to imply that any one of the "variants" is as good as any other receives any direct support from the variation and selective retention model. Indeed, I have been at pains to emphasize that variants are selected for, both in terms of initial plausibility and in terms of ultimate acceptability. Admitting the existence of conceptual diversity is not equivalent to a rampant subjectivism. Utilizing the variation and selective retention model does not mean urging that anything goes; rather, it focuses attention away from both dogmatic orthodoxy and unbridled subjectivity onto reflective equilibrium.

There is also a general intellectual enterprise which might seem at first sight to be reinforced by the account I have been defending. I refer to the sociology of knowledge. In one sense there can be no objection to a sociology of knowledge where this is conceived of as the description and explanation of the social genesis, justification, and growth of knowledge claims, or as the description and explanation of the operation of knowledge-generating social systems. It is only when such social processes are taken in a strong way as identical with the justification of knowledge that problems arise. For then truth is likely to come to be identified with elite opinion, and the political formation and perpetuation of an elite will replace critical thought as the path to truth. Such a position is clearly unacceptable, and yet sociologists of knowledge who make such strong claims appeal to considerations very similar to those in this book. Indeed, I have myself suggested that we must find out what the best collective understanding in any area is by appealing to the experts in those areas, and the experts are to be identified by sociological criteria. Does the variation and selective retention account give any support to identifying truth with expert opinion?

Expert opinion does indeed serve as part of the selection mechanisms for knowledge variants, but it does not constitute the truth of the field. At most it is one way of representing it. The criteria deployed by the experts have themselves been subjected to selective retention and thus have some claim to represent the wisdom we have accumulated thus far as a result of human enquiry. Given the socialization mechanisms that serve to perpetuate such wisdom, the experts will surely be the most reasonable deployers of the selection criteria of each field. Truth is not expert opinion, but an account of expert opinion, its genesis, growth, and change, will be very nearly an account of the operations of a variation and selective retention model in the genesis, growth, and change of knowledge in that field. Thus sociology of knowledge as a descriptive science can contribute to an evolutionary epistemology, but it is not identical with it.

The variation and selective retention model actually gives results incompatible with a too-easy acceptance of radically different conceptual schemes. We cannot go around just changing the norms of reason, for example, more or less at will. We probably cannot even change very many lower-order principles more or less at will. It is not that any logical incoherence would result, but rather the supposition that we could make such changes runs counter to the results given by an evolutionary epistemology. I have already noted that the norms of reason, for example, embody very abstract representations of extremely robust nodes of stability in the world. A large number of alternative descriptions of those nodes focus on the same boundaries, and although the descriptions may change, the boundaries must be dealt with. It may always be in order to propose an alternative knowledge variant, but whether the variant is ultimately acceptable depends upon whether or not we can reach a reflective equilibrium that takes into account (even if it redescribes) our observational systems and the norms of reason, and that allows us to deal with the anomalies which prompted the variant in the first place. As in the case of pluralism, the recognition of an alternative conceptual scheme does not by itself constitute an argument for its acceptability; the scheme must also be elaborated and defended by submitting it to systems of selection. Thus the sociology of knowledge cannot be used to defend an attitude of "anything goes" in curriculum matters.

There is, however, one educational change that does seem to follow from an evolutionary epistemology, and this is a relocation of the burden of proof for justifying educational interventions in the lives of children and adults. As long as we operate solely with an old-knowledge approach to the *Meno* dilemma, the basic knowledge postulated by such an approach is used to justify further enquiry and growth in knowledge. If we as educators already possess this basic knowledge, curricular decisions will follow automatically for any student. On the other hand, once we shift to an evolutionary epistemology with its emphasis on reflective equilibrium, we will have to justify to the student *in the student's terms* why we are asking for an accommodation to the new conceptual scheme embodied in, say, the formal disciplines. Sometimes we will be able to justify successfully to the student the necessity to modify his or her conceptual scheme, and sometimes we will not. In cases when we cannot, the individual autonomy of the student will have to be allowed sway in educational decisions. Even when the burden of proof *can* be carried, there will have been a shift away from a reliance on dogmatic orthodoxy in education.

7 | Learning

1. Enquiry vs. Learning

Although on occasion the preceding discussion has utilized examples from individual learning and the psychology of individuals, the major emphasis has been on enquiry in general. The *Meno* dilemma was cast in terms of enquiry and not in terms of an individual's learning. The examination of old- and new-knowledge approaches was an examination of attempts to solve the problem of enquiry in general. The discussion of the analogies between current problems in the philosophy of science and problems of conceptual change had to do not with a single student learning science, but with how we are to understand the growth of scientific knowledge. The control system model of action is intended as a general account of human behavior. The variation and selective retention model was concerned with the knowledge processes, not of the individual, but of human beings in general.

There are undoubtedly some educational insights to be gained from the discussion of enquiry in general which has occupied me so far. To the extent that the forms of knowledge structure our ways of knowing, we can see the importance of disciplined study. To the extent that there is conceptual diversity involved in the growth of knowledge, we can provide an implicit justification for teaching students about alternative ways of looking at the world. To the extent that conceptual change is important in science, we can criticize the standard textbook presentation of science as a static, ahistorical model of the world. To the extent that the control system model of action provides a synthesis of perception, rules, and behavior, a whole new perspective on, for example, testing for learning can be suggested. To the extent that the variation and selective retention model accounts for accommodative changes, we can find a middle ground between a dogmatic orthodoxy and an unbridled subjectivity in curricular matters. These and many other examples could be cited of the importance for education of a consideration of the *Meno* dilemma of enquiry.

However, education is, at base, concerned with an individual's learning and not with enquiry in general, except perhaps at the upper reaches of university-level research. The growth of human knowledge will be of concern to most people only if it affects them personally (e.g.

155

if a cure of cancer is found). Few, however, will ever participate in those kinds of knowledge processes. On the other hand, every individual is intensely interested in his or her own individual knowledge processes, that is, in the growth of his or her individual knowledge. And it is this latter area, the growth of an individual's knowledge, that is of primary concern for education, whether we are speaking of the formal processes of schooling or the more informal educational processes in which an individual might be involved.

Accordingly, there seems to be a prima facie distinction between enquiry, concerned with the growth of human knowledge, and learning, concerned with the growth of an individual's knowledge. Since both enquiry and learning are concerned with the acquisition of knowledge, they both have the normative aspect noted in the first chapter. That is, we ordinarily think of both enquiry and learning as aimed at knowledge in some fairly broad sense (see Hamlyn, 1973a; Green, 1971). Broad empirical accounts of mere "changes in behavior" on either the collective or the individual level do not seem to capture the notions of enquiry and learning. Such accounts include too much, and hence need to demonstrate the relevance of their concern with behavior change in general to the educator's concern with desirable and worthwhile behavior change.

Despite their common concern with the growth of knowledge, enquiry and learning can be distinguished by the processes of knowing appropriate to the two different cases. In the case of learning, since what is being learned is already known to humanity at large, the knowledge processes of the student may include recognition of a teacher's authority, or even an appeal to the knowledge of the community. "It is known that. . . ," a textbook in physics might run. Known by whom? Physicists, one supposes. Does each and every student have to become a physicist to know likewise? That seems too restrictive. The question thus becomes to what extent it can be assumed that an account of enquiry as adaptation in terms of assimilation, accommodation, and reflective equilibrium can simply be carried over whole and applied to learning. It seems that very different knowledge processes may be operative in the two cases, to say nothing of the differences among individual students.

The problem can be put in the form of an objection.* Whatever we might say about the *Meno* dilemma of enquiry, there simply is no analogous dilemma of learning—at least not about the kind of learning ordinarily encountered in schools and even in other, more informal, educational settings. Enquiry is something very few people ever engage

---

*This objection was suggested to me by Robert Ennis.

in, but in ordinary cases of learning quite clearly we can and do find out what we do not know. The teacher tells us, we read in an authoritative text, we look it up in the encyclopedia, we have someone demonstrate a skill for us and correct our efforts, and so on. Put in another way, virtually all of an individual's learning is of things that are already known to humanity, and, thus, for the dilemma of learning as opposed to the dilemma of enquiry, the old-knowledge horn is trivially grasped. What am I to make of this claim?

The short way with this objection is to point out that, strictly speaking, it is a non sequitur. The condition for grasping the old-knowledge horn of the *Meno* dilemma involves showing how it is that what is to be learned is already known and yet how learning can be nontrivial. However, the objection equivocates on this condition. What is known is already known to humanity and not to the student; yet it is the student whose learning is supposed to be nontrivial. The old-knowledge horn has not been trivially grasped.

However, to take the short way with the objection would be to miss an extremely important educational question. What, if anything, can be said about the relationship between knowledge processes in general and the knowledge processes of an individual student? How does a student, who does not know, come to participate in our public modes of understanding and knowledge? Notice that this question has particular urgency in that I have discarded old-knowledge models of "handing over" knowledge and new-knowledge models of the unconstrained creation of knowledge. If rational enquiry itself is a matter of adapting our public modes of understanding to the twin constraints of our purposes and the way the world is, what is rational for an individual student to do?

2. Knowledge and Understanding

The objection I am considering claims that knowledge is not justified by anything that the student believes or does, but rather by its place in the established wisdom and practice of humanity. I accept the claim that for anything to be known in general, it must be justified by appropriate criteria for enquiry in that field. However, for any *individual* to know something, that person must understand it in his or her own terms, in terms of the level of rules he or she can grasp. Indeed this is the epistemological insight behind the educational dictum that we must begin with the student's current cognitive and intellectual state. Just because something is reasonable does not mean that it is reasonable for the student. And unless it is made reasonable for the student, the student will not learn it, although the student may learn to parrot some noises. For learning to occur, the learner's understanding is logically presupposed.

This connection between knowledge and understanding has often been noted by philosophers of education. Even someone as committed to collective understanding and public rules as Israel Scheffler (1960, p. 57) has written: "To teach, in the standard sense, is at some points, at least, to submit oneself to the understanding and independent judgment of the pupil, to his demand for reasons, to his sense of what constitutes an adequate explanation." Likewise Hamlyn (1973b) urges:

> No one could be said to have come to understand a subject, to have learned it, without some appreciation of general principles, some idea of what it is all about. But knowing and understanding general principles is not just a matter of being able to recite the relevant general propositions. Nothing is contributed by way of understanding when people are made to recite general propositions, even if these are fundamental to a subject. Thus, to present a very young child with, say, the general principles of number theory or algebra would be a futile business; for, he must be capable of cashing such general principles in terms which mean something to him, if understanding is to follow.

Scheffler's point seems directly related to propositional learning. That is, we must give explanations, evidence, and reasons that are accessible to the student for any propositions that we are attempting to teach. Hamlyn's point has more to do with the acquisition of concepts and their role in learning the general principles of a field of study. However, he too emphasizes the necessity that for the student to understand the concepts and general principles, they must mean something to the student. We might also note that even the learning of skills, to the extent that it departs at all from mere habit acquisition, also involves understanding. "Knowing how" to do something as opposed to merely being able to do something seems to imply some level of understanding.

Whatever analysis of knowledge is adopted, the element of understanding in knowledge is crucial (Petrie, 1970; Waks, 1968). First, to believe *any* proposition involves assent to the proposition, and we cannot assent to something that we do not understand, at least at the minimal level of comprehending the words. The point is almost too obvious to state, and yet it is of crucial educational importance. It is not that a proposition must be understandable in general, but rather that before a given person can be said to know the proposition, that particular person must actually understand it. The claim that motion is relative may be understandable with reference to relativity theory, but it will not be understood by a person until it fits into that person's mode of understanding. Second, and perhaps even more importantly, understanding on the classical analysis of knowledge as justified true belief arises in conjunction with the justification condition. That is, not only must there be a justification in order for any proposition to be known, but also in order for us to say that any given person knows the proposition, that person must be justified in believing the proposition. The person's justification need not always be that found in a discipline, but it must be a justification that the knower possesses. That is, *my* justification for the relativity of motion conceivably may not be in terms of relativity theory. My grounds may be authority, but, nevertheless, even authority must be something that I understand as justificatory in order for me to be said to know.

Jane Martin (1970) suggests that this understanding amounts to seeing connections or relations. She analyzes the seeing of connections into two parts: an internal understanding which amounts to an analysis of the item to be understood, and an external understanding which amounts to a placing in context. Or, to oversimplify, understanding for Martin consists of distinguishing and classifying. Robert Halstead (1975) has argued convincingly that distinguishing and classifying are but two sides of the same coin. In distinguishing one thing from another, we are always doing the distinguishing relative to the assumed classification of the thing. The Civil War is distinguished from other events on the basis of the classification of events as wars. Conversely, we classify items on the basis of certain distinguishing features.

The main point is that on either Martin's or Halstead's view, understanding is an *activity* in which people engage with conceptual frameworks. Whether distinguishing and classifying are separate or connected, they are activities, and they are relative to concepts, modes of application, background knowledge, categorical schemes, and so on. Distinctions and classifications can be made for different purposes. A given traffic accident can be understood quite differently depending on whether it is from the point of view of the insurance investigator, the highway engineer, the automotive designer, or the social critic of our reliance on the private automobile. At the beginning of the previous chapter, I urged that our concept of rationality be extended to include the purposes and activities of the people involved in any rational enterprise. There is no "general understanding" to be had of the accident independent of these special kinds of purposes and activities.

Although neither Martin nor Halstead says much about it, it seems clear that their analyses could be applied at two very different levels: first, the level of collective understanding or enquiry, and, second, the level of an individual's understanding, or learning. In both cases, coming to know presupposes understanding which in turn depends upon doing things with our conceptual schemes. Thus, prima facie, a thing might be understood, without a given person's understanding it. Put another way, the very existence of the phenomena of learning or coming to know seems to require adjustments in the conceptual frameworks of individual students.

The claim that the *Meno* dilemma with respect to learning is trivial is, therefore, based on a conflation of something's being understandable with its being understood by a given person. Merely pointing to the fact that what children come to know is already known in general is no solution to the dilemma. From the students' points of view, they will not know until *they* understand, until *they* can distinguish and classify with their conceptual frameworks. From the students' perspectives they either already know in their terms, in which case learning is otiose, or they do not know in their terms, in which case, *they* will be unable to understand, or hence, learn the very subject that they are to master, even though others, including the teacher, may understand the material. Yet students *do* learn. How is this possible?

Before answering this question it is necessary to mention a variety of related concerns simply to set them aside as not germane to the central question of how learning is possible. In the first place, we can ask whether or not the sense in which a given proposition or concept can be said to be understood in the collective understanding is at all similar to the ways in which the proposition or concept is said to be understood by an individual. I have already pointed out in chapter 2 that Hirst seems to identify these two modes of understanding, yet surely that is an inadequate account of the matter. Halstead (1977) has convincingly argued against Hirst that whether we locate the collective understanding in formal features and rules of the discipline or in the activities of the disciplinarians, cases abound in which the student can be said to understand the material without having learned the explicit rules of the discipline and without behaving precisely as the disciplinarian behaves. We can reason correctly without appeal to the explicit rules of formal logic and without making all the methodological moves of the fully trained logician.

Another extremely important set of questions concerns the different kinds of barriers that might stand in the way of an individual's understanding. Ralph Page (1977) has identified five: sensory, psychological, developmental, theoretic, and ontological. Clearly it is crucially important for educators to know which of these kinds of barriers may be impeding understanding in any given case, for different barriers will have to be overcome in different ways. Since I am concerned with the structure and changes in the organization of an individual's conceptual scheme, I shall be concentrating here primarily on developmental, theoretic, and ontological barriers. At any given time, for a particular individual, a rough distinction can be drawn between the organization of the individual's conceptual scheme and individual occasions of use of that scheme. Organization reflects those patterns of use that seem to have a kind of stability or unity over the diverse instances of the application of the structure. Controlled quantities in control systems, for example, represent stable features of the organization of an individual's conceptual scheme. The ability to perform the basic arithmetic operations in a variety of circumstances is a part of the organization of an individual's conceptual scheme, while figuring the change from dinner the night before is a particular application of that scheme. My concern will be primarily with the influence of developmental, theoretic, and ontological factors on the organization of conceptual schemes.

Yet another set of concerns involves the possibility that the organization of an individual's conceptual scheme may be such that a given belief is unreasonable even from the individual's own point of view. This is the kind of case in which we might criticize someone for being unreasonable, not because the person does not possess our collective understanding, but because the person has made what would be a mistake from the person's own point of view. An example here might be someone who fudges the interpretation of an astrological chart so that the interpretation will conform to a desired result. Such cases are of educational significance because if we want to criticize the individual, it can be on internal grounds as well as by appealing to our collective understanding.

Finally, there are the questions of when it is justifiable, ethically and epistemologically, to initiate changes in the organization of an individual's conceptual scheme. On my view an individual's conceptual scheme has a kind of integrity which must be appreciated in any educational decision. On some occasions it may not be justifiable to force conformity of an individual's understanding to our collective understanding (even though it may be justifiable to have educational institutions *tend* in such a conservative direction). The clearest example of such a case is the scientific genius who achieves a breakthrough in scientific understanding precisely because of challenging the collective understanding of the time. However, there are also more prosaic situations in which we may not be justified in changing students' conceptual schemes. An example of this might be the Amish and their desire to limit, primarily on religious grounds, the schooling of their youngsters to the eighth-grade level. Again the importance for educational decisions of considering when and under what conditions we are justified in changing a student's conceptual scheme is obvious.

There are two distinguishable but related perspectives that must be taken in considering changes in the organization of an individual's conceptual scheme. In the first place there is the external perspective, external in that the primary concern is with how, through education and schooling, an individual's understanding comes to approximate our collective understanding. That is, what are the constraints and problems involved in moving from the personal point of view of the student to the public point of view of accepted knowledge? This is an external perspective in that it is heavily influenced by the current keepers of collective wisdom, curriculum planners and individual teachers. In a sense this perspective bears an affinity to old-knowledge approaches to the *Meno* dilemma. The knowledge and understanding are assumed to be there; the question is, how are they passed on to the student?

The second perspective from which we must view alterations in the student's cognitive apparatus is from the standpoint of the student as autonomous individual. From the student's perspective the knowledge and understanding that the curriculum planner and teacher wish to impart are by hypothesis external and not yet grasped. So from the student's point of view they are not yet accepted as knowledge. Thus the student's point of view bears an affinity to new-knowledge approaches to the *Meno* dilemma. The student must apply to the public knowledge selection criteria which the student accepts, or can be brought to accept, if the student is ever to learn the publicly accepted material.

As with the old- and new-knowledge approaches to the *Meno* dilemma on the level of human enquiry, so too in considering an individual's learning, problems result from not taking into account both the external perspective of the curriculum planner or teacher and the internal perspective of the student. On the level of enquiry in general I have argued that old- and new-knowledge approaches are connected through the processes of assimilation, accommodation, and reflective equilibrium. On the level of individual learning both the process of initiating the student into the public forms of understanding and the process of an individual's cognitive development and change must be considered. I shall consider these two processes in the next two sections.

3. Individual and Collective Understanding

Let me first adopt the external, or teacher's point of view and consider the question of how it is possible to initiate the student into the public forms of understanding. One plausible suggestion (Green, 1971) is that the acquisition of the public forms of understanding must be through the operation of the individual's mode of understanding and sense of reasonableness. The problem with this suggestion, as I have already shown in considering old-knowledge approaches to the *Meno* dilemma, is that if we are limited to existing knowledge structures in assessing reasonableness, it becomes extremely difficult to see how any new-knowledge variant could ever come to be seen as reasonable. Suppose that what is at issue is teaching the student Newtonian mechanics when the student's current framework for understanding motion is that of impetus. On the view that the student must judge a new framework for reasonableness in terms of her of his old framework of reasonableness, how could change of organization ever occur?

Green (1971, pp. 43–55) attempts to meet this challenge by claiming that knowledge variants can be assessed from the perspective of an evidential style of belief. An evidential style of belief involves believing for good reasons. Yet it is ambiguous whether this means good reasons from the student's point of view or good reasons from the public point of view. If it is the former, then the student already has an evidential style of believing, and it is unclear how, from the student's standpoint, any changes in that style could be reasonable. If it is the public sense of reasonableness, then the problem has simply been redescribed, since we must begin with the student's current style of belief.

We could, of course, simply insist that the student be forced through repetition to master the modes of thought that characterize current public methods of understanding. And, in many cases, this is indeed what we do, and perhaps what we must continue to do. We teach spelling by rote, we insist that arithmetic must be done in such and such a way, we claim that certain modes of historical explanation are irrelevant, we assert that experiments in magnetism must be conducted in the manner prescribed in the laboratory manual, and so on. Even in graduate education there remains a certain basic level at which we simply train the student to behave as the teacher does. Even at the graduate level where tolerance of divergent viewpoints and the appeal to reason is the strongest, we do not allow the student to depart *too* far from the canons of the discipline and still be counted as a disciplinarian. Thus in a sense there is an empirical method, stemming from Aristotle, which shows how it is possible to get students to have an evidential style of belief. Aristotle said that to become virtuous, one should act as the virtuous person acts, habitually, and one will become virtuous. We can insist that the student think as we do, and if the student fails, we will count that student as beyond the pale. People do in fact learn to reason under that kind of tuition, but problems of understanding just what is happening remain.

In the first place, there seems to be an ethical problem involved in constraining people to behave in certain kinds of ways. Prima facie, it would seem that we must justify interfering with another person's life and forcing certain kinds of behavior from that person. Perhaps a justification could be given in terms of how an evidential style of belief will contribute instrumentally toward the student's later self-realization. That is, if we believe reasonably, we are more likely than not to be able to assess means to our ends. Furthermore, an intrinsic justification might be attempted. An appeal to reason as part of what it is to be human could be made. Such a justification could perhaps be given, although the more usual practice in education is to assume that the student bears the burden of proof of showing why any deviation from the public curriculum should be allowed.

Yet the intrinsic justification clearly appeals to public criteria of reasonableness and ethical standards. We are not justifying to the student why we are thus interfering in his or her life, and somehow that seems intuitively questionable. A justification appealing solely to public criteria might have been acceptable had we ever found the self-evident, absolute criteria of rationality and reasonableness for which philosophers have been searching all these years. But it has been the thesis of this book that we must give up such a search, and, once we have, once we have recognized the existence of conceptual diversity and conceptual change, then we cannot simply ignore the potentially different conceptual scheme of the student. We will have to justify inducting the student into public canons of reasoning in terms of the student's current canons of reasoning. The claim, "It's for your own good," has been invoked far too often in dubious and improper situations in the past to be taken at face value. If something really is for the student's own good, then to some extent we should be able to make that clear to the student.

This consideration leads to the second problem with simply asserting that empirically we do, at least sometimes, get students to form an evidential style of belief by forcing them to behave in the appropriate manner. Recall that in the first chapter I mentioned that the paradox of moral education seemed to be a close kin to the *Meno* dilemma (Peters, 1974b). The paradox of moral education involves the apparent necessity of having to inculcate certain behavioral habits that are not fully moral in order to reach the stage of full morality which involves critical reflection on moral rules. To be fully moral we must act *because* we know the rules are right and not merely because we have been trained to act. Yet this is paradoxical, for how can amoral behavior which seems to be required prior to moral behavior turn into moral behavior? What I want to suggest here is that there is an exactly analogous paradox which can be constructed with respect to the initiation of students into an evidential style of belief.

The paradox is this. Children do not innately think rationally and critically; they must learn these skills. A part of this learning involves making certain kinds of moves in the rationality game. It involves being open to evidence, being able to tell when a piece of information is evidence, being consistent, being able to entertain alternative hypotheses and points of view, and so on. Yet it is not merely acting habitually in these kinds of ways that constitutes rationality, but rather doing these things *because* they are seen to be the most reasonable things to do. However, such critical reflection on the rules and norms of reason is not present when we begin learning how to reason. So the empirical approach of saying we merely train people in the moves of being rational and they then become rational, while true, leaves the paradox standing. How is it possible that the habits of making certain intellectual moves without understanding them to be rational nevertheless turn into rationality which involves making the intellectual moves *because* they are seen to be rational? How can we rationally teach students to be rational?

One approach to this second question has already been mentioned in another connection in chapter 4. Recall Paul Hirst's claim that to have a rational mind involves having our experience structured by the forms of knowledge. These forms of knowledge enable us to articulate what it is to be rational, and our individual experience is conceived of as rational only insofar as it reflects a structuring by the forms of knowledge which in turn constitute our collective understanding.

Thus, Hirst's answer to the question of what the connection is between the student's individual mode of understanding and the collective mode of understanding is that it is a conceptual one. That is, we will be able to call a given student's conceptual apparatus reasonable only if it partakes of or prefigures the public objective sense of understanding explicated in terms of the forms of knowledge. Modes of thought and reasonable behavior on the part of any student will be modes of *thought* and *reasonable* behavior only if they contain in some way a structuring by means of the forms of knowledge. On Hirst's view, there is no mystery in passing from the student's understanding to the public understanding, precisely because the latter comprehends the former and lends the student's understanding its purchase on being appropriately called reasonable in any sense.

Educationally such a view is characteristic of most discipline-centered theorizing. When children's thought processes diverge from adult standards, they are typically not seen as reasonable in a different way, but are rather viewed as mistaken or at best as potentially reasonable insofar as they approximate to the public objective understanding. Contrast this approach with those views that see a relatively self-contained reasonableness in the child's way of looking at things. Clearly this latter view, if not allowed to degenerate into a radical subjectivism, is more nearly in harmony with the emphasis on conceptual diversity and change argued in this work.

In any event, a conceptual connection between the forms of knowledge and an individual's mode of understanding is not defensible (see Halstead, 1977). It may well be true that in some sense or other we describe the student's mode of understanding in our more public terms, but that is similar to the situation with respect to our historical view of conceptual changes in human enquiry in general. I have already argued that although we now comprehend historical conceptual changes from our current perspective, it is simply false to the historical record to suppose that somehow those earlier concepts were rational or reasonable only insofar as they approximated our current views. How could combustion as the driving off of phlogiston have approximated combustion as the taking on of oxygen? Once we look at the historical record in some detail, the existence of real conceptual change becomes hard to deny. And this is so even though a fine-grained historical analysis can often show how the knowledge variants were plausible as proposed and were ultimately justified by reasonable selection criteria. The evolutionary model enabled me to show the unity and rationality in diversity and change. The situation seems entirely analogous in the case of an individual's learning. The mere fact that we describe the status of the student's current cognitive structure in our terms should not blind us to the fact that this structure undergoes radical changes over time.

Indeed this point is clearly recognized by anyone who has reflected seriously on any individual's learning history. It is simply not necessary for anyone to learn explicitly the norms characterizing the public mode of understanding in order for the person to be correctly described in terms drawn from the public mode of understanding. People reasoned correctly long before logic was formalized as a way of characterizing correct reasoning. And there have clearly been historical changes in the concepts of logic. A student can learn to write well without learning the rules of good writing, and so on. The fact that we describe rational and reasonable behavior in ways derived from our currently accepted sense of what is reasonable and publicly understood does not imply that what is being done by an individual is the explicit following of those rules, or even anything conceptually connected with those rules.

This point is often given lip service, even by Hirst. The order of logic is not necessarily the order of pedagogy. For example, the most perspicuous way we currently seem to have of representing the foundations of arithmetic is in terms of set theory (although that too is a matter of controversy). Because of this, most, if not all, of the new math developed during the 60s more or less explicitly taught arithmetic in terms of set theory. After all, if there is a conceptual connection between the ordinary activities of adding and subtracting on the one hand and operations among sets on the other, then operations among sets must be what is "really" occurring on a basic level when we are adding and subtracting. However, this supposed conceptual connection eluded tens of thousands of teachers who needed to be retrained in the new math and millions of parents who could no longer help their children with homework. If, on the other hand, teachers and new math professors possessed divergent representation systems, the difficulty might actually have been a clash of two different modes of understanding. It is wrong to close off a priori the possibility that the difficulty of learning new math was due to the fact that the modes of understanding characteristic of the activity of adding are different, although perhaps related to, the modes of understanding characteristic of the activity of taking the union of two sets. The analogous mistake in the philosophy of science was to insist that earlier science had to be viewed either as a mistake or as a logical precursor of current ways of viewing the world. Contemporary history of science seems to have demonstrated that there have been structural changes in science as well as mistakes and mere elaborations.

As I shall urge in the next section, Piaget has begun to do for education what Kuhn has done for science, namely, show that we cannot a priori foreclose the possibility that some learning is due to structural changes in a child's cognitive apparatus and not merely to elaborations of an existent apparatus. At a minimum it is at least sensible to suppose that alternative conceptual structures account for such examples as Piaget's conservation experiments. If even this much be granted, then a part of the argument for whether we should accept the hypothesis of alternative conceptual structures or the hypothesis of mistakes and precursors is to be found in the plausibility of the elaborations of these two views.

In concluding this section on the problem of bringing a student's mode of understanding into line with the publicly accepted mode of understanding, I want to forestall one objection and pose the problem in a form to be considered further in the next chapter. The objection is that by insisting on the relative autonomy of the student's mode of understanding I have committed myself to a radical subjectivism and left no room for the influence of public modes of understanding on any individual's cognitive structure. In short, it might be objected, I have rendered respectable the student's response, "That's just your opinion." Alternatively I could be said to have debased the public mode of understanding to a simple sum of all the individual modes of understanding. Or perhaps the objection might take the extreme form that by questioning the effect of public criteria of rationality on an individual's modes of believing, I have committed myself to the essential incommensurability of individuals' cognitive schemes.

Not at all. Indeed, this objection sounds suspiciously like the one raised in the context of enquiry and conceptual change at the beginning of the preceding chapter. It simply does not follow that we must give up objectivity in order to recognize that individuals may have relatively autonomous modes of understanding and senses of what it is reasonable to believe. As in the case of enquiry in general, what does follow is that we must characterize objectivity otherwise than in terms of an independent, unproblematic access to the way things really are and instead substitute the notion of a reflective equilibrium reached through a process of adapting our individual representational schemes, theoretical and observational, to the demands placed on them. The individual, too, must assimilate and accommodate. If we assume that we are justified in some cases in altering an individual's cognitive framework, the question then becomes how the public standards of objectivity and understanding can be brought to bear upon an individual's relatively autonomous conceptual scheme. The answer, to be elaborated in the concluding chapter, is through a triangulation of thought and action that will help the student to see his or her individual life in terms provided by the public modes of understanding.

4. Individual Development and Learning

Introducing the idea that an individual must also come to a reflective equilibrium as a process of adapting to the ecology leads to a consideration of the internal perspective of the student. All of the influences on the individual student, from the causal influences of the physical world to the social influences of public notions of what it is objectively reasonable to believe, will be mediated through the individual's representational systems, both theoretical and observational. Thus, we must consider the individual's point of view and ask how the individual's system changes in response to what kinds of demands. The external perspective of the teacher or curriculum planner is analogous to that of the historian of science. Both have a picture of conceptual change that comprehends both beginning and end. Both can see where we start with a conceptual change and where we end up. On the other hand, the scientist currently on the frontiers of knowledge is analogous to the student facing intellectual problems which may or may not call for structural changes. It is to a consideration of such internal perspectives where neither participant yet has the benefit of hindsight that I wish to turn in this section.

The analogies between the individual case and enquiry in general are striking. We seem to have to satisfy the same criteria of adequacy already elucidated for the *Meno* dilemma of enquiry. First, we must allow for conceptual diversity. This diversity occurs across individuals and across time within individuals. Examples of the former range through differential reaction to optical illusions in different cultures to differential ways of experiencing by differently trained people. The electrician seems to have a different set of concepts concerning residential wiring than does the average homeowner. Conceptual differences within an individual range from the striking phenomena of religious conversion to the difference between my concept of philosophy now and when I was in high school. They also would include the kinds of differences noted by Piaget between concrete and formal operations, for example, and by Kohlberg between different stages of moral development.

Second, there is a conceptual continuity within these changes. Although there are vast differences between what I thought about philosophy in high school and what I think about it now, there seem to have been no radical conversion experiences. Each step of the way seemed plausible, and although I now see certain initial motivations for pursuing philosophy as irrelevant, they were operative at the time. Compare this with the development of science in which anomalies may end up being solved by being dissolved.

As active individuals utilizing our conceptual and representational frameworks for dealing with the world, the sources of changes become important to us. We bump up against our representations of the world and society, and we are not always able to carry out our individual purposes without changing these representations. The changes must be plausible and adequate. We do not usually consider wild variants until we have exhausted more plausible ones, and any variant must ultimately be selected as adequate for our purposes. If we do consider wildly improbable variants, they are less likely to be ultimately selected as adequate.

At the same time our individual purposes and choices are insufficient to condition our representational schemes in any wholly subjective way we wish. Our purposes will guide the development of our cognitive structures, but the structures will also be conditioned by the physical and social world with which we must interact. Put in evolutionary terms, selective criteria will be drawn from individual and social purposes and from representations of the physical and social world which have survived earlier selective pressures and thus will reflect distinctions which people have found it worthwhile to make throughout history. In short, the conditions on a solution of the *Meno* dilemma of individual learning are quite similar to the conditions on the solution of the *Meno* dilemma of human enquiry.

Probably more than any other contemporary psychologist, Jean Piaget can be construed as having concerned himself with precisely this problem of the changes of cognitive structure in the individual through learning and development. (See, for example, Piaget, 1948, 1951abc, 1952, 1954, 1968b, 1972.) And although in many respects Piaget's work is in harmony with the position being developed in this book, I have purposely avoided discussing him in depth until now. There are two reasons for this. First, once one starts on Piaget there is no stopping, for making sense of his own output is a mammoth task to say nothing of the overwhelming secondary literature. This book would have turned into yet another commentary on Piaget, and while that might have been useful, I feel that the approach I have taken via the *Meno* dilemma allows me to place Piaget within a larger historical framework and, therefore, to assess his work in a comparative way. Second, as will become apparent below, although Piaget's genetic epistemology is akin to the evolutionary epistemology I have been advocating, there are crucial differences. These would have been obscured, I think, had I chosen the route of commenting more directly on Piaget.

Very briefly, Piaget's view of cognitive development involves the passage of the child through a number of stages in a fixed order. These have been characterized at one point by Piaget (1968a, pp. 5–6) in the following terms:

1) The reflex or hereditary stage, at which the first instinctual nutritional drives and the first emotions appear.
2) The stage of the first motor habits and of the first organized percepts, as well as of the first differentiated emotions.
3) The stage of sensorimotor or practical intelligence (prior to language), of elementary affective fixations, and of the first external affective fixations. These first three stages constitute the infancy period—from birth till the age of one and a half to two years—i.e., the period prior to the development of language and thought as such.
4) The stage of intuitive intelligence, of spontaneous interpersonal feelings, and of social relationships in which the child is subordinate to the adult (ages two to seven years, or "early childhood").
5) The stage of concrete intellectual operations (the beginning of logic) and of moral and social feelings of cooperation (ages seven to eleven or twelve, or "middle childhood").

6) The stage of abstract intellectual operations, of the formation of the personality, and of affective and intellectual entry into the society of adults (adolescence).

These stages involve varying kinds of conceptual structures which enable the child to make sense of the world. At different stages, different structures are utilized. For example, the difference between concrete operations and formal operations for Piaget lies essentially in the fact that the operations or actions in the fifth stage are upon concrete problems—one actually tries out various problem solutions—whereas, in the formal operations stage, the alternatives can be represented in thought and the alternative solutions tried out abstractly rather than concretely. There are similar differences between the other stages.

Piaget accepts many of the points I have been emphasizing in this book. He recognizes the importance of schemata for structuring and organizing experience. He recognizes conceptual diversity in that he urges that there are different stages which progress into each other. Indeed I have borrowed my terms assimilation and accommodation from him. He, however, seems to envisage them slightly differently. For Piaget, assimilation seems to be a response to internal factors of cognitive processing, while accommodation is an alteration of cognitive processing in response to external factors, with both proceeding together. My own characterization of assimilation as removing disturbances by an existing control system, and accommodation as changing control systems in response to anomalies, makes no such internal-external distinction, or at best a relative one, relative to what the control system is controlling. Furthermore, the two processes need not go on simultaneously for me.

The crucial feature of Piaget's system is that he believes that an individual's development is explained in terms of the equilibration of assimilation and accommodation. Piaget asserts that development can be viewed as so many progressive forms of equilibrium, each an advance on the last. If we could understand how the equilibrium of assimilation and accommodation explains development, we would understand the development of cognitive structures from the internal point of view of the individual. If we could obtain such an account of the internal development of an individual's cognitive structure, the outstanding problem from the previous section of how to understand the transformation of an individual's mode of understanding to the publicly accepted mode of understanding (in those cases where that is a reasonable goal) would be amenable to solution. Indeed, my own suggestion at the end of that section was that we must look at the development of an individual's conceptual scheme from the point of view of a reflective equilibrium among its parts. Piaget's views are very promising here.

Clearly, Piaget does start with the child's perspective. He is concerned not to describe the schemata being utilized by the child as deviations from adult norms. The child's schemata appear to have a relative autonomy and distinctive mode of functioning at any given stage of development, and that mode of functioning changes as the child moves from stage to stage. Equilibration for Piaget is a process that operates both within a given stage of development and between stages of development. Within a given structure of action schemata, behavior is originated in response to needs which can be anything from physiological deprivation to theoretical puzzles, and the behavior continues until the need is satisfied. This description of equilibrium operating within a given stage is close to the more detailed control system analysis I have given of assimilation. However, for Piaget this equilibration continuously involves both the assimilation of reality to the existing schemata and the accommodation of the schemata to the disruption. Thus, while I explain accommodation in terms of anomalies that overwhelm existing systems and require structural alteration so that equilibrium can again be reached, that route is not open to Piaget. Accommodation, since it occurs constantly for him, cannot be used as I do to explain stage transition. He must explain in another way how it is that we ever pass from one stage with its distinctive contents and structures to another stage with its different contents and structures.

He says (1968b, p. 4): "We must, however, introduce an important distinction between two complementary aspects of the process of equilibration. This is the distinction between the variable structures that define the successive stages of equilibrium and a certain constant functioning that assures the transition from any one stage to the following one." That is, Piaget asserts that there is a constant functioning underlying the transition from stage to stage such that each equilibrium is an advance on the one which went before. Each equilibrium is more stable than the preceeding. This is in sharp contrast to my own view in which there is absolutely no guarantee, especially prior to the transition from stage to stage that the succeeding stage will be more stable in any ultimate way than the preceding one. Yet for Piaget the greater stability is taken to explain transition between stages.

What is the nature of this greater stability for Piaget? The most stable structures seem to be the logico-mathematical ones. Once they are reached in mental development, they do not change. They may enter into other structures, but their stability seems perfect. If this is so, Piaget seems to be suggesting that the ultimate stability is to be found in such structures and that greater stability is defined as approaching nearer and nearer to such structures. Indeed it is clear that Piaget (1968b), p. 105) accepts the theory-ladenness of observation and in particular believes that "it would be impossible to discover any content without a structuring involving at least a partial isomorphism with logic." Logic is, however, the perfect expression of reversible compensations and thus seems to be definitive of equilibrium. Piaget (1968b, p. 105) is careful to say that logic itself is not to be found everywhere, but, nevertheless, the structures that do exist are prototypes of logical structure, and "logical structures result from the progressive equilibration of the pre-logical structures which are the prototype of the later structures."

Notice what has happened here. Piaget has shifted from the internal perspective of an individual's developing mental structures and an equilibrium understood from such an internal perspective to a perfect objective equilibrium to be found in logico-mathematical structures. But these logico-mathematical structures are the inevitable end product of the progressive equilibration of the early structures which are protypes of the logico-mathematical structures. As Toulmin (1972, pp. 423–25) has pointed out, Piaget is a developmental Kantian. Unlike Kant, Piaget insists that the universal a priori forms of understanding are not to be found in every stage of thought. But the structures that are to be found there are the prototypes of the fully rational thought to be found in the logico-mathematical structures, and the development toward those structures is guaranteed by the process of progressively more stable equilibrations which turn out to be defined by the logico-mathematical structures.

So Piaget spans the gap between an individual's mode of understanding and the public mode of understanding, with a conceptual bridge after all. He began by looking at individual development but explained its course by bringing in the collective objectivity of logico-mathematical structures and the progressively more adequate equilibration of earlier structures prototypical of the logico-mathematical ones. The conceptual link is stretched out over the period of development for Piaget, unlike Hirst's direct conceptual link, but it is, nevertheless, a conceptual link. A more adequate equilibration is defined as one that approaches more closely to the logico-mathematical structures. We had hoped to obtain from Piaget an account of equilibration from the internal perspective of the individual. He ends up smuggling a developmentalized Kantianism into the process, thereby guaranteeing the transition to the ultimate objective understanding given in logico-mathematical structures, but denying the relative autonomy of the internal perspective. Once more we see an old-knowledge approach to the dilemma of learning with all the usual attendant problems. In this case the real conceptual diversity we find among students and within students at different times would have to be illusory on Piaget's account. This shortcoming accords with the standard criticism of Piaget that his stages are not so rigid and necessary as he would have us believe, and that his attempts to handle embarrassing empirical facts smack significantly of the ad hoc.

In attempting to avoid the skepticism of an empiricism that relies on direct access to given atomistic bits of experience, Piaget embraces a Kantian view that reason, at least as an end product, must be found to structure all our experience. In addition to such objections as I have raised, Piaget is open to the charge (e.g., Hamlyn, 1973b) that his psychological explanation of development in terms of equilibration merely redescribes the phenomena in a misleading way. Piaget "explains" the development of more rational structures of thought by progressively more adequate equilibration, where the adequacy of the equilibration is defined by logico-mathematical structures which in turn are constitutive of more rational thought. Thus, Piaget has made a conceptual point in misleading psychological or biological terms. As I have already argued, my own account of equilibrium does not assert a conceptual connection between individual and collective understanding. Rather it depends upon control system theory and the variation and selective retention model, and is, therefore, not open to the objection of explanation by redescription.

Although Hirst (1965), too, invokes a conceptual bridge between the individual and the public senses of reasonable to believe, his bridge is more direct. Perhaps Hirst would allow a developmental stretching out of the process, as does Piaget, but his view differs in another, even more important, respect. For Piaget the ending structures are perfectly equilibrated, a deliverance of pure reason. For Hirst the forms of knowledge are not capable of any absolutist justification. They are simply the best we currently have. Nevertheless they provide the structures and bounds of sense in describing our mental activities. In this sense Hirst is following Strawson's (1959, 1966) modification of Kant. This modification amounts to recognizing that no transcendental justification can be given of the categories of understanding. We cannot justify such structuring of our experience on the basis of the deliverances of pure reason. Nevertheless, Strawson asserts we can *describe* what in fact seem to be our current basic categories of understanding and these in fact do structure our experiences.

The problem with the Strawsonian approach is that while it looks as if it recognizes conceptual change and diversity, it leaves the process of such change wholly mysterious. For either this approach gives no account of conceptual change, or it leaves the question of the adequacy of alternative structurings untouched. But what are we to say of alternative structurings of experience, alternative bounds of sense? Are they better or worse than ours, or simply incomprehensible? If comprehensible, what sense can then be given to changes in our concepts? Even if we have good reason to believe that our current bounds of sense apply to all humans in the circumstance in which we currently live, how could we make any rational, even plausible, decisions about changes in such structures in the face of changed circumstances? Strawson and Hirst lack the full-blooded Kantian justification, and so these questions are appropriate, but they are not answered. Indeed, it is hard to see how they could be answered since the bounds-of-sense position seems essentially committed to recognizing only assimilation as an adaptive process and denying the adaptive nature of accommodation (in my, not Piaget's, sense of those terms).

My own view of the logico-mathematical structures differs from both Piaget's and Hirst's in that both conceptual change and the relative autonomy of an individual's cognitive structures are taken seriously, as is the necessity of accounting for the continuity in conceptual change. On my view there is a kind of equilibrium to be found in control system theory. Control systems remove disturbances to perception, where the behavior is accounted for in terms of existing structures. There is another related equilibrium, reflective equilibrium, which is what serves on the variation and selective retention model to explain when a conceptual variant is better than a competitor. If the variant removes an anomaly and allows assimilation to proceed with the new structure, where all the selection criteria have been satisfied, then the new system is in reflective equilibrium, from an *internal* point of view.

I have argued that observational systems and the norms of reason, including the logico-mathematical structures, comprise two sets of relatively stable, albeit quite different, representational systems and, hence, serve as selection criteria for conceptual variants. I have claimed that such twin stabilities at the "concrete" and "abstract" ends of our cognitive schemes are to be expected on the variation and selective retention model, even though these stabilities are neither guaranteed nor impervious to future changes. What this means is that logico-mathematical structures will in fact exert a very powerful effect both on the growth of knowledge in general and on the course of individual development. I have already shown how logico-mathematical structures will form a core selective system on the level of general enquiry. They will likewise be centrally implicated in an individual's learning and development because of their evolutionary success for human beings. These systems can be implicated in a variety of ways. There is the obvious fact that we socially inculcate logic, mathematics, and reasoning skills into our children (although the account of how this occurs thus far remains elusive). Perhaps we can properly construe other systems of thought that are not characterized by explicit logico-mathematical formulation as nevertheless conforming to the norms of reason, e.g., different cultural or individual reasoning processes. It may also be that some other such structures are really "prototypes" of Piaget's logico-mathematical structures and as such will prove tremendously important to an individual's cognitive development.

What has emerged thus far from the discussion of an individual's learning and development from an internal perspective has not been very fruitful. Although Piaget's descriptions of development and stage transitions may be helpful in understanding the relatively autonomous development of an individual's conceptual scheme, his explanation of this development in terms of equilibration (as he understands the term) was not helpful. I have suggested that the notion of reflective equilibrium which I have been developing might help, but that suggestion needs to be spelled out in more detail.

5. Robustness Again

The supposition of the existence of robust nodes of stability in the ecology of the individual can be pressed into the service of an account of the internal view of learning and development. Recall that a node of stability is a point in the ecology that is stable enough so that it can form the basis for the controlled quantity of a control system. In other words, we can *represent* a node of stability and behave in ways to correct disturbances to our representation of it. A node is robust if it can support a variety of control system representations. Another way of making this point is to say that the different boundaries given by the different representational systems are largely congruent. Disturbances in one boundary representation will likely be disturbances in another boundary representation. This single supposition, surely a plausible one, provides the basis for constructing an account of how it is possible that from an internal perspective an individual's cognitive scheme could develop in roughly the ways it does. We can also give an account of the conditions under which we can make sense of the notion of leading individuals to the public mode of understanding by getting them to assess the situation by means of their personal modes of understanding (see Green, 1971).

The process is that of a kind of pattern matching or triangulation. (See Campbell, 1959, 1966.) The progress from one Piagetian schema to a later more adequate one can be seen as a transition between two successive control systems focused on the same node. However, instead of Piaget's conceptual link between the two systems, on the present view the connection will be the empirical one involving the fact that the boundaries defined by the first control system largely overlap the boundaries defined by the second control system. A disturbance in one will likely be a disturbance in the other. This feature is what gives the clue to the judgment that the later control system is focused on the same node as the earlier one. The two triangulate on a single "object."

What does this triangulation look like in specific examples? A striking, literal example of triangulation is to be found in ordinary binocular vision. Psychologists have explored binocular vision utilizing a device known as a stereoscope. This device presents a separate field of stimulation to each eye. It turns out that the patterns presented have to be very similar in order for the familiar fusion into a single image to take place. Thus if two vertical lines are presented to each eye, but differently separated, the patterns do not fuse, but rather are superimposed, and three or four lines will be seen. The pattern node is not robust enough. On the other hand, if highly patterned but very different presentations are made to each eye, one or the other will be totally suppressed. The nodes, although individually very robust, are different and hence cannot be triangulated upon. The necessity of robustness is further illustrated by the use of a reduction screen. This allows only very small parts of a larger pattern to be presented to the eyes. When the same small piece of the pattern is presented to each eye, it is impossible to tell if it is the same piece when the reduction screen is in place, but easy when it is removed and we can utilize the whole pattern to locate the part. A part of triangulation thus involves the ability to discriminate the node of stability from surrounding nodes.

Memory patterns form another illustration of triangulation: we can triangulate across time on the same node of stability. First we observe a node with a given control system and store the perceptual pattern thus received; then, on a subsequent occasion, the use of the same control system generates a perception similar to the memory and justifies the judgment of sameness. (Note here that the account is not question begging because similarity has already been accounted for in terms of control systems. In this case, we have a system triangulating on both the memory and the present perception to see if there is a norm that comprehends them both.)

The preceding examples of triangulation have been within the realm of assimilation. However, what is at issue here is an individual's accommodation. That is, how is it possible for the individual to change conceptual structures and yet preserve a continuity between the structures? Consider several typical Piagetian experiments. Assume that the baby in the crib possesses both visual and tactile control systems.

How are they put together? There are bound to be innumerable opportunities, but, for ease of explication, suppose there is a mobile hang-
ing in the crib and the baby bumps into it while viewing it.

Clearly the disturbances of the boundaries of the two systems, visual
and tactile, coincide; what disturbs one disturbs the other. The requisite
robustness is present for the two systems to overlap and focus on the
"same" object. We might well suppose that what has occurred is a
change of conceptual schemes from visual objects and tactile objects
to a single object with visual and tactile qualities. The continuity consists in a very large similarity between disturbances to a "tactile-object
control system" and disturbances to a "tactile-qualities-of-a-physical-
object control system." For most purposes we behave in similar ways
to the two controlled quantities, although perhaps not entirely. We
have to learn that we cannot walk through a glass door.

Another Piagetian example involves not merely tying together the
various qualities of a physical object, but its permanence when those
qualities are not being perceived. Thus Piaget reports children's apparently not realizing that a toy passed behind an opaque screen still
exists and is the same toy when it appears on the other side rather
than being a new toy. Later, children do come to see the permanence
of the object and hunt for the toy behind the screen. (Again, of course,
alternative explanations can and have been offered, but I am here
concerned with demonstrating how we are to understand the Piagetian
explanation in terms of changing mental structures.) Once more the
possibilities for such situations are virtually limitless, but suppose the
child is holding a toy which is accidentally put out of sight, under a
blanket, say. Assuming that the child already controls for physical
object, then a tactile quality remains while the visual quality is absent.
Is there a new object or are objects permanent when some of their
qualities are not being perceived? Perhaps the object looks and feels
the same when it emerges from underneath the blanket. Once again
the continuity is provided by the fact that the boundaries of potential
disturbances of the object-existing-only-when-perceived coincide largely
with the permanently-existing-object, although again, perhaps not entirely. It would be hard to understand how the existing-only-when-
perceived control system could handle objects that change their look
or feel, like a fire that burns out with no one in the room. (I assume
here that no one is attributing to a child the sophisticated idealism of
a Bishop Berkeley who tried to explain even the fire without presupposing object permanence.)

Finally, consider the conservation experiments. When a child comes
to realize that the water poured from the shallow container to the tall
container is the same, then the concept of more or less matter will

have changed. Again, however, there is a triangulation on the same node of stability, and the disturbances to the two control system representations of the node will largely overlap. Thus, it may well be that originally "more stuff" means for the child "more vertical height," and, of course, even with the new view of conservation, more height usually will indicate more stuff, especially with objects that are constrained in their horizontal spread. That is, taller trees generally contain more stuff than do shorter trees, taller buildings more stuff than shorter buildings, and taller heaps of sand, more stuff than shorter heaps of sand. The boundaries defined by the different representational systems overlap and are partially congruent.

Overlapping boundaries then provide the condition for how we can understand the continuity in an individual's development without presupposing a conceptual connection between later and earlier. But the question remains, why should an individual change? Once again, the answer must be given not merely in terms of our collective understanding of the felicitous nature of the change, but also from the individual's point of view. Of course, as curriculum planners, we will need to appeal to our collective understanding for justification of our programs, but we will also have to appeal to the student's point of view—because that will make us more effective, *and* because ethically we must justify changing a person's conceptual scheme, *and* because epistemologically we must if we wish the student to understand what we are teaching. Indeed, the necessity for reconciling the external justification in terms of our collective modes of understanding with the internal justification in terms of an individual's mode of understanding, without reducing one to the other, forms the central challenge to educational epistemology. It is nothing less than the *Meno* dilemma at the level of individual learning.

From the student's point of view, then, a change of structure will be motivated by an anomaly. An anomaly is a disturbance which cannot be removed by the ordinary operations of the existing framework but neither can it be ignored for it is a disturbance and thus something humans are concerned about. It is defined in terms of the existing framework and because of that guides at least the initial selection of variants proposed to remove the anomaly. Recall the discussion of this process in scientific discovery in chapter 4, section 4. Initially the individual, much as the normal scientist, will attempt to assimilate the disturbance to the existing conceptual schemes and structures, and it is only when the disturbance continues to resist such efforts that it becomes an anomaly and variant changes of structure become likely.

Now, of course, for the young child the variants may not be the outcome of any conscious reflective hypothesis as they probably are for both the scientist and the older student, but they are seemingly pursued in a quite deliberate, experimental way. Piaget reports that new structures are explored and experimented with in the process of development. The continual tactile, visual, gustatory, and auditory explorations of the environment by the young child seem to give ample evidence of this. Thus if a toy gets covered by a blanket for a child who does not yet have the concept of object permanence and the child wants something to play with, there is an anomaly. Various exploratory movements are emitted; these in the past have often led to a toy; they may result in finding the toy under the blanket. Has the child created a new toy? Possibly this is what the child believes. But if so, the child may attempt to create a new toy by looking under the blanket again, when the toy has been knocked out of the crib. The "creating movements" of search are unsuccessful in this instance and the anomaly remains. A new structure must be sought. These sorts of situations must confront the average child almost continuously, and the range of potential variants is already highly focused by prior evolutionary selection of what is available for variation and by the particular focusing effect of the anomaly. Thus, the idea of object permanence is likely to be hit upon, and, as it is used, it seems to coincide with the boundaries of earlier representational systems in most instances and allows the control, in some way or other, of the situations which were anomalous under the earlier conception. A reflective equilibrium has been reached from the child's point of view.

Notice that this reflective equilibrium is no guarantee of the truth. Some equilibria that are reached, although they remove the instigating anomalies and work tolerably well for most succeeding cases, may yet be slightly off. And this corresponds well with the known facts of development. Vertical height as an indication of "more" works pretty well most of the time, but in some cases it fails. There is the well-known fact that in early language learning children utilize systematic, yet wrong, rules. The stage of forming all past tenses in a regular way by adding -ed is familiar. Faced with the anomaly of not being allowed by parents and teacher to talk about the past with present-tense constructions, children hit upon the technique of forming past tenses in a regular way. It works for a lot of cases, but not all. Or finally consider the effects of being brought up in a sheltered home environment and then facing, say, a modern college experience. The inadequacies of the reflective equilibrium achieved earlier in the face of the new ecology are well known to college counselors.

The point here is not that truth is determined by reflective equilibrium, but rather that unless the ecology upsets a given reflective equilibrium, thereby creating anomaly, we will not know that our current reflective equilibrium is not completely adaptive. Our only approach to truth is through reflective equilibrium; and reasonableness, in contradistinction to truth, is a function of reflective equilibrium. This is to say in yet another way that if we wish our students to understand what we are teaching them, we must focus on the reflective equilibrium, or what can come to be a reflective equilibrium from the student's point of view. We must start with where the student conceptually and behaviorally is.

But this raises another important point. If we do not pay attention to the students' reflective equilibria and their relation to the reflective equilibria we believe characterize our collective understanding, some strange and unwanted reflective equilibria can and do arise in the students' minds as a result of our educational efforts. I have already mentioned the almost inevitable shift from learning as a goal to grades as a goal, given our current misguided emphasis on measuring outcomes rather than seeing if disturbances are corrected (chap. 5, sec. 8). If we introduce disturbances to the students' conceptual schemes and then provide an educational ecology selecting variants that lead to getting good grades as opposed to variants that emphasize learning, can we really be surprised when the students reach a reflective equilibrium that views grades as the purpose of their learning?

The examples can be multiplied ad infinitum. The point is crucial. When faced with anomalies to their current ways of dealing with things, students will vary their mental structures to reach a new reflective equilibrium, but what equilibrium they reach will depend heavily on the ecology which selects among the variants. It is thus essential to the inculcation of a critical, evidential style of belief that we provide an educational ecology that will select for evidential styles of belief when such are tried out by the students. Moreover, if we do not know what the students' current reflective equilibria look like, we will be unable to tell if a given educational ecology will actually select variants leading to an evidential style of belief or not. To take one current and troubling example, we might well think that an educational environment that models the critical examination of issues would help select variants leading to an evidential style of belief. Yet, I think it has been the experience of many educators that given the widespread subjectivism and lack of understanding of reasoned argument on the part of many contemporary students, just the opposite effect may result. That is, suppose a student possesses some set of values or other along with the belief that values cannot possibly be discussed rationally. Suppose we, as teachers, cause a disturbance by presenting alternative values or drawing out some undesirable consequence of the student's set of values. Suppose, we also stand ready to engage in critical discussion of both the student's values and our own challenge. Now if we fail to appreciate that the student believes that it is impossible to engage in such a discussion, our attempts to do so are likely to reinforce the belief that a commitment to critical argument is just another value on a par with all the others and no more "objective" than any of the others. An insistence on critical argument by the teacher will be seen as demonstrating that teachers are really just authoritarian after all. Paradoxically the student may well come to believe that critical argument, an evidential style of belief itself, is just a sophisticated way of masking basically authoritarian attitudes. Our honest attempts at inculcating a rational style of belief will lead to just the opposite result because we have not fully appreciated what our efforts might look like from the student's point of view, and it is from the student's point of view that a reflective equilibrium must emerge.

6. Appreciating the Student's Point of View

Given the model of learning propounded in this book, and assuming that the question of the justifiability of teaching the student a given piece of material has been settled affirmatively, the teacher must determine if the lesson being taught is one that the student will assimilate or whether it will require an accommodation. This must be done by considering the current cognitive structure of the student or students. Ideally, of course, we would tailor our instruction to individual students' cognitive structures at any given time, but with a few exceptions, e.g., doctoral study, this is generally not possible. However, since we must make some kind of group estimate, it becomes clear that groupings of students with homogeneous conceptual structures with respect to any given lesson are epistemologically justified. Thus to the extent that age grading, or tracking, or course prerequisites, or self-selection guarantees some cognitive homogeneity for a given lesson, such rule-of-thumb practices may be epistemologically justified. Of course, I am not suggesting that merely because there is this epistemological point in favor of, say, tracking, that we ought, therefore, to track. There are other considerations, primarily of a social nature.

For lessons which are largely capable of being assimilated in terms of currently existing cognitive structures, teaching strategies and techniques such as practice, lectures, homework, programmed texts, are all useful for this kind of didactic function (Broudy, 1972). The logical point is to determine what the nature of the learning process is likely to be—assimilation or accommodation—and then to choose the teaching technique on those grounds. The same lesson may require assimilation by one group of students and accommodation by another. So simple-minded assessments of teaching techniques which consider only the subject matter being presented and do not take account of the cognitive development of the students in relation to the goals of both teachers and students are largely useless.

Yet many teaching studies concentrate on variables such as authoritarian style of teaching, inductive style of learning, open classroom, and so on. Such variables are wholly inappropriate because they are not placed within the integrated view of learning I am here advocating. The variable of authoritarian teaching style, for example, is currently conceived of as a relatively independent stimulus in the learning process. On the view I am developing, it can be seen that if the material is largely an addition to existing structures, if it has been determined that the students already possess the requisite organizing structure, if the goals of the students are largely to flesh out that structure, and so on, then an authoritative presentation of facts (possibly even in an authoritarian style) may be appropriate. Whereas, if the problem is one of changing students' cognitive structures, if the students need to be motivated to change, and so on, authoritarian teaching styles may be wholly inappropriate. The point is that variables like "authoritarian teaching style" do not seem to cut up the field of teaching in very useful kinds of ways. Even when variables that might be relevant are studied, such as organization of material, seldom are they seen in light of the stage of cognitive development of the students. As we all know, beautifully organized material will occasionally fall completely flat. On the assimilation and accommodation model this will occur if the students do not already possess the framework for appreciating the organization the teacher imposes. If the students do possess the proper framework, then well-organized material will probably be effective.

When we consider cases in which accommodation seems to be the proper learning response, the situation is even more complex. In the first place, in cases requiring accommodation a simple presentation of the information to be acquired by the student will by hypothesis be ineffective if the information is represented as it appears in the public collective modes of understanding, because it is precisely such modes of understanding to which the student must accommodate. The basic concepts of limits in calculus, philosophical questioning of previously taken-for-granted presuppositions, and atomic physics all seem to be examples typically requiring accommodation. If this kind of material is presented by lecture, for example, ample opportunity must be provided for the student to try out variants which are hypothesized by the student as appropriate, to see if such variants really do focus on the nodes the teacher is trying to get across. Put in slightly different terms, in accommodative learning, new systems of representation and perception are at issue, and the teacher must not simply assume the student will automatically perceive things the way the teacher wants (Petrie, 1974b).

The basic teaching techniques for accommodative learning are probably heuristic (Broudy, 1972). That is, the teacher is primarily concerned to help the student master new modes of representation and new ways of dealing with material. It is not simply a matter of the accretion of facts and skills to an already established base. Rather it involves changing the base. Discussion and discovery techniques will typically provide useful tactics, although here, too, there will be no one-to-one correspondence between accommodative learning and particular tactics. Discussion is useful because it typically provides greater opportunities for the student to try out variants. Practice and homework are also important, not so much to fix material which is presumed to be understood as to eliminate plausible but inadequate variants the student may be trying out; in short, to help the student understand. In both assimilation and accommodation the student's active participation is essential, for the goal is either eliminating disturbances or reaching a new reflective equilibrium, both of which are active processes.

One other feature is of particular importance to the teacher. The student will try to assimilate everything presented. If assimilation is the goal, the material must be couched in terms the student can grasp. If accommodation is the goal, then assuming the teacher does disturb the student's schema sufficiently to cause an accommodation, the educational ecology must be such as to promote the right kind of accommodation. The student will change cognitive structures to reach a reflective equilibrium, but since the student, by hypothesis, does not know what the proper equilibrium looks like, the possibility exists that an equilibrium will be reached that is quite different from the one desired. The phenomenon of underprivileged children being completely turned away from school and yet being able to cope very well with their street environment can almost surely be explained by the lack of an educational ecology which would or could select for the desired equilibrium. I am not here necessarily blaming the schools. The selective pressures of the streets may be much sharper for such a child in our society than any formal school ecology which we might be able to provide.

From the point of view of the student, assimilation will be attempted with all material. The student will attempt to remove any disturbance to extant representational systems by utilizing those systems. If the material can be handled in that way, all will be well. If, however, the teacher wants an accommodation, but has not sufficiently analyzed the student's conceptual scheme to see that the student might instead assimilate the material, misunderstanding will result. The student will think the material is understood, and if there is significant overlap in the student's way of processing the material and the teacher's way, the mistake may remain hidden for some time.

So if accommodation is the goal, the disturbances must become anomalies for the student, and the search for a new reflective equilibrium must begin. But in such cases, the student needs to be willing to try out the variants that come to mind, for only by subjecting the variants to the educational ecology are we likely to achieve the desired outcome. What the student will have to realize, contrary to much popular talk about good teaching, is that in such cases, the teacher will *not* be able to lay out the ultimate learning goals in terms the student can understand in the beginning, and that this is not a deficiency on the part of either teacher or student. It is a logical point about accommodation. The student will literally not know where he or she is going. Confusion about the course will be the standard experience. The remark is familiar: "I was lost for almost the whole course, but then it all fell into place." Currently such a remark is taken to mean either the teacher could have done a better job or the student was somewhat slow. In either case it is assumed that the situation could be corrected. On the assimilation and accommodation view such an experience on the part of the student is to be expected, and is in principle unavoidable. It simply reflects the existence of anomalies to the student's current representational schemes, the trying out of variants, and ultimately the new reflective equilibrium reached by the selection mechanisms. In accommodation, i.e., in grasping the new-knowledge horn of the learning dilemma, the student literally does not know that which is being learned, but there are selection mechanisms in the student and in the educational ecology which will lead to a new reflective equilibrium.

I turn now to the question of the justification of educational practice. (See, for example, Oliver, 1976.) As long as we are operating under the assumption that we can give a completely general account of rationality and somehow or other ground the account in certain knowledge whether it be of concrete particulars, abstract universals, or methodological principles of enquiry, the justification of educational practices will assume a kind of transcendental form. By this I mean that the principle of justification will be somehow located independently of actual adaptive human behavior in a changing environment. I have examined such an example in Hirst's justification of liberal education. The transcendental nature of the justification is particularly revealing in Hirst's case since, as I have shown, he does admit that rationality depends on the bounds of sense within which human beings find themselves. That is, in some sense, reasonableness depends on the kinds of contingent beings we are and the contingent world in which we happen to find ourselves. Nevertheless, Hirst explicitly denies that any account of reasonableness can be found outside of or even pushing against the bounds of sense. As I have argued, such a view cannot account for the fact of conceptual change.

Once we give up the search for a general account of rationality and instead focus on the processes by which people in general and individuals in particular manage to cope with their environments, we are faced with a corresponding shift in the nature of educational justification. No longer will we be able to appeal *simply* to our current collective wisdom without also taking into account the reasonableness of potential changes in such wisdom and the reasonableness of individuals whose wisdom is at variance with our collective wisdom. In short, we will have to take seriously the autonomy of the individual, and the burden of proof will shift from the individual, who will no longer have to justify deviations from the educational system, to the educational system, which will have to justify changing an individual's already-achieved reflective equilibrium.

Often the burden of proof can be carried. We justifiably do not let three-year-olds ride their tricycles in the street, and we are probably fully justified in our insistence that everyone learn to read, write, and do arithmetic. At the other extreme, it is almost surely wrong to direct adults into various social slots based on some central planner's estimates of social needs. In between lies a vast gray area. Are we justified in requiring a distribution of studies in a liberal arts curriculum among science, social science, and humanities? What, if anything, is justifiably required of a high school student with respect to English? Literature? That the students be able to write? What? The knowledge of explicit grammatical rules? Why?

Clearly, detailed decisions will depend on a detailed consideration of the specific instances, but a few general points can be made. If there are some general principles of individual development that show, for example, that certain ways of looking at things will change as the child develops, then we need not allow considerations taken from such earlier stages to weigh decisively in curriculum decisions. We need not, for example, allow the kind of reasonableness of the nonconserving child to dictate the views of physics that child should ultimately hold. At the same time, we would not be justified in possibly inculcating counterproductive learning habits by treating such nonconserving views as simply mistakes.

For some subjects we might well decide that typically individuals' purposes and goals for their educational activities coincide almost wholly with the purposes of people in general as these are embodied in collective rational enterprises such as science, the law, and so on. In such cases we would probably be justified in presuming to initiate everyone into such modes of thought although we would have to distinguish carefully between the way those modes of thought are carried on explicitly by the expert practitioners of them and the way they might figure in other people's development. This is the point urged earlier that the mode of understanding embodied in an explicit form of knowledge need not necessarily be simply copied in the student in order to inform the student's thought. We would also have to be careful to allow individual exceptions when a plausible case can be made that despite the generally accepted and pervasive nature of certain general purposes embodied in rational enterprises, a given student does not really have such purposes and goals. For example, it might be argued that to be successful a musician or performing artist must devote so much time to the development of the requisite technical skills that a liberal education on top of that is just not possible. Hence, we ought to segregate such people at early ages into arts academies and train them accordingly. I do not necessarily advocate such a policy, but it could conceivably be justified in this kind of way.

A third general principle has to do with the question of whether we are justified in compelling students to transcend a given mode of thought in order to attain a stance from which, were they then to choose the original mode of thought, we would be satisfied. This kind of question is what lies behind our uneasiness when certain narrow kinds of decisions are taken at impressionable times. Thus we do not so much mind someone's choosing to believe in astrology if the person has knowledge of, and a critical attitude toward, the alternatives. We do feel uneasy if somehow an early induction into astrology forecloses the investigation of alternatives, and somehow the charge does not ring true that such a reliance on rational consideration of the alternatives is itself just one more narrow kind of bias, on a par with astrology.

The evolutionary perspective provides some guidance here. While recognizing the fallibility of current collective wisdom, it insists that an overall strategy of pursuing each and every variant no matter how wild is not ultimately adaptive. That is, the variation and retention mechanisms must be in some kind of balance for evolution to be at all adaptive. If too much time and energy are spent generating variants, then not enough time and energy will be left for selecting the variants. If too much time and energy are spent on selection and retention, none will be left for variation in response to changing ecological conditions. If a variant is pursued *after* we have considered the alternatives, we seem to be giving some room to the demands of both retention and variation.

The upshot is that it may be justifiable to insist somewhere in our educational system that individual forms of reasonableness give way to the collective forms of reasonableness which we hope are embodied in the educational system, provided that at other points decisions to reject the collective understanding are honored. Without such provision the possibility of conceptual change in the collective reasonableness would seem to be effectively foreclosed. For the only source of such potential change are individual forms of reasonableness. To put the point in terms of the *Meno* dilemma, the collective understanding preserves the insights of the old-knowledge horn while the relative autonomy of individual understanding captures the insights of the new-knowledge horn. Without in any way sanctioning either dogmatism or license, the evolutionary approach reminds us of the possibility of both conceptual change and conceptual continuity.

7. An Objection Considered

D. W. Hamlyn (1978), among recent philosophers, has been most explicit about considering the epistemological problem of the growth of knowledge. His book, *Experience and the Growth of Understanding,* is a conscious attempt to grasp the old-knowledge horn of the *Meno* dilemma. Despite its improvement on most old-knowledge approaches and the many presuppositions it shares with my own account, I have argued that Hamlyn's position is radically incomplete. It does not take account of conceptual change, diachronically and synchronically. Hamlyn is correct in his emphasis on the social setting in which the development of knowledge takes place, but he errs in not appreciating the fact that societies, too, must be placed in the context of the historical development of the growth of knowledge in general.

However, because of Hamlyn's explicit recognition of the importance of the *Meno* dilemma, he canvasses alternative positions and raises objections to them. In particular, he objects to Piaget's implicit attempt to solve the *Meno* dilemma. According to Hamlyn, Piaget's account of genesis with structure fails to solve the puzzle for a variety of reasons. My own account, although differing at crucial points from Piaget's, can also be fairly characterized as an account of genesis with structure. For this reason it will be useful to rehearse Hamlyn's objections to Piaget to see the extent to which my own account overcomes them. In passing, it should be remarked that Hamlyn admits (p. 49) that Piaget's account of genesis with structure blocks the potential infinite regress of knowledge that Hamlyn found fatal to the rationalist's structure without genesis. Thus an account of genesis with structure is prima facie a promising candidate for explaining the growth of knowledge and understanding.

One of Hamlyn's objections to Piaget's view of the development of structures is the vagueness that surrounds the criteria of identification of structures (p. 47). This is a standard criticism of Piaget, and, given his emphasis on a stage development theory, it is crucial. My own account does not depend upon a stage theory, but rather upon the view that structures are to be explicated in terms of control theory. On my view, the identification of a control system is in principle straightforward. Introduce a disturbance to the hypothesized controlled quantity and see if the disturbance is counteracted. If it is, there probably is a control system in operation controlling the hypothesized quantity.

A second challenge that Hamlyn raises is that Piaget gives no account of where the structures come from in the first place. I have already commented that Hamlyn's own account of the origin of knowledge does nothing more than repeat the truism that knowledge does, in fact, have an origin. My account of the origin of such structures is twofold. I have tried to give an evolutionary account of the growth of knowledge in general that makes use of the blind variation and selective retention model of explanation. Thus, this part of my account goes beyond Hamlyn's in taking into consideration the historical context in which any society finds itself. With regard to the origin of an individual's knowledge, I have relied upon both the capacities that individuals possess as a result of the learning of the race, and the notion of triangulation as well. The triangulation is of thought and action and, thus, does go further than Hamlyn's account. At least the outlines of a model of how basic knowledge can come about are present in my position, whereas with Hamlyn, knowledge just occurs.

Closely connected to this last point concerning the origin of knowledge structures is Hamlyn's claim that Piaget does not give an account of how agreement in judgments is possible (p. 56). Since I, too, believe that agreement in judgments is crucial for an account of the growth of knowledge as opposed to the mere origin and development of cognitive structures, I must meet this challenge (p. 48). I have essentially agreed with Hamlyn that when a change of knowledge structures is not at issue, a reference to the possibility of agreement among persons pursuing the same mode of knowing is crucial. Where I believe I have improved upon Hamlyn here is in also giving an account of the triangulation of thought and action, thus providing another access to the world besides the cognitive structures themselves. Objectivity does have a toehold. In cases where what is in question is a change in the mode of knowing, I have given an account both for the race in terms of evolution and for the individual in terms of triangulation.

My evolutionary account also meets Hamlyn's objection that much traditional epistemology, including Piaget's, concentrates on one's own case without taking account of the social nature of knowledge (pp. 54–55). I have already argued that Hamlyn himself is too parochial in concentrating only on a single society and not considering the fact that a society's modes of knowing change and develop over time. Despite Hamlyn's disparagement of biological accounts (see below), an evolutionary perspective of blind variation and selective retention is manifestly *not* an individualist position. It requires not only a social perspective at this point in time, but a historical social perspective as well. Hamlyn sometimes seems to conflate his objections to an individualist perspective on the growth of knowledge with his objections to a biological account that he believes cannot meet the epistemological requirements for understanding the growth of knowledge. I think it is clear that my evolutionary account is not individualist in tone. It does, however, run together the biological and the epistemological, and it is to this objection that I now turn. Hamlyn says (pp. 56–57):

> In adopting his biological approach Piaget often uses terms such as "biological knowledge," but the justification for the use of such terms rests only on the general analogy that he sees between cognitive development and more general biological development. The acceptability of that analogy itself, however, turns on whether the concept of knowledge can be construed in strict biological terms; hence, unless further considerations were adduced, the argument would be circular. It might be argued that the further considerations lie in the detailed working out of the analogy that Piaget provides in *Biology and Knowledge;* but in fact that working out is merely a detailed extension of the analogy and does not bring forward independent considerations. The idea that the cognitive development of the individual can be seen as a sequential succession of equilibrations brought about through assimilation and accommodation is at least commensurate with the idea that it can also be seen as a progressive structuring of the world by the individual. All that is lacking in the second idea to make it strictly commensurate with the first is the idea that the structuring must follow certain necessary paths if it is to result in the mature way of structuring things. A mature way of structuring things, however, is not *eo ipso* the *right* way of structuring things; yet it should be this if it is to be knowledge.

Hamlyn does not claim that, in principle, a biological approach to the concept of knowledge must be mistaken. His objection seems rather in the nature of a challenge. Any approach to the growth of knowledge must in fact account for why it is knowledge. In arguing in some detail for a naturalized epistemology, I have been arguing that it is at least in principle possible to give a biological account of knowledge. The question then becomes whether or not my own account does provide the further considerations Hamlyn claims are lacking from Piaget's account.

It is at this point that Hamlyn's concern for the possibility of agreement in judgments enters in. He claims (p. 59):

> When, therefore, it is said that Piaget seriously underestimates the social in his approach, it is not just that he underestimates the efficacy of social factors in producing deviations from the normal pattern of development which he thinks necessary for the reasons given; it is also that he ignores the necessity of bringing others into the picture as part of the context in which alone the concept of knowledge can get a purchase. Thus a purely biological model and the epistemological approach which is commensurate with it must prove inadequate for the task in hand.

Does my biological approach fare any better than Piaget's? Does my account allow us to give application to the concept of objectivity?

Hamlyn's objection to Piaget's biological approach seems to be that Piaget's notions of reversibility and decentration do not sufficiently get us away from the case of the individual. They provide at best necessary conditions for objectivity but not sufficient conditions (pp. 55–56). The conditions could, in fact obtain, and yet we could fail to have knowledge because we have not taken into account the contribution of the world to our knowledge. Hamlyn seems to be claiming that it is a conceptual point after all that objectivity entails truth.

In a sense this is a strange condition for Hamlyn to place on an account of the growth of knowledge. In other places he claims that knowing does not entail knowing that we know. For example, he says (p. 91):

> Nevertheless, it is possible for us to come to take things in a certain way without this being counted by us or recognised by us as knowledge, and yet for it to be recognised later that this is what it indeed was. We may say "I came to know at that point that it was so, although I did not recognize at the time that I did know it."

If Hamlyn really is presupposing that the epistemological problem is not simply to trace the logic of the concepts of the growth of knowledge and understanding, but to give sufficient conditions for their employment, then he is clearly an epistemologist of the old school after all. He wants a certain and absolute basis for knowledge and will not be satisfied until he has laid skepticism to rest entirely. I have spent this whole book in arguing that such certainty is not to be found, and I can only hope that my arguments for a naturalized epistemology may have given at least a sketch of a plausible alternative to such an extreme position.

On the other hand, if, as appears more likely, Hamlyn is simply saying that a sketch of how objectivity is *possible* is required, then his objection to Piaget is a challenge rather than an outright rejection. In this case, the challenge applies equally to Hamlyn's own account. For Piaget, it is possible that an individual's acquiring the concepts of reversibility and decentration is insufficient to guarantee the possibility of knowledge. For Hamlyn, an individual's having been taught to agree in judgments with a given parochial society is equally insufficient to guarantee the possibility of knowledge. That society's modes of knowing may be inadequate. What my evolutionary account provides is an explanation of *why* agreement in judgment with others in a society gives objectivity a purchase. Any given society is a product of a long evolutionary process of selective retention of the judgments that have allowed human beings to deal with their world. The concept of the social is crucial to the possibility of the objectivity of knowledge precisely because when knowledge is conceived of as adaptation, the social is the analogue of the species, and it is the species which adapts. The social is, therefore, the repository of adaptation, and, ipso facto, of knowledge and objectivity.

It is, I must admit, in the last analysis possible that the agreement in judgments of the human race may be insufficient to guarantee objectivity and knowledge. After all, species do die out in the evolutionary scheme of things. But what is at issue is the *possibility* of objectivity and knowledge, and I believe that my evolutionary account with its model of the triangulation of thought and action does show how knowledge and objectivity are possible. Both our thoughts about the world and the world's influence on us contribute to our experience in ways that can be distinguished.

It is because of the failure of people to have found an absolute guarantee for knowledge that I have urged we should accept an account of rationality conceived of as adaptation, including assimilation and accommodation. This account, unlike Piaget's, does successfully combine a biological strand with an epistemological strand. Hamlyn's challenge has been met.

8 | Education

If the arguments of the preceding chapter are at all persuasive, then as well as the more usually stated *Meno* dilemma of enquiry, there is a *Meno* dilemma of individual learning. How is learning possible? This is clearly one of the central concerns of education. As I have shown, the only way to overcome the *Meno* dilemma is through grasping both the old-knowledge horn and the new-knowledge horn, i.e., through a reflective equilibrium between assimilation and accommodation. There are two immediate educational implications. First, most educational thought simply does not distinguish between these two different ways of reaching a reflective equilibrium. Indeed most educators seem implicitly to take an old-knowledge approach and assume that the cognitive and perceptual structures of students are not really at issue and that the only serious concern is how to design material to be assimilated by these presupposed structures. Second, the actual case, however, seems to be that a large and important segment of learning will require changes in cognitive and perceptual structures. Merely to note that the desired end structures are presumably already known to teachers and scholars does nothing to help the student. From the student's point of view, the question still is one of accommodative change. Thus if the student is to be brought to the collective understanding of any subject, the student's internal point of view must be considered.

In the preceding chapter I argued that it was in principle possible to account for individual accommodative change without presupposing a conceptual link between our collective modes of understanding and an individual's mode of understanding. Reflective equilibrium can take place given an anomaly, and the resulting variation and selective retention of knowledge variants. Indeed such a view seems to accord with the occasional odd, yet understandable, equilibria which are reached by students. Such idiosyncratic, yet coherent, adaptation seems mysterious on the view that treats the connection between a student's mode of understanding and the collective understanding as conceptual. Yet, because the adaptation "makes sense," we hesitate simply to label it a mistake. Forming past tenses by adding -*ed* to every verb is one such well-known adaptation. Every teacher has experienced others. The case is analogous to the history of science. Without an evolutionary perspective, earlier theories can be viewed only as logical precursors or out-and-out mistakes, but neither account seems to accord with the historical facts.

One of the most important implications of the view developed in this book is that these "odd" equilibria reached by the students may be odd only in that they do not match the reflective equilibria enshrined in our current collective modes of understanding. It does not follow from such a mismatch that the student must be wrong and that we must be right. Given the evolutionary nature of both individual and collective modes of understanding, progress is often made when an individual refuses to accept the current collective mode of understanding. Not only must we leave open the possibility that the student's mode of understanding may be better than the current collective mode, but we must also allow for the possibility that we may not be justified in attempting to change the individual's understanding to match the collective understanding. The equilibria reached by individuals through their own particular histories of learning and development may render their ways of looking at things as reasonable as the history of enquiry has left the equilibria to be found in our collective understanding. That is, there may be cases in which, although it is reasonable in general to ask students to learn the collective mode of understanding, yet for this particular student, it may not be.

Even on general grounds we may be unable in some instances to prefer the collective understanding to an individual's understanding. This clearly happens on at least some occasions in the growth of scientific knowledge. Given the analogy I have drawn between the scientist on the frontiers of knowledge and the student about to learn something brand new to the student, it may be best for a given student *not* to learn the material. These judgments are complex and difficult to make, and many features other than the epistemological ones of assimilation and accommodation may enter into the decision process. A great deal more work needs to be done in this area. (See, for example, Oliver 1976.) However, the epistemological considerations highlight the way in which we must take account of the individual's mode of understanding, both in deciding if we are justified in attempting to change that mode of understanding and in devising effective ways of achieving that goal.

For the purposes of this chapter, however, I shall assume that these complex decisions have been made of when and under what conditions accommodation by a student is appropriate and justifiable. The questions then are: How in principle is accommodation educationally possible? Can anything be said that would aid our teaching in cases when an accommodation and not an assimilation is appropriate? Can we design educational ecologies which have a better than average chance of providing selection mechanisms which will in turn lead to individual reflective equilibria in line with our collective understanding?

1. Bending, Breaking, and Constructing Rules

Let me begin this section by quoting a parable from Donald Campbell (1963, pp. 101–2).

> Let us pose to a hypothetical animal psychologist the problem of diagnosing the habits of an aged and experienced rat shipped to him from another laboratory. What would happen? The process would be a hit-or-miss, random, trial-and-error procedure. The foreign rat under varying degrees of deprivation would be placed in all the likely pieces of apparatus available in the diagnostic laboratory. Knowledge that the rat shared some common culture, i.e., that it was a university-psychology rat, would make the selections of apparatus somewhat less random. The rat would be tried in a lever-pressing Skinner box, while buzzers buzzed and lights flashed, and any combinations that resulted in increased lever pressing would be taken as symptoms of some habit. The rat might be placed on a Lashley jumping stand while various colors and designs were placed in the card slots; and if jumping occurred, an effort would be made to find to which cue cards the jumping was most consistent. Multiple T and Y maze segments would be tried. The process would be one of random search, and the presence of a common culture merely serves to limit the range of things tried or to make certain guesses more probable. And no matter how clever the research, there would still be the possibility that important and highly routinized habits of the rat went unnoticed by the diagnostician.
>
> The diagnostician makes the initial definition of stimuli and the initial classification of response. They represent classes of objects and behaviors which the experimenter can consistently discriminate, and which he guesses the animal might also. Once he finds some evidence of the stimulus-response consistency on the part of the rat, the experimenter would typically start varying stimuli and varying his classification of muscle movements in order to approximate more closely the appropriate genus proximum for the habit; that is, he would try and find out whether certain subtleties discriminable by him were also discriminable and being discriminated by the rat. Thus, if he found that the rat jumped to a yellow circle, he would start varying the shape and the color of the stimulus card to find which degree of yellow, if any, maximized the response, which shape maximized it, or whether shape made any difference. At the same time, he would strive to learn the appropriate classification of the consistency of response. Was it a consistency of muscle contraction,

or a consistency of locomotor achievement, an object consistency, etc.? Gradually, by trial and error, the diagnostician would obtain a more specific and appropriately labeled stimulus-response correlation. The final classification, however, would still be in the scientist's terms, and would be limited to discriminations that the scientist could make.

This parable could be used as an analogy to illustrate the problems of a teacher in diagnosing a student's conceptual scheme so that lessons and learning experiences could be designed accordingly. However, I want to suggest that it is even more fruitful to look at the parable as an analogy to the student's position in being faced with a teacher attempting to pass on a part of our collective understanding which requires not merely an elaboration of the student's existing conceptual scheme, but rather a fundamental change in that conceptual scheme. Furthermore, in accepting the theory-ladenness of observation, I am forswearing any "building block" attempt to teach the student. Rather, any "building blocks" would themselves have to be constructed or modified in the course of the learning experience. On this view the student is analogous to the animal psychologist and the professor to the university rat whose habits the psychologist is trying to establish. Such a switch in the more usual way of looking at teacher and student may be salutary in itself. With this in mind, how might Campbell's parable read?

Let us pose to a student the problem of diagnosing the habits of an aged and experienced professor teaching a new course for the student where the student has no information about prior environments and reinforcements of the teacher. The process would be a hit-and-miss, trial-and-error process. Knowledge that the professor shared some common culture, i.e., that it was a university philosophy professor, would make the selections of apparatus somewhat less random. The professor would be placed in a classroom while questions would be asked about different aspects of the course, and any combination of types of questions which produced increased enthusiasm and nods of the head by the professor would be taken as symptoms of some habit. The professor might be placed at a desk while various student papers were used as discrimination cards and if any markings of *A* occurred, an effort would be made to find which paper was most frequently marked in that way. In similar fashion, office visits, and examination answers would be explored by the student. The presence of the university culture would serve simply to limit the range of things tried by the student or to make certain guesses more probable. But no matter how clever the research by the student, there would still be the possibility that important, highly specific, and stable habits of the professor would go unnoticed by the student.

The initial definition of stimulus and classification of response are the student's. They represent classes of objects and classes of behaviors which the student can consistently discriminate, and which he guesses the professor can also. Once some evidence of stimulus-response consistency on the part of the professor were found, the student would typically start varying stimuli and varying the classification of movements in order to approximate more closely the optimal description of the habit. Thus, if the student found that the professor marked "good" at a place in the paper which questioned suppositions, the student would start varying suppositions questioned and the depth of the questioning to find what maximized the contingency. Likewise, an attempt would be made to try to discern the appropriate classification of response. Does the professor want clarity or originality, or what? Gradually by trial-and-error, the student would obtain a more specific and appropriately labeled conceptual map of the subject being taught. The final classifications would still be in the student's terms, however, and would be limited to classifications which the student could make.

What I believe this parable illustrates is the kind of triangulating of thought and activity which can lead through a succession of iterations from a given way of conceiving a situation to a radically different way of conceiving the situation. And all the while, the modes of representation are the scientist's or student's. There is no direct contact with the world "as it is." There is only conjecture and correction in a process which ultimately focuses, not necessarily on "the truth," but on a representational structure which is adequate for the scientist or student in dealing with the world. It is, I believe, in this way that we learn something radically new.

There seem to be several more or less distinct stages to this process of triangulation by means of which new rules of interpretation are constructed. In the first place the student will simply try to understand the subject in terms of structures already possessed. It is only if these structures prove inadequate for dealing with the material that any change of structure will occur. For example, when undergraduate education students are first questioned about why they favor a certain curriculum practice, they tend to say that they *feel* it is best. They become flustered when asked why their feelings should be a reason for doing what they are doing. They are not used to justifying or questioning their presuppositions, yet it is just such questioning that they are called upon to do in a course in philosophy of education or social foundations. So only if the ordinary ways of dealing with the world prove inadequate will changes be made. In short, an *anomaly must be sensed* from the students' point of view.

The second step in the process involves *trying out alternative sets of rules* or structures in terms of which to interpret the situation. If the experience cannot simply be processed in terms that immediately suggest themselves, then perhaps some alternative structure is appropriate. It is here that direct teaching is of crucial importance. Either another structure already extant in the student must be elicited, or the process of bridging from the structures the student does possess to the structures being taught must be started. The philosopher of education can begin pointing out to the student that it is not because of feelings that curriculum is justified, but because those feelings represent critical professional judgments about what children need to learn, what they can learn, and how best to go about that.

But a new set of rules by itself will not suffice. The bent, broken, or newly constructed rules of interpretation provide at most a new way of viewing the situation—one leg of the triangulation. Third, there must be *action in accordance with the rules* to see what happens. Activity provides the other leg of the triangulation. The student needs to respond and to try out this notion of critical professional judgment as a justification for curriculum decisions. For example, the student might say to the philosopher, "Well, then if it is a matter of judgment, then anyone's opinion is as good as anyone else's."

Such a response illustrates the need for the fourth step of the process—*correction*. Does the new conceptualization plus the activity in accordance with the conceptualization remove the anomaly? If not, a correction must be made. "No, no," replies the philosopher of education. "Critical professional judgment is not merely anyone's opinion, else my opinion on a student cello player would be the equivalent of Casals's." And so the process would have come back to another anomaly. The student does not quite have the concept right, and that was shown by the active response that was made, but the correction does indicate that there has been some progress. Judgments have become the focus of discussion rather than feelings.

Notice that despite the fact that I have focused on what the philosopher might do in such a situation, the process is essentially a learner-centered one. The philosopher's response to the student's initial justification was anomalous *to the student*. It might not have been. The student might simply have written off the philosopher as "weird." The student grasped the concept of critical professional judgment—at least to some extent—as evidenced by the activity of interpreting it as just anyone's opinion. The correction would be a correction only if the student sensed the difference between the philosopher's judgement of cello playing and Casals's judgment of cello playing. The process is profoundly one of the *learner's* bending, breaking, and triangulating with new rules of understanding. The teacher and the classroom are a part of the students' ecology and, hence, have only indirect influence.

And the process is iterative. The last correction in the example becomes a new anomaly to be resolved. The corrected activity provides another triangulation on the problematic situation and reflects back on the new conceptualization, beginning to show in what sense the ultimately correct conceptualization will differ from it. Likewise, the corrected activity reflects back on the original conception of the situation as anomalous, showing the extent to which the anomaly is being removed by the corrected activity and its evolving conceptualization. And then the process starts all over again. To what extent is there still an anomaly? The anomaly is now defined by the extent to which the new conceptualization is still inadequate; this points to a modification of conceptualization which in turn brings about slightly modified activity with a new balance of triangulation on the problematic situation. To the extent that corrections are still needed, the process may be repeated several more times. It is essentially the iterated process of triangulation of conceptualization and activity, powered by the perception of remaining anomaly, which enables the student gradually to change conceptual schemes to accommodate totally new experiences.

The same process is present when we consider the situation from the external point of view of the teacher, but the steps look somewhat different. The teacher must pay special attention to both the initial intelligibility to the student of the new conceptualization and the appropriateness of the activity for triangulation on the new material. The teacher must also consider the ecology in which corrections leading ultimately to a reflective equilibrium in the student take place. In triangulating on the new material, the student will stop when conception and activity have combined to remove the anomaly. There are equilibria which do not match the collective understanding the teacher is trying to impart, and these are the ones which must be avoided. Probably the best way in general to avoid such a possibility is to provide an ecology rich in opportunities to apply the student's newly established equilibrium of conceptualization and activity. For if the student's triangulation is just a bit off, such errors are more likely to become apparent to the teacher if there is a variety of cases.

The conceptual power of the notion of successive triangulation can be brought out in the following way. Recall that I have rejected the view that we attach language to the world through some kind of direct perceptual access which in turn provides the foundations for observation terms. On the contrary, observation is itself a mode of representing reality, and it depends on the concepts we use. Observational categories can and do change over time. If this is so, then both observational and theoretical representational systems will be intimately bound up with our conceptual frameworks. I believe that a kind of equilibrium among these systems is the best we can hope for under these conditions. However, a great number of people believe that such a perspective seriously threatens the objectivity of science and knowledge (e.g., Scheffler, 1967). They ask, "How can we change our equilibria in response to the way the world is, if observation is theory dependent?" The answer which I have suggested is that we triangulate on reality with our representational schemes, and some of these representational schemes require activity in the world which may well be frustrated if the observational representation is inadequate. If all we had to do was think about the world, then, indeed, we might fear for objectivity, but since we must act in the world and coordinate our activity with our thought so that activity and thought triangulate on nodes of stability in the world, objectivity and conceptual change are possible at the same time.

In the following sections I shall consider a variety of educational contexts in which we can see this process of anomaly–alternative conceptualization–activity–correction at work. Some of the contexts— homework, discussion, and textbook writing—will be old standbys, but seen from the new perspective of how they contribute to conceptual change in a student. The other three, use of metaphor, training research scientists, and the phenomena of cult conversions and brainwashing, more obviously require significant conceptual changes on the part of the student.

2. Homework

Is homework merely busywork, overlearning so that the lesson will be remembered, a method of social control, a pain for parents, or what? No doubt homework is all of these things at different times and in different contexts. But it is also a way of changing conceptual structures. An incident with my stepdaughter's homework will illustrate the point.

The subject matter was fractions in arithmetic, and the particular skill had to do with multiplying and dividing fractions. Even more specifically, this lesson had to do with the word problems that come as close as school arithmetic ever seems to in getting children to begin using arithmetic in their daily lives. The homework consisted primarily of a series of problems such as the following: "Sarah had a board seven and one-half feet long and cut it into thirds. How long was each piece?" "Mike regularly jogs one and one-half miles. When he had run half his regular distance, what fraction of a mile had he run?" "The

Smiths had two-thirds of a ton of coal to heat their house. They used one-half of it during the first two weeks of December. What fraction of a ton did they have left?" The pattern was clear. The student was to multiply the given fraction or whole number by the fraction "used up" to get the answer.

However, the authors of this particular drill sheet were just a little bit sneaky. Immediately following the last problem cited above was another one. "The Joneses had three-fourths of a ton of coal to heat their house. They used one-half ton of coal during the first two weeks of December. What fraction of a ton of coal did they have left?" Now the student had to *subtract* one-half ton from three-fourths of a ton instead of taking one-half of the total coal available.

This homework assignment doubtless fits into the middle of a complex learning experience involving fractions. For example, I have no idea how the whole subject matter was set up by teacher or textbook, or what initial conceptualizations may have been employed or modified by my stepdaughter. But this episode does, I believe, represent one cycle in the iterative process of anomaly, alternative conceptualization, activity, and correction.

Probably what the homework was designed to do was to guard against the students' simply memorizing a formula and repeating it without understanding it. Let me assume that was indeed the conceptualization my stepdaughter had. Put into words, it might have run, "Whenever I have a fraction or a mixed number of units of something and then another fraction enters into the problem, multiply the two together." The subtraction problem constituted an anomaly, but notice it was an anomaly only when the wrong answer was pointed out as being wrong by parent or teacher. In short, homework must be corrected if it is to stand any chance of being useful.

The alternative conceptualization was provided by my saying something such as, "You have to distinguish between one-half *of* a certain amount of coal and one-half ton of coal. One-half ton of coal always stays the same, but one-half *of* a given amount of coal would differ depending on how much you had to begin with. If you use one-half *of* a certain amount then you would multiply by one-half to see what is left, but if you used one-half ton, you would subtract that from the amount with which you started."

I next suggested analogous problems with whole numbers. These were the *activities*. "How much coal would the Smiths have left if they had four tons to start with and used one-half of it?" "How much coal would the Joneses have left if they had four tons of coal and used one ton?" "What did you do to find the answer in the two cases?"

And finally, I corrected these and other answers she gave to my sample problems until I was reasonably certain she had removed the initial anomaly. There appeared to be a triangulation between her conceptualization and her problem-solving activity, at least on this minor point. Of course, other homework or other tests might reveal the need for further differences and corrections.

The point is that homework can be an extremely effective tool in the process of changing a student's conceptual scheme. It probably is not very useful in presenting an initial conceptualization or an alternative conceptualization, but it is tremendously helpful in locating slight errors in conceptualization. Even here, however, it will be useful only if it is corrected and gone over with the student by someone who knows what the right answer is and why it is right. It would have done no good for the teacher simply to have marked the problem incorrect (the anomaly step) without having gone on to explain why (the alternative conceptualization step), and having provided more practice (activity), and further instruction (correction) as needed.

I am, of course, not denying that homework may also aid memorization, for example. However, in this particular case, the memorization seems far less important than the correction to the conceptual scheme that seemed to occur. Indeed, if we were to focus on the memorization aspect, we would be more apt to try to get the "recipe" stated so precisely as to ensure that mistakes of the kind illustrated could not occur. But that would simply push the problem back to how the children could ever learn to "apply" the tremendously complex recipe. I have already argued that the question is not one of learning how to apply the theory to practice but rather one of experiencing in terms of the theory.

3. Discussion

If homework is the bane of "progressive" teachers, then discussion modes of instruction are likely to be believed to be a panacea. Of course discussion is no more to be universally praised than is homework to be universally condemned. It depends on the context. In this section I want to illustrate the kinds of contexts in which discussion as an instructional device can be used to aid in changing or adding to a student's conceptual scheme.

This example is drawn from a university discussion section in which the topic was the distinction between facts and values. The teaching assistant explained that factual statements were those that describe what is the case, the way the world in fact is. Value claims, on the other hand, say something about the way the world ought to be or how nice it would be if the world were that way. Value claims involve pro and con attitudes toward the world. He next gave several examples of each and then started down a list of examples, asking the class about each one. He came to one, "Evolutionary theory explains the origin of life," and there was quite a mixed reaction. Some students claimed it was a value; others claimed it was a fact.

As it turned out, this example, and the discussion that ensued, changed quite a number of conceptual schemes. Let me first talk about the changes for the teaching assistant. First of all, the response from the class was an anomaly for him in that he felt the example was clearly a fact as opposed to a value. The assistant first attempted to assimilate the response to the category of simple student mistake. The students were adamant, however. They said, "Yes, we know what your definition was, but the example concerns certain people, believers in evolutionary theory, who think it would be nice if the world were that way. It clearly doesn't describe the way the world is, because we just don't know. Therefore, it's a value." Others in the class were as adamant on the other side.

From the discussion and further probing and examples, the teaching assistant hit upon the following changed conceptualization: these students associate "fact" only with those statements that are known for certain. Anything that is controversial is not for them a fact. So, the teaching assistant said, "All right, I will grant that the example is not a fact because we're not sure of its truth. It may be a mere opinion. But, what I was trying to get at was the distinction between what we *claim* is the case and what our attitudes are toward those claims. So, let me call both what we're sure of, and our opinions, *fact-like* claims, for they both *purport* to describe the way the world is, and let me call *value-like* those claims which purport to say something about how the world ought to be, whether we agree with the particular value claim or not. Now, with that distinction, is the evolutionary theory example fact-like or value-like?" There was now fairly general agreement that the example was fact-like, although one student still claimed it was value-like.

The assistant next constructed another series of examples involving both controversial fact-like claims and unpopular value-like claims. There was much more agreement from the students on the proper classification of the examples, and the few disagreements were usually handled by other students in the class pointing out how the new classification of fact-like and value-like applied. Sometimes the disagreements came because of sloppy wording of the examples by the assistant as in, "Astrology is a discredited theory." Some students felt that was value-like because it referred to people's attitudes toward astrology. These students were happier to call "Astrology does not meet the criteria for being a scientific theory" fact-like, although many of them added that they thought the issue was not settled.

All the stages of conceptual change for the teaching assistant were present in this episode. There was the anomaly of bright students answering differently than he had expected. There was the new conceptualization of what "fact" meant for these students and probably for most people. There was the activity provided by the newly constructed examples. Note how the choice of the new examples of controversial fact-like claims and unpopular value-like claims was guided by the new conceptualization of what "fact" meant for these students. Finally, there were the corrections made in the assistant's new conception of what "fact" ordinarily means.

Fairly obviously, the students' conceptual structures changed, too. They were faced with the anomaly of having the teaching assistant disagree with their classifications of the evolutionary example. They were finally given a new, broader conceptualization of "fact" by the assistant. They tried it out in new examples and were corrected. They probably left the class with a sharper categorization of facts, opinions, and values, and how they may be related.

The general point is that the discussion mode of instruction encouraged the introduction of anomalies into both students' and teacher's conceptual schemes; it facilitated the search for new conceptualizations, and provided some opportunity for activity in accordance with the new conceptualization. Finally, it gave ample opportunity for correcting mistakes in a highly individualized way, for it provided immediate feedback to new conceptualizations and activities. Indeed, if the class had not run out of time, it might have provided an opportunity to pursue why the one student refused to classify the evolutionary example even as fact-like. Because of this extreme openness to conceptual modification, discussion modes of instruction are particularly suited to introducing new concepts and exploring the frontiers of our conceptual maps. Of course, discussions can also be misused by teacher and student alike when they mask a series of monologues which never allow anomalies to be recognized and dealt with.

4. A Textbook Example

One of the interesting features which seems to characterize most people's unreflective concept of motion is that there is no difficulty in deciding whether something is in motion or not. One simply looks and sees. Yet an essential feature of motion is that it is properly describable only relative to a coordinate system. Where the observer happens to be located when trying to decide whether something is in motion is essential to understanding motion. To acquire the concept of motion relative to a coordinate system requires a change of conceptual structure on the part of most students and not merely an assimilation of experience to existing structures.

How do secondary school science texts approach this problem? Let me illustrate in some detail how one randomly chosen text treats relative motion (Fisk and Blecha, 1966, p. 217–18). After noting several examples of motion, the text suggests that one look at a nearby object, e.g., a chair, and decide whether or not it is moving. The authors assume the answer will be "no," and then they point out that the chair is on the earth's surface, and the earth is moving, so the chair must be moving after all. This question introduces an anomaly into the student's conceptual scheme. Does the chair move or does it not?

The authors have to assume two things about the student; first, that the standard unreflective judgment of the student will be that the chair is not moving, and, second, that the student knows that the earth moves. Without those two assumptions the attempt to introduce an anomaly into the student's view of the world will fail, for the student will simply reject one of the things he or she is being invited to consider, probably the claim that the earth moves. What this illustrates is that an anomaly will *be* an anomaly only from the standpoint of a conceptual scheme. If the student does not know about the earth's movement, no anomaly will occur.

The authors of the text seem implicitly to recognize this problem, for their next paragraph straightforwardly reminds the student about the earth's movement, both rotational and orbital. They are not sure how many of their students will have the appropriate knowledge to recognize the thought experiment as creating an anomaly. The authors are also still a bit worried about the students' really understanding that the chair moves in virtue of its being on the earth. So the next paragraph is concerned with making the same point in terms of a book on the seat of a moving car. Does the book move or not? From the point of view of the car, no; from a point of view outside the car, yes. Surely, most modern students will have had experience with cars, both inside of them and outside of them.

Next, the authors try to make the anomaly explicit by suggesting that it may seem strange to say the book is both moving and not moving. Here they are relying on the idea that everyone probably finds contradictions anomalous. The conceptualization to be used to solve the anomaly is then introduced. The book's moving and not moving seem strange only because the book is being observed from two different *frames of reference*. I take it that the new concept is "frame of reference."

The authors next define "frame of reference" as "a place or position from which an object's motion may be observed and described" (p. 218). It might be objected at this point that since "frame of reference" is being explicitly defined, it is not a brand new concept at all. I grant that "frame of reference" probably *is* a technical literal term for people who already know how to use it. The student, however, may not be capable of building up the concept from more basic parts. Does it mean, for example, that the student is to put up a picture frame and block out part of his or her experience? That would be one "literal" meaning of the phrase. Alternatively, if the student has not yet grasped the notion of different points of view, then "a place or position from which an object's motion may be observed" and described may literally mean to the student, the student's *own* place or position. Thus, unless we presuppose that most of the work of grasping the new concept has already occurred, a literal building block definition may not do the trick at all.

This point can be brought out in another way. I have suggested that activity guided by the new concept is what comes next. In the current case, that activity is largely confined to thought experiments (as it necessarily must be in most written materials). The student is asked to imagine the chair on the earth's surface and the book on the car's seat as both moving. The former experiment is capable of being performed *only* as a thought experiment given current technology, while the latter, the book on the car seat, is something that virtually all students will have experienced. In this way, the thought experiments take on the logical role of the activity which helps us to triangulate on motion. The concept "frame of reference," however that is initially understood by the student, provides the other leg of the triangulation. If the thought experiments do not provide sufficient activity for the student to get a triangulation on the idea of relative motion, they could be supplemented by actual activities of the same type.

The fourth requirement is correction. The first attempts at triangulation may result in fairly gross approximations, and corrections may be needed. The authors in this text refer back to the chair example and now, using frame of reference language, explicitly suggest that we look at the chair from a position in space near the moon and, as they put it somewhat hopefully, "You would probably say that the chair is moving because the earth is moving" (p. 218). They are implicitly correcting the possible mistake about the chair's movement which they anticipate some students may have initially made.

The text also uses an interesting diagram to supplement in a perceptual way the new conceptualization suggested by the term "frame of reference" (The diagram is reproduced in figure 5). Through the

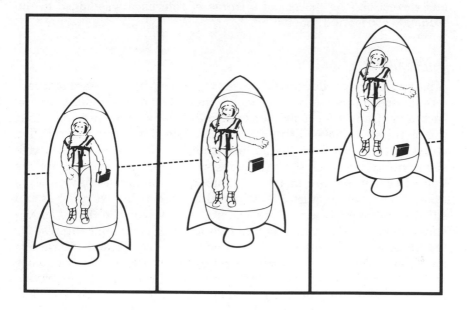

Figure 5. Frame of Reference. Redrawn From Franklin G. Fisk
and Milo K. Blecha, *The Physical Sciences* (1966). By permission
of Laidlaw Brothers, A Division of Doubleday & Company, Inc.

sequence of pictures, the authors try to show how important "point of
view" is. They take it for granted the student would, if in the spaceship,
say the book fell to the floor. By presenting a schematic series of pictures
of the spaceship ascending, an anomaly is created, for the floor is also
rising. But the pictures also illustrate the alternative conceptualization
which can solve the problem. The pictures quite plainly demand that
we take up a point of view outside the spaceship, and it is that "other
point of view" which is the point of the lesson. Again the activity is
left to thought experiments. Both "book falling" and "floor rising" seem
appropriate from the point of view from which the pictures are seen.
For the students to check out their ideas on this fairly subtle point
provides opportunity for correction and successive triangulations.

My overall point in this example is that, if successful, the student's
conceptual framework has been changed in a fundamental way through
the use of the concept "frame of reference." The notion was given a
literal definition in terms of place of observation, but the appropriateness of that definition depended upon the *nonlinguistic* ability to take
up alternative points of view, so that place of observation did not simply
mean to the student "where I happen to be at the time." Through the
by now familiar process of anomaly, new conceptualization, activity,

and correction, the concept of a frame of reference was added to the student's conceptual scheme.

5. Metaphor

A particularly apt educational device for extending or changing a conceptual scheme is metaphor. Indeed, metaphor is a paradigm case of such a device in that it provides a familiar lens which demands that the material be looked at in a new way. "Sleep knits up the ravelled sleeve of care" demands, as a start, that we view sleep as an active agent and care as possessing (or being) a garment which could become unraveled and require mending. Thus, good metaphors have always taken a familiar linguistic phrase and applied it in a surprising and edifying manner to a new subject matter. One of the issues in the voluminous literature on metaphor which is of particular interest for my purposes is the distinction between comparative and interactive metaphors. On the comparative view of metaphor, what a metaphor does is to say implicitly that two apparently dissimilar things have a similarity in common after all. Thus, in speaking of sleep and someone who knits, it is held that there is a fundamental similarity—they both make things whole again. On this view a metaphor is an implicit comparison whereas a simile or an analogy is an explicit comparison (Green, 1971). Metaphors would thus transfer meaning and understanding by comparison. It should be noted that comparative metaphors would not serve to make intelligible the acquisition of radically new knowledge. By hypothesis, radically new knowledge is knowledge that results from a change in cognitive structures, whereas comparisons must occur within a given cognitive structure which renders the comparison sensible. The comparative level of metaphor might allow for extensions of already-existing knowledge, but it would not provide a new form of understanding.

There are, however, problems with attempting to construe all metaphors as implicit comparisons. Consider the example from Haynes (1975), "Virginity is the enamel of the soul." Is the implicit comparison to be between the positive features of clarity, strength, and protectiveness, or the negative features of rigidity, brittleness, and enclosure? Nothing in the metaphor tells us, and only nonlinguistic contextual knowledge of speaker or hearer seems useful. For reasons such as this, many writers have claimed that there is also an interactive level of metaphor. Black (1962, p. 37) says, "It would be more illuminating in some of these cases to say that the metaphor creates the similarity than to say that it formulates some similarity antecedently existing." The interactive level of metaphor is peculiarly appropriate for my purposes, because if it *creates* similarities, then it could provide the bridge between a student's earlier conceptual and representational schemes and the later scheme of the totally unfamiliar subject to be learned by the student. Interactive metaphor would allow truly new forms of knowledge and understanding to be acquired by the student without presupposing that the student already knows, in some sense, that which is being learned.

Another issue is whether or not a metaphor can be identified by some set of linguistic features independent of its use on particular occasions. The appropriate category for metaphor, at least for educational purposes, seems to be not that of formal linguistic sentence meaning, but rather that of utterance meaning or speech act (Searle, 1969, p. 16). Such a categorization is suggested by the necessity of taking account of the context of understanding in deciphering a metaphor. In the current typology of speech acts there is not one which corresponds to speaking metaphorically. We could probably add such a category and give conditions for its employment (Loewenberg, 1975b); however, I am more concerned at present to look at the connection of uttering a metaphor with making an assertion.

Assertions are speech acts which are properly assessed in the true-false domain. Considered as a potential assertion, a metaphor will always turn out to be false because the world just is not the way it is represented as being by the words in the utterance if those words are given their literal interpretation. A basic convention of language is that people intend to utter meaningful, useful, and, in the case of assertions, true, statements. When a teacher utters a metaphorical statement in a typical educational context, the student's first thought tends to be that the teacher is asserting something. That is, the student tries to assimilate the utterance to literal schemata, rules, and conventions. But when the student attempts such an assimilation, the statement turns out to be fairly obviously false. In short, a metaphor is anomalous on its face.

If the student already possesses a cognitive structure sufficient to render intelligible the implicit comparison contained in a comparative metaphor, then the disturbance caused by the recognition that the statement is false is easily removed. The student transfers the literal features being singled out for comparison to the new subject matter. Thus, the mending characteristics of a knitter are transferred to sleep. This is a case of extending one's existing cognitive schemes to cover new cases. There is no radically new knowledge, for the cognitive structures remain the same; only their field of application has changed.

Sometimes, however, the student does not possess the cognitive structure which would enable him or her to interpret the metaphor in a comparative way. In these cases the disturbance created by the recognition that the metaphorical statement is literally false becomes an anomaly in that it cannot be assimilated to the student's existing cognitive structure. The student will have to accommodate his or her cognitive structure to account for the anomaly. If the student is somehow "in the presence" of the new material to be learned, then the student can try to deal with the material as if the metaphor were literally true. In the case of the virginity example, this would involve looking at theories of the soul, social pressures for virginity, the protective qualities of enamel, and so on. As the student attempts such a literal focusing on the material, the teacher and the material itself can provide corrections to the knowledge which does not transfer directly.

It is the anomalous character of an interactive metaphor, anomalous in terms of the student's current set of rules for understanding, that distinguishes the way metaphor transfers chunks of experience from the way in which literal language or comparative metaphor transfers chunks of experience. Literal language requires only assimilation to existing frameworks of understanding. Comparative metaphor requires simple extensions of the framework in the light of a more comprehensive framework. Accommodation of anomaly requires changes in the framework of understanding. It is this general requirement of a change in cognitive framework that provides the distinction between the ways interactive metaphor and literal language are to be understood and secures the importance of metaphor in considering how radically new knowledge is acquired.

Consider finally a metaphor provided by my high school geometry teacher. She began the course by holding up a pencil. "Think about this pencil being sharpened as sharp as it can be and then much, much sharper than that. That is a geometric point." Then grasping this imaginary pencil point between her right thumb and forefinger, she drew it horizontally in front of her, saying, "And that's a line." Then grasping both ends of the "line," she pulled the line vertically down in front of her, continuing, "and that's a plane."

A pencil point sharper than it can be sharpened? Surely that is anomalous, and yet it conveys dimensionless geometric location very well. And if that location is drawn straight out it clearly becomes a one-dimensional line, and next a two-dimensional plane. Of course it was working with those concepts throughout the rest of the geometry course, proving theorems, solving problems, doing homework, and so on, that provided the other legs for triangulating on the material. There were plenty of chances for corrections, too, but the initial metaphor began the bridge from familiar, tangible points to unknown, ideal geometric locations.

6. The Growth of Science

The foregoing description of how an interactive metaphor creates an anomaly for a student and leads the student toward changes in cognitive structure bears a striking analogy to Kuhn's (1970b) description of the workings of science during scientific revolutions. During the periods of normal science, puzzles and problems are solved by the use of the accepted paradigm of the moment. Occasionally such problems or disturbances resist current paradigm efforts to solve them, and they become anomalies. The scientist then searches for a new metaphor or model which can remove the anomaly. The main difference between the scientist on the frontiers of knowledge and the student is that in the student's case the metaphor provided by the teacher, if it is a good one, is likely to be more immediately helpful than are the variants tried out by the scientist. But except for a kind of trust in the teacher, the student does not really know any more about where he or she will end up than does the scientist. This seems to me to go directly against the educational dogma that we should always lay out in advance for the student exactly what the goals of the learning experience are taken to be. In cases where the goals are to *change* significantly the student's current cognitive structure, it will not be possible to lay out in advance learning outcomes the student can presently understand. Only metaphorically can the student be brought to understand the goals expressed in terms and categories of the to-be-learned subject matter.

One of the crucial senses of "paradigm" for Kuhn is what he calls an exemplar. An exemplar is a concrete problem which together with its solution constitutes one of the scientific community's standard examples. Acquiring these exemplars is a critical part of the scientist's training, and they serve the absolutely central function of allowing the student to "apply theory to practice," although this is a misleading way of making the point. The exemplar is what enables the student to deploy the symbolic generalizations of the theory being learned in particular problem situations. This role is extremely important because on Kuhn's view we do not always link up theory and observation statements by means of correspondence rules, nor is there any direct access to the world independently of our theoretical language. In sum, once we have denied a direct perceptual link to the world "as it is" and accepted the fact that observation is theory-laden, another account of the link between our beliefs and nature must be provided. Kuhn's suggestion is that in an important sense exemplars serve this function.

How do exemplars work? Kuhn (1974) has given an extended example of a young boy learning to recognize ducks, swans, and geese by repeated ostensive definition and correction of mistakes. His account goes no further than the simple observation that this is indeed how such learning often happens. Kuhn claims that the boy has learned not "rules" of application, but rather a primitive perception of similarity and difference. This perception precedes any linguistic formulation of the similarity relations. Can these nonlinguistic similarity relations be spelled out in more detail? If so, perhaps a way of accounting for the link between observation and nature or between theoretical language and observational language about nature can be found after all.

What I wish to suggest is that understanding an interactive metaphor includes as an essential part activities similar to those involved in acquiring an exemplar. For when a metaphor has effected a change of cognitive structure (where the "rules" of the cognitive structure need not be explicitly formulated or formulatable), the student has a new way of dealing with, describing, and thinking about nature, just as the science student in acquiring an exemplar has a new way of deploying symbolic generalizations in nature.

The key to both processes is that they are bound up with *activities* on the part of the student. It is not simply a case of hearing words, understanding them literally, and applying them directly. It is a case of *acting* in their ecology. For the science student this is brought out by Kuhn's insistence that in acquiring exemplars the student requires diagrams, demonstrations, and laboratory exercises and experiments. Even the young boy learning about ducks, swans, and geese is doing something. He is classifying and being corrected. Of course, language is involved, not as a kind of labeling, but as a prod to *activities* of sorting, classifying, and perceiving similarities and differences.

These are the activities that provide one of the crucial legs in the triangulation of conceptualization and activity on the subject area. Such problem solutions are indeed how the science student learns to deploy the disciplinary matrix in dealing with the world. The four-step process I have outlined of anomaly, new conceptualization, activity, and correction can be seen as construing Kuhn's ostensive definition as an activity in which the student must construct the experience the definition is to apply to. At the same time if the process of learning a new paradigm is at all like what I have described as the process of a student's coming to change conceptual frameworks, then the process of paradigm shift is both intelligible and intelligent. It is intelligible as an iteration of triangulations of thought and action on the world. It is intelligent in that it proceeds from the rules of reasonableness currently held by the scientist/student at any point in the historical process. Thus, charges of radical subjectivism leveled against my interpretation of Kuhn do not stand. Language bumps into the world at those places where our activity runs up against similar boundaries in diverse situations.

7. Brainwashing and Cult Conversion

As a final example of the application of my model of reflective equilibrium, I shall venture outside of the normal processes of formal education to an area of great practical and personal importance—thought reform and cult conversion. It is not fashionable or popular to talk about the phenomenon of thought reform, or "brainwashing," as a serious educational problem. Indeed, the very name sets it apart from "real" education and seems to imply something mechanical and beyond the influence of reason. Yet thousands of Westerners and millions of Chinese, Koreans, and Russians have been "brainwashed." Surely the image of all these people under the control of puppet-master leaders strains credulity. A plausible alternative hypothesis is that the typical Western reaction is ethnocentric and defensive. Since it is not *our* way, it cannot be right. Yet the mere existence of such widespread, radically different ways of viewing the world provides a prime example of the existence of the radical conceptual diversity I have been arguing throughout the book, and the phenomenon of the transition to such a new perspective should provide an excellent real-life example of massive conceptual change. Furthermore, if the theory of adaptation through assimilation and accommodation which I have advanced in this book can point the direction to understanding "brainwashing," then that will be an indication of new research directions which my theory provides and competitors do not.

Similar remarks can be made about cult conversions. Despite the acknowledged pain and suffering of parents whose (sometimes adult) children are lured into cults, current ways of describing and dealing with the problem seem wholly inadequate. Using such language as "programming" for the conversion exerience, and "deprogramming" for the sometimes forcible abduction and treatment which some parents undertake to regain their children, is not very helpful. Such language implies that the whole process is mechanical and something to which no reasonable person could succumb. Such a view is incapable of explaining, first, why programming and deprogramming do not always work; and, second, why the courts are mixed in their response to parents' abducting and deprogramming their children. Just where and how is the line to be drawn between mechanistic "programming" and a truly different belief system? The phenomenon cries out to be illuminated by my model of assimilation and accommodation.

Recall my initial distinction between an analysis and description of behavior change in general and an analysis of enquiry and learning where the latter are seen as having to do with standards of correctness, reasonableness, and validity. The *Meno* dilemma applies only to the latter. However, current ways of describing thought reform and cult conversion tend to assimilate them to mere causal mechanisms. What I want to suggest is that a more fruitful way of viewing these phenomena is in terms of radical conceptual changes where the convert clearly believes in the correctness of the new view and believes it *because* it is seen as correct. As Robert J. Lifton, the acknowledged authority on thought reform, says (1961, p. 15): "In all of this it is most important to realize that *what we see as a set of coercive maneuvers, the Chinese Communists view as a morally uplifting, harmonizing, and scientifically therapeutic experience.*" There could scarcely be a clearer signal that we are dealing with radically different conceptual frameworks.

Lifton (1961, pp. 65–85), a personality theorist, describes the psychological steps involved in thought reform in terms of death and rebirth of personality structures. It takes no great leap to see this death and rebirth in terms of a radical change of conceptual frameworks. The particular sequence of anomaly, new conceptualization, activity, and correction doubtless takes place any number of times during the protracted period of thought reform. Nevertheless, the major psychological steps identified by Lifton can be usefully viewed as contributing primarily to one or another of the stages in the cognitive process I have described for acquiring radically new knowledge.

The first four steps in the process involve an assault upon the person's identity, the establishment of guilt feelings, a betrayal of self (and others), and reaching a breaking point, where the threat of total annihilation becomes dominant. These four steps fairly clearly exemplify the introduction of an anomaly into the person's conceptual framework. A sense of personal identity is closely connected to one's total cognitive and affective modes of behaving. An attack on the one is an attack on the other. Guilt is a feeling of inadequacy and failure with regard to one's thoughts and behavior. The greater the guilt, the more obvious is it that an anomaly is present for the person. To betray oneself is to introduce even greater strains into one's cognitive and affective structures. It is a virtual admission that I cannot, as I now function, even be true to myself. Finally, the threat of annihilation would constitute the ultimate anomaly if cognitive systems truly are evolutionarily grounded. If my way of dealing with the world has led me to a position in which I may be annihilated, then surely something must be wrong with my way of dealing with the world. Or, at least, so it will appear to the person being threatened—especially if there appears to be an alternative which holds promise of allowing the removal of the threat and once again dealing with the world in an effective way.

The notion of an alternative leads to Lifton's next three steps—leniency and opportunity, the compulsion to confess, and a rechanneling of guilt. At or near the breaking point, thought reformers show some kindness and compassion, a glimpse of what could be if the subject actually is successful in adopting the new perspective. The compulsion to confess combined with a channeling of one's guilt by means of the new conceptual framework fairly clearly parallels my discussion of a new conceptualization. Both a new lens for looking at one's past and future activities, and the motivation for using it, are present at these stages.

Lifton calls the eighth step, "Re-education: Logical Dishonoring." By this he means both detailed reinterpretation of past experience by means of the new conceptual framework, as well as the analysis of the old framework in its own terms to show its inadequacy. This stage is somewhat analogous to reaching not only an appreciation of the theory of combustion, but also the feeling that the phlogiston theory which preceded it must have been fatally flawed internally. How could any rational person have believed it? It is in this sense that the old conceptual scheme has been "logically dishonored." For my purposes, this stage involves a myriad of activities and corrections. As the person reexamines in thought experiments the old ways of believing and acting, he or she is constantly corrected by the instructor so that the new way of looking at things becomes firmly entrenched.

The last four psychological steps in thought reform identified by Lifton are progress and harmony, the final confession, rebirth, and release to the larger society. These steps reflect the iteration of conceptualization, activity, and correction, leading eventually to a new reflective equilibrium which has removed the initial anomaly. Progress and increasing harmony show clearly the iterative nature of the process. The final confession is a kind of final examination, while rebirth indicates a new reflective equilibrium and release symbolizes the ability once again to deal with the world, although now a radically reconstituted world.

Special notice should also be given to the series of confessions characteristic of thought reform. These confessions illustrate starkly the iteration of triangulations of thought and action on the world which ultimately lead to a new reflective equilibrium. The new theory or conceptualization is propounded, and the thought experiments of applying it to one's experience provide the other leg of the triangulation.

The resulting confession is then criticized and corrected, and another attempt is made. There is a lot of "homework" in thought reform, and the teachers meticulously correct that homework.

It is also important to see that although Lifton describes the steps using coercive language, coercion is not essential, as even he observes. Lifton studied two groups of subjects for his book—Westerners imprisoned by the Chinese communists and later released, and Chinese intellectuals who later defected. Thus, in all cases he looked only at those for whom thought reform failed in some sense. Nevertheless, the descriptions these people, especially the Chinese, give of the process show how what is essential is not the coercion but the process of perceiving the inadequacy of one conceptual scheme and then replacing it with another. Thought reform for Chinese intellectuals takes place in revolutionary universities, not in prisons, and the threat of physical annihilation is replaced by the threat of the inability to find a place in the new social order. But is that latter threat really much different from the threat, implicit in our own society, that unless one learns to read, one will not find a job?

My point, of course, is not to endorse Chinese communism. Rather, it is to show that a view of learning as assimilation and accommodation can help us to understand why thought reform is as successful as it is. Furthermore, the crucial feature is that thought reform is not a psychological mechanism which is, or can be, used for questionable ends, but rather a process which engages our rationality. People believe, not because they have been "manipulated," but because by believing they can more adequately deal with their environment, and that, I have argued, is the essence of rationality.

This last remark also points to the ultimate arbiter between, say, liberal capitalism and communism. That arbiter will, on my account, necessarily be the ecology, both natural and social. Will the reflective equilibrium reached by communism be adequate, or will it require an impossibly strict control of the environment, including physical threat as well as propaganda? Will liberal capitalism be able to balance the demands for freedom, equity, and increased industrial productivity, or will our system become either a total welfare state on the one hand, or a fascist society on the other hand? The advantage of the assimilation and accommodation model is that it forces us to consider ideologies, environment, and their interactions in order to answer these questions.

I turn now to the painful phenomenon of conversion to cults, or even fringe religions. Indeed, the inability to draw the line between a "cult" and a religion which is simply different is bedevilling both heartsick parents and the courts. On the one hand, the word *cult* again calls to mind an irrational form of commitment, perhaps enforced by fear, mass hypnosis, and charismatic leadership. Whereas *religion* is a term which commands toleration, no matter how we might disagree with a particular set of beliefs.

Ted Patrick and Tom Dulack (1976, pp. 224–25) give a perspective on the conversion phenomenon that is remarkably similar to that of those who view thought reform as brainwashing: "Brainwashing came from Korea during the Korean War when many of our prisoners of war were subjected to intensive political indoctrination, using the same methods so many of the cults . . . employ today, namely fatigue, psychological fear, isolation, repetition of political dogma, and so forth." That is, cult conversion is viewed by Patrick and Dulack as a largely mechanistic, nonrational process. Elsewhere, the initial phases of the conversion are described as "on-the-spot hypnosis" (p. 37), and it is claimed that the converts sound like zombies (p. 33). Patrick calls his own work with converts "deprogramming," clearly implying that only his way of looking at things is a rational one. The cults program; he deprograms so that a person's reason can once again take over.

However, I want to urge that my model of assimilation and accommodation provides an alternative, and, I believe, more helpful, way of looking at the phenomenon of cult conversion. The alternative is to view the experience as a radical conceptual change, with the iterative operation of anomaly, alternative conceptual scheme, activity, and correction as descriptive of both conversion and deprogramming. This view would then help us focus on the basic question—namely, which reflective equilibrium is most adequate?

A secondary question, of course, is the means used both to convert people and to deprogram them. Both the cults and Patrick rely heavily on fatigue, isolation, and repetition of dogma. Without endorsing these methods, we see that they focus on the critical role of control of the environment in the sense that the dogma and the environment must be brought together in a reflective equilibrium. This, in turn, refocuses our attention on why we tend to disapprove of a heavily controlled environment, whether it be the creation of the cult or of the deprogrammer. Much work remains to be done, but the evolutionary assimilation and accommodation model at least suggests an outline of a research program. We currently denounce tightly controlled environments as an abrogation of human freedom. But this approach leaves us uneasy about how to justify the tightly controlled environments upon which we do agree, from enforcing certain kinds of social behavior to a "return to the basics" in school. Are we not just indoctrinating, too?

The evolutionary approach redefines the question. Freedom is a good, to be sure, in that it allows for new knowledge variants. On the other hand, if rationality is ultimately to be understood in terms of adaptability, then old knowledge cannot be slighted either. Freedom is good in so far as it promotes reflective equilibrium, which, in turn, is the essence of rationality. But freedom may, in cases such as the paradox of moral education, have to be limited by what we already know. On the other hand, we do not know so much that we can provide a definitive, dogmatic answer to all of our questions. Freedom is necessary for rationality.

The reflective equilibrium approach also casts new light on research into the characteristics of those most susceptible to either conversion experiences or brainwashing. If a reflective equilibrium between the old-and new-knowledge horns is the way to escape the *Meno* dilemma, then it could be predicted generally that those who attempt to grasp one horn of the dilemma to the exclusion of the other will have conceptual schemes most subject to anomalies. It follows that if a cult can so completely control an environment and provide an ideology which rationalizes the environment, then in that situation, anomalies will be removed for either someone who is constantly trying out new variants, or someone who has a long history of involvement with rigid orthodoxies. And this is exactly what one finds. The most susceptible converts are those who come from either very rigid backgrounds, or overly permissive backgrounds. A hardheaded pragmatism seems to provide the best, although not infallible, antidote to cult conversion experiences.

I will conclude this discussion with two suggestions for the kind of further research and study on thought reform in general which might be suggested by my evolutionary model. In the first place, thought reform makes very real the possibility of alternative conceptual schemes, with different kinds of reflective equilibria from that of our unreflective common wisdom. Furthermore, on the evolutionary model, we cannot simply use words such as *brainwashing, programming,* and *deprogramming* to describe the phenomena of thought reform. Such terms imply a mechanistic view of a process which may rather be highly adaptive, and, hence, rational in certain ecologies. In short, we must take differing ideologies and cults seriously and examine them in their own terms. This examination goes far beyond a plea for tolerance, however, for the evolutionary model points to the necessity of examining the processes of knowledge of a given ideology *in* its ecological context.

Of more specific importance for education, the success of thought reform throws into basic relief some of the inadequacies of our own educational practices. Whatever may be said about the unethical means employed by some thought reform practitioners, at least they appear to recognize that they are dealing with a radical change of conceptual schemes. They appreciate the necessity for a thoroughgoing critique (introduction of anomalies) of current ways of dealing with the world. They are careful to present both their way of looking at the world and the opportunity for seeing that theory in practice (alternative conceptualization and activity). Finally, they are meticulous in correcting early attempts by the converts.

By contrast, our current educational system "intellectualizes" its content far too much. We seldom recognize that there are occasions on which we wish to change a student's conceptual scheme radically and are justified in so doing. We, therefore, present the new scheme, but give little or no attention to the anomaly, activity, and correction stages of the process. What we teach, thus, makes no real contact with the student's way of dealing with the world, and we are constantly bedeviled by the fact that our students do not practice what we preach. But how can they? By our lack of attention to several of the important steps of radical conceptual change, we ensure our failure. Our students often simply continue to assimilate what we teach to their old ways of thinking and acting.

Nor need we adopt the more extreme and questionable practices of the communists and the cults. We can appreciate the necessity for introducing anomalies without having to destroy a student's entire self-identity. We can present positions which we believe are justifiable without catechising. We need not send our intellectuals to the farms to incorporate the necessity for triangulating activity with the new conceptual scheme we wish to teach. We can correct mistakes without coercion. A research program guided by the evolutionary model will enable us to design and assess effective instructional strategies for both assimilative and accommodative kinds of change.

Finally, the evolutionary model highlights the profound limits to our ability to mold students as we will. Learning is a process of successive reflective equilibria between human thought and action. No one can make the world, including other human beings, conform to his or her desires simply by wishing it so. Neither, however, can anyone justifiably claim to have access to reality as it really is. In the long run, if our attempts at teaching do not allow the student to deal more effectively with his or her world, we will fail. Human freedom consists precisely in the fact that in a varied and changing world, the reflective equilibria needed may also be varied and changeable. It is this feature that underlies the growth of understanding, both for humanity in general, and for the individual student in particular.

8. Conclusion

This work began with the question "How are enquiry and learning possible?" The answer I have given is that it is only if we focus on the processes of learning and coming to know rather than on the products of learning or knowledge structures will we be able to answer this question. This means that much more emphasis must be placed on processes of knowing than on structures of knowledge. In a fundamental sense, we need to know more about how people reasonably change their knowledge structures than we need to know about what those knowledge structures look like at any given time. A static snapshot of a knowledge structure in the process of transition is useful primarily for what it can tell us about the transition and not so much for what it can tell us about the structure. I think this emphasis on knowledge processes is useful for epistemology in general, but it is absolutely crucial for educational epistemology.

Once the shift is made to focusing on knowledge processes rather than knowledge structures, an interesting picture emerges. There are two quite different types of knowledge processes corresponding to the two horns of the *Meno* dilemma. The knowledge process that adds to and fleshes out an existing conceptual framework I have called assimilation. Those who would grasp the old-knowledge horn of the *Meno* dilemma tend to try to assimilate all coming to know to elaboration of existing conceptual schemes. On the other hand there is the knowledge process that involves changing our conceptual schemes. The knowledge process that changes our existing conceptual framework I have called accommodation. Those who would grasp the new-knowledge horn of the *Meno* dilemma tend to try to assimilate all coming to know to changes in conceptual schemes. Neither approach tells the whole story, and what I have been urging throughout this book is that learning and enquiry are possible only by attaining a reflective equilibrium between assimilation and accommodation.

These two knowledge processes are not well recognized in current educational thought. Still less recognized is the necessity for dealing with them simultaneously, i.e., for slipping between the horns of the *Meno* dilemma. What educators must begin to do is ask what knowledge process is of concern in any given situation. The answer may well dictate quite different educational practices and policies. If the process is assimilation, there still remains the necessity for understanding the ways in which experience is processed by existing knowledge structures. A great deal of adaptiveness can be found simply in how we deal with situations which are similar to but never quite the same as situations we have dealt with before. Behaviorism seems bankrupt in this regard. Control system theory looks promising, especially in that it gives a radically new view of how to test for learning. Look not at the outputs of the student but at what disturbances to inputs the student resists. If, on the other hand, the process of concern is accommodation, the problem becomes one of how we rationally change our cognitive structures to account for recalcitrant experience. Here I have urged a much greater reliance on variation and selective retention processes. From the student's point of view it will be logically impossible in cases of accommodation to specify in advance in terms intelligible to the student what it is that is to be learned. Rather we must concentrate on getting the students to try out knowledge variants which have as their sources the students' current knowledge structures and arrange the educational ecology so that the reflective equilibrium the student reaches is roughly what is required by our collective understanding. The autonomy of the students' reason is necessarily respected in this approach, for it is the student's equilibrium which will control the knowledge processes of that student.

The problem in educational thought is that this reflective equilibrium is seldom maintained, and the educational pendulum oscillates wildly between new- and old-knowledge approaches. Not so many years ago, we were inundated with cries for the reform of dull, drab, irrelevant schooling. The curriculum of the schools was outmoded and uninspiring; we were told that we needed to open up our schools and classrooms and allow far more student participation. I have no doubt that this reform movement was reacting appropriately to schools and schooling that seemed to deny that conceptual structures were ever rationally alterable. In our time, however, the reform is "back to the basics." I have no doubt that this movement is reacting appropriately to excesses of open schools that seem to deny that the human race has collectively learned something of value that should be passed on to our children.

But neither the new- nor the old-knowledge horn of the *Meno* dilemma can be grasped to the exclusion of the other. I confidently predict that the "back to the basics" movement will effectively deny that concepts do change and will ultimately be challenged for its inability to integrate conceptual change with the movement's emphasis on conceptual continuity. Not until we recognize the necessity for a reflective equilibrium between assimilation and accommodation will education avoid impaling itself first on one and then on the other horn of the *Meno* dilemma.

An unfriendly critic might accuse me of having said nothing new about learning and enquiry. Indeed, we knew all along that the *Meno* dilemma was solvable—we see it solved every day as people learn new things all around us. It might also be said that I have not really added anything to our knowledge except perhaps some technical jargon we could easily do without. Surely we have always known that we must start with the student's current cognitive state, that new conceptual structures are occasionally necessary, that rule-governed activity is central to education, that trial-and-error learning does sometimes take place, and even, perhaps, that there is such a phenomenon as conceptual change.

One might raise such an objection, but to do so would be to miss the central point of this work. And that is that we do manage to move, collectively and individually, from current knowledge and ways of knowing to new knowledge and ways of knowing, and it is that movement which must be of central concern to education. Of course I have utilized what is already known about learning and ways of knowing. One must not deny the old-knowledge horn of the *Meno* dilemma. But neither have I simply summarized what we already know. I have pointed to some new and different directions; I have suggested a new conceptualization, if you will, for understanding how our existing knowledge and ways of knowing can and do change. The ideas presented here have implications for future study and research in education which are significantly different from the directions of much current educational thought. In that sense this book is at least a sketch of a new educational theory.

The central thrust of that theory can be seen by returning to the *Meno* itself. Most scholars have focused on Plato's theory of recollection as his intellectual answer to the *Meno* dilemma. Such a focus presupposes that knowledge *structures* are the chief area of concern. What has recently been done in the context of Platonic scholarship has been to look at the *activity* that the dilemma engendered in the dialogue, namely, the active searching for and trying out of knowledge variants (see, for example, Sternfeld and Zyskind, 1978). The theory of recollection is followed in the *Meno* by Socrates' active demonstration of its truth with the experiment with the slave boy. The Socratic method as exemplified within the experiment with the slave boy itself makes essential use of the *activities* of the slave boy in propounding new ideas, correcting them, and iterating the process. As Klein (1965, p. 172) anticipated, "It is *the action of learning* which conveys the truth about it. The answer to the question about the possibiltiy of learning is not a 'theory of knowledge' or an 'epistemology' but the very *effort* to learn."

Near the end of the *Meno* Plato says (98A):

> True opinions are a fine thing and do all sorts of good so long as they stay in their place; but they will not stay long. They run away from

man's mind, so they are not worth much until you tether them by working out the reason. Once they are tied down, they become knowledge, and are stable. That is why knowledge is something more valuable than right opinion. What distinguishes one from the other is the tether.

This book has attempted to work out the tether for a new theory of education. It is a tether that requires us to alternate in a constantly adaptive way between what we already know and what we do not yet know. It requires us to act in the world as well as think about it, and in that way we shall be able at last to step between the horns of the *Meno* dilemma of enquiry and learning.

References

Acton, H. B. "Hegel, Georg Wilhelm Friedrich," in *The Encyclopedia of Philosophy*. New York: Macmillan, 1967.

Anderson, John R., and Gordon H. Bower. *Human Associative Memory*. Washington, D.C.: V. H. Winston and Sons, 1973.

Anderson, R. C.; R. J. Spiro; and W. E. Montague, eds. *Schooling and the Acquisition of Knowledge*. Hillsdale, N.J.: Lawrence Erlbaum Associates, 1977.

Blachowicz, James. "Discovery and Cross-Checking." Unpublished article, Loyola University, Chicago. (a)

————. "Discovery and Intuition." Unpublished article, Loyola University, Chicago. (b)

Black, Max. *Models and Metaphors*. Ithaca, N.Y.: Cornell University Press, 1962.

————. "Rules and Routines," in R. S. Peters, ed., *The Concept of Education*. London: Routledge and Kegan Paul, 1967.

Bluck, R. S., ed. *Plato's Meno*. Cambridge: Cambridge University Press, 1961.

Broudy, Harry S. "Didactics, Heuristics, and Philetics." *Educational Theory* 22, no. 3 (1972):251–61.

Brown, Malcolm, ed. *Plato's Meno,* translated by W. K. C. Guthrie. New York: Bobbs Merrill, 1971.

Bruner, J. S.; J. J. Goodenow; and G. A. Austin. *A Study of Thinking*. New York: Wiley, 1956.

Brunswik, Egon. *The Conceptual Framework of Psychology*. Chicago: University of Chicago Press, 1952.

Butterfield, H. *The Origins of Modern Science*. London: G. Bell and Sons, 1957.

Campbell, Donald T. "Common Fate, Similarity, and Other Indices of the State of Aggregates of Persons as Social Entities." *Behavioral Science* 3, no. 1 (1958): 14–25.

————. "Methodological Suggestions from a Comparative Psychology of Knowledge Processes." *Inquiry* 2 (1959): 152–82.

————. "Pattern Matching as an Essential in Distal Knowing," in Kenneth B. Hammond, ed., *The Psychology of Egon Brunswik*. New York: Holt, Rinehart and Winston, 1966.

————. "Objectivity and the Social Locus of Scientific Knowledge." Presidential Address to the Division of Social and Personality Psychology, American Psychological Association, 1969.

————. "Evolutionary Epistemology," in P. A. Schilpp, ed., *The Philosophy of Karl Popper. The Library of Living Philosophers,* vol. 14. LaSalle, Ill.: Open Court, 1974.

———— and Donald W. Fiske. "Convergent and Discriminant Validation by the Multitrait-Multimethod Matrix." *Psychological Bulletin* 56, no. 2 (March 1959): 81–105.

Carnap, Rudolf. *Logical Foundations of Probability.* 2d rev. ed. Chicago: University of Chicago Press, 1962.

Chomsky, Noam. "Review of B. F. Skinner, *Verbal Behavior. Language* 35 (1959): 26–58.

————. *Language and Mind.* New York: Harcourt, Brace and World, 1969.

Cornfield, J., and J. W. Tukey. "Average Values of Mean Squares in Factorials." *Annals of Mathematical Statistics* 27 (1956): 907–49.

Cornford, F. M., "Anamnesis," in Malcolm Brown, ed., *Plato's Meno.* New York: Bobbs Merrill, 1971.

Cronbach, L. J.; G. C. Gleser; H. Nanda; and N. Rajaratnam. *The Dependability of Behavioral Measurements.* New York: Wiley, 1972.

Davidson, Donald. "Actions , Reasons, and Causes." *Journal of Philosophy* 60, no. 23 (Nov. 7, 1963): 685–700.

————. "On the Very Idea of a Conceptual Scheme." *Proceedings of the American Philosophical Association* 47 (1973–74): 5–20.

Dewey, John. *Logic: The Theory of Enquiry.* New York: Henry Holt, 1938.

Duhem, Pierre. *Aim and Structure of Physical Theory.* New York: Atheneum, 1954.

Feyerabend, Paul. "Against Method: Outline of an Anarchistic Theory of Knowledge," in M. Radner and S. Winokur, eds., *Analyses of Theory and Methods of Physics and Psychology.* Minnesota Studies in the Philosophy of Science, vol. 4. Minneapolis: University of Minnesota Press, 1970.

Fisk, Franklin G., and Milo K. Blecha. *The Physical Sciences.* River Forest, Ill.: Doubleday, 1966.

Fodor, Jerry. *The Language of Thought.* New York: Crowell, 1975.

Goffman, E. *Relations in Public.* London: Allen Lane, The Penguin Press, 1971.

Green, Thomas F. "Teaching, Acting, and Behaving," in B. Paul Komisar and C. B. J. MacMillan, eds., *Psychological Concepts in Education.* Chicago: Rand McNally, 1967.

————. *The Activities of Teaching.* New York: McGraw-Hill, 1971.

Halstead, Robert E. "Teaching for Understanding," in *Philosophy of Education, 1975*. Philosophy of Education Society, 1975.

——. "Cognitive Structures and Forms of Knowledge," in *Philosophy of Education, 1977*. Philosophy of Education Society, 1977.

Hamlyn, D. W. "Epistemology and Conceptual Development," in T. Mischel, ed., *Cognitive Development and Epistemology*. New York: Academic Press, 1971.

——. "Human learning," in R. S. Peters, ed., *The Philosophy of Education*. Oxford: Oxford University Press, 1973a.

——. "Logical and Psychological Aspects of Learning," in R. S. Peters, ed., *The Philosophy of Education*. Oxford: Oxford University Press, 1973b.

——. *Experience and the Growth of Understanding*. London: Routledge and Kegan Paul, 1978.

Hanson, N. R. *Patterns of Discovery*. Cambridge: Cambridge University Press, 1958.

——. *Perception and Discovery*. San Francisco: Freeman, Cooper, 1969.

Harré, R. " 'Rule' as a Scientific Concept," in Theodore Mischel, ed., *Understanding Other Persons*. Totowa, N.J.: Rowan and Littlefield, 1974.

Haynes, Felicity. "Metaphor as Interaction." *Educational Theory* 25, no. 3 (Summer 1975): 272–77.

——. "Reason and Insight in Learning." Ph.D. dissertation, University of Illinois, Urbana, 1977.

Hempel, Carl G. *Aspects of Scientific Explanation and Other Essays in the Philosophy of Science*. New York: Free Press, 1965.

Hirst, P. H. "Liberal Education and the Nature of Knowledge," in R. D. Archambault, ed., *Philosophical Analysis and Education*. London: Routledge and Kegan Paul, 1965.

——. "The Forms of Knowledge Re-visited," in P. H. Hirst. *Knowledge and the Curriculum*. London: Routledge and Kegan Paul, 1974.

Holton, Gerald. *The Project Physics Course Reader, Unit 2: Motion in the Heavens*. New York: Holt, Rinehart & Winston, 1970.

——. *Introduction to Concepts and Theories in Physical Science*. 2d ed. rev. with new material by Stephen G. Brush. Reading, Mass.: Addison-Wesley, 1973a.

——. *Thematic Origins of Scientific Thought; Kepler to Einstein*. Cambridge, Mass.: Harvard University Press, 1973b.

——. *The Thematic Component in Scientific Thought: Origins of Relativity Theory and Other Essays*. Austin: University of Texas at Austin, 1973c.

———. *Science and Its Public: The Changing Relationship.* Edited by Gerald Holton and William A. Blanpied. Boston Studies in the Philosophy of Science, vol. 33. Dordrecht, Netherlands: D. Reidel, 1976.

———. *The Scientific Imagination: Case Studies.* Cambridge, England, and New York: Cambridge University Press, 1978.

Hume, David. *A Treatise of Human Nature,* edited by L. A. Selby-Bigge. Oxford: Clarendon Press, 1964.

Kant, Immanuel. *Critique of Pure Reason,* translated by Norman Kemp Smith. London, Macmillan, 1961.

Katz, Michael. *Class, Bureaucracy and Schooling.* New York: Praeger, 1971.

Keat, R., and J. Urry. *Social Theory as Science.* London and Boston: Routledge & Kegan Paul, 1975.

Klein, Jacob. *A Commentary on Plato's Meno.* Chapel Hill, N.C.: University of North Carolina Press, 1965.

Kuhn, Thomas. "Reflections on My Critics," in I. Lakatos and A. Musgrave, eds., *Criticism and the Growth of Knowledge.* Cambridge: Cambridge University Press, 1970a.

———. *The Structure of Scientific Revolutions.* Enlarged edition. Chicago: University of Chicago Press, 1970b.

———. "Second Thoughts on Paradigms," in Frederick Suppe, ed., *The Structure of Scientific Theories.* Urbana, Ill.: University of Illinois Press, 1974.

Lakatos, Imre. *Criticism and the Growth of Knowledge.* International Colloquium in the Philosophy of Science, Bedford College, 1965. Edited by Imre Lakatos and Alan Musgrave. Cambridge, Eng.: University Press, 1970.

———. *Proofs and Refutations: The Logic of Mathematical Discovery.* Edited by John Worrall and Elie Zahar. Cambridge and New York: Cambridge University Press, 1976.

———. *Philosophical Papers.* 2 vols. Edited by John Worrall and Gregory Currie. Cambridge, Eng., and New York: Cambridge University Press, 1978.

Lévi-Strauss, Claude. *The Savage Mind.* London: Weidenfeld and Nicolson, 1966.

Lifton, Robert J. *Thought Reform and the Psychology of Totalism.* New York: W. W. Norton, 1961.

Loewenberg, Ina. "Truth and Consequences of Metaphors." *Philosophy and Rhetoric* 6, no. 1 (1973): 3–46.

———. "Denying the Undeniable: Metaphors are *Not* Comparisons." *Mid-American Linguistics Conference Papers* (1975a): 305–16.

———. "Identifying Metaphors." *Foundations of Language* 12 (1975b): 315–38.

MacIntyre, Alasdair. "Existentialism," in *The Encyclopedia of Philosophy*. New York: Macmillan, 1967.

Martin, Jane Roland. *Explaining, Understanding and Teaching*. New York: McGraw-Hill, 1970.

Melden, A. E. *Free Action*. London: Routledge and Kegan Paul, 1961.

Miller, George A. "Four Philosophical Problems of Psycholinguistics." *Philosophy of Science* 37 (June 1970): 193–99.

Miller, Ralph M. "The Dubious Case for Metaphors in Educational Writing." *Educational Theory* 26, no. 2 (Spring 1976): 174–81.

Nagel, E. *The Structure of Science*. New York: Harcourt, Brace, 1961.

Oliver, Russell Graham. "An Epistemological and Ethical Justification of Educational Research and Practice." Ph.D. dissertation, University of Illinois, Urbana, 1976.

Ortony, Andrew. "Why Metaphors Are Necessary and Not Just Nice." *Educational Theory* 25, no. 1 (Winter 1975): 45–53.

———. "On the Nature and Value of Metaphor: A Reply to My Critics." *Educational Theory* 26, no. 4 (Fall 1976): 395–98.

Page, Ralph. "Reasonable Beliefs and Personal Points of View." *Philosophy of Education, 1977*. Philosophy of Education Society, 1977.

Paivio, A. *Imagery and Verbal Processes*. New York: Holt, Rinehart, and Winston, 1971.

Patrick, Ted, with Tom Dulack. *Let Our Children Go!* New York: Ballantine Books, 1976.

Pearce, Glenn, and Patrick Maynard, eds., *Conceptual Change*. Dordrecht: Reidel, 1973.

Peters, R. S. *The Concept of Motivation*. 2d edition. London: Routledge and Kegan Paul, 1960.

———. *Education as Initiation*. London: Evans, 1963.

———. "The Development of Reason," in *Psychology and Ethical Development*. London: Allen and Unwin, 1974a.

———. "Reason and Habit: The Paradox of Moral Education," in R. S. Peters, *Psychology and Ethical Development*. London: George Allen and Unwin, 1974b.

Petrie, Hugh G. "Rote Learning and Learning with Understanding." Ph.D. dissertation, Stanford University, 1965.

———. "Learning with Understanding," in Jane R. Martin, ed., *Readings in the Philosophy of Education: A Study of Curriculum*. Boston: Allyn and Bacon, 1970.

———. "A Dogma of Operationalism in the Social Sciences." *Philosophy of Social Science* 1 (1971a): 145–60.

———. "Science and Metaphysics: A Wittgensteinian Interpretation," in E. Klemke, ed., *Essays on Wittgenstein*. Urbana, Ill.: University of Illinois Press, 1971b.

———. "Action, Perception, and Education." *Educational Theory* 24, no. 1 (Winter 1974a): 33–45.

———. "The Believing in Seeing," in Lindley Stiles, ed., *Theories for Teaching*. Center for the Teaching Professions, Northwestern University. New York: Dodd, Mead, 1974b.

———. "Can Education Find Its Lost Objectives under the Street Lamp of Behaviorism," in Ralph Smith, ed., *Regaining Educational Leadership: Essays Critical of PBTE/CBTE*. New York: Wiley, 1975a.

———. "That's Just Einstein's Opinion: The Autocracy of Students' Reasons in Open Education," in David Nyberg, ed., *The Philosophy of Open Education*. London: Routledge and Kegan Paul, 1975b.

———. "Evolutionary Rationality: Or Can Learning Theory Survive in the Jungle of Conceptual Change?" *Philosophy of Education, 1976*. Philosophy of Education Society, 1976a.

———. "Metaphorical Models of Mastery: Or How to Learn to Do the Problems at the End of the Chapter in the Physics Textbook," in R. S. Cohen, et al., eds., *PSA 1974*. Dordrecht, Holland: Reidel, 1976b.

———. "A Rule by Any Other Name Is a Control System." *Cybernetics Forum* 8, nos. 3 and 4 (Fall/Winter 1976c): 103–14.

———. "Science and Scientists, Technology and Technologists, and the Rest of Us," in Richard LaBrecque and Vincent Crockenberg, eds., *Culture as Education*. Dubuque, Iowa: Kendall-Hunt, 1977.

———. "Against Objective Tests: A Note on the Epistemology Underlying Current Testing Dogma," in M. N. Ozer, ed., *A Cybernetic Approach to the Assessment of Children: Toward a More Humane Use of Human Beings*. Boulder, Colo.: Westview, 1979.

Phillips, Bernard. "The Significance of Meno's Paradox," in Alexander Sesonske and Noel Fleming, eds., *Plato's Meno: Text and Criticism*. Belmont, Calif.: Wadsworth, 1965.

Phillips, Denis. "Response." *Philosophy of Education, 1976*. Philosophy of Education Society, 1976.

Piaget, Jean. *The Moral Judgment of the Child*. Glencoe, Ill.: Free Press, 1948.

———. *The Child's Conception of Physical Causality*. London: Routledge and Kegan Paul, 1951a.

———. *The Child's Conception of the World*. London: Routledge and Kegan Paul, 1951b.

———. *Judgment and Reasoning in the Child*. London: Routledge and Kegan Paul, 1951c.

———. *The Language and Thought of the Child*. London: Routledge and Kegan Paul, 1952.

———. *The Construction of Reality in the Child*. New York: Basic Books, 1954.

————. "The Role of the Concept of Equilibrium in Psychological Explication," in J. Piaget, *Six Psychological Studies*. New York: Vintage Books, 1968a.

————. *Six Psychological Studies*. New York: Vintage Press, 1968b.

————. *The Principles of Genetic Epistemology*. New York: Basic Books, 1972.

Polanyi, Michael. *Personal Knowledge*. Rev. ed. Chicago: University of Chicago Press, 1962.

————. *The Tacit Dimension*. Garden City, N.Y.: Doubleday, 1966.

Popper, Karl. *The Logic of Scientific Discovery*. London: Hutchinson, 1959.

————. *Conjectures and Refutations: The Growth of Scientific Knowledge*. 2d ed. New York: Basic Books, 1965.

Powers, William T. *Behavior: The Control of Perception*. Chicago: Aldine, 1973a.

————. "Feedback: Beyond Behaviorism." *Science* 179 (26 January 1973b): 351–56.

Quine, W. V. O. "Two Dogmas of Empiricism." *Philosophical Review* 60, pp. 20–43. Reprinted in W. V. O. Quine, *From a Logical Point of View*, 2d ed. Cambridge Mass.: Harvard University Press, 1962.

————. "Epistemology Naturalized," in *Ontological Relativity and Other Essays*. New York: Columbia University Press, 1969a.

————. "Natural Kinds," in *Ontological Relativity and Other Essays*. New York: Columbia University Press, 1969b.

Rathbone, C. H. "The Implicit Rationale of the Open Education Classroom," in Rathbone, C. H., ed., *Open Education: The Informal Classroom*. New York: Citation Press, 1971.

Rorty, R., ed., *The Linguistic Turn*. Chicago: University of Chicago Press, 1967.

Rosemont, Henry, Jr. "On the Concept of Indoctrination." *Studies in Philosophy and Education* 1, no. 3 (Spring 1972): 226–37.

Rosenshine, Barak. "Enthusiastic Teaching: A Research Review." *School Review* 72 (1970): 499–514.

Rummelhart, D. E., and A. Ortony. "The Representation of Knowledge in Memory," in Anderson, R. C.; R. J. Spiro; and W. E. Montague, eds., *Schooling and the Acquisition of Knowledge*. Hillsdale, N.J.: Lawrence Erlbaum Associates, 1977.

Russell, Bertrand. *Logic and Knowledge: Essays, 1901–1950*. Edited by R. C. Marsh. London: George Allen & Unwin; New York: Macmillan, 1956.

Ryan, Alan. *The Philosophy of the Social Sciences*. New York: Pantheon, 1970.

Ryle, Gilbert. *The Concept of Mind*. London: Hutchinson, 1949.

Scheffler, Israel. *The Language of Education*. Springfield, Ill.: Charles C. Thomas, 1960.

———. *Conditions of Knowledge*. Chicago: Scott, Foresman, 1965.

———. *Science and Subjectivity*. New York: Bobbs-Merrill, 1967.

Searle, John. *Speech Acts*. Cambridge: Cambridge University Press, 1969.

Slack, W. V., and D. Porter. "The Scholastic Aptitude Test: A Critical Appraisal." *Harvard Educational Review* 50 (1980): 154–75.

Sneed, Joseph. *The Logical Structure of Mathematical Physics*. Dordrecht, Holland: Reidel, 1971.

Snook, I. A. "The Concept of Indoctrination." *Studies in Philosophy and Education* 7 (Fall 1970): 65–108.

———, ed. *Concepts of Indoctrination: Philosophical Essays*. London: Routledge and Kegan Paul, 1972.

Spodek, Bernard, and Herbert J. Walberg, eds. *Studies in Open Education*. New York: Agathon, 1974.

Stegmuller, Wolfgang. *The Structure and Dynamics of Theories*. Translated by W. Wohlheuter. New York: Springer-Verlag, 1976.

Sternfeld, R., and H. Zyskind. *Plato's Meno*. Carbondale and Edwardsville, Ill.: Southern Illinois University Press, 1978.

Strawson, P. F. *Individuals*. London: Methuen, 1959.

———. *The Bounds of Sense*. London: Methuen, 1966.

Strike, Kenneth. "Learning by Discovery." *Review of Educational Research* 45, no. 3 (Summer 1975): 461–83.

Suppe, Frederick, ed., *The Structure of Scientific Theories*. Urbana, Ill.: University of Illinois Press, 1974.

Tarski, Alfred. "The Semantic Conception of Truth," in Leonard Linsky, ed., *Semantics and the Philosophy of Language*. Urbana, Ill.: University of Illinois Press, 1952.

Tomko, T. N. "The Logic of Criterion-Referenced Testing." Ph.D. dissertation, University of Illinois, 1980.

Toulmin, Stephen. *Foresight and Understanding*. New York: Harper and Row, 1963.

———. *Human Understanding*. vol. 1. Princeton, N.J.: Princeton University Press, 1972.

———. "Rules and Their Relevance for Understanding Human Behavior," in Theodore Mischel, ed., *Understanding Other Persons*. Totowa, N.J.: Rowan and Littlefield, 1974.

Tunnell, Donald. "Open Education: An Expression in Search of a Definition," in David Nyberg, ed., *The Philosophy of Open Education*. London: Routledge and Kegan Paul, 1975.

van Heijenoort, John. "Logical Paradoxes," in Paul Edwards, ed., *The Encyclopedia of Philosophy*. New York: Macmillan, 1967.

Veatch, Henry. *Two Logics: The Conflict between Classical and Neo-analytic Philosophy*. Evanston: Northwestern University Press, 1969.

Waks, Leonard J. "Knowledge and Understanding as Educational Aims." *The Monist* 52, no. 1 (January 1968): 104–19.

Weimer, Walter B. "Psycholinguistics and Plato's Paradoxes of the *Meno*." *American Psychologist* (January 1973): 15–33.

Weitz, Morris. "Analysis, Philosophical." *The Encyclopedia of Philosophy*. New York: Macmillan, 1967.

Wilson, Edward O. *Sociobiology*. Cambridge, Mass.: Harvard University Press, 1975.

Wimsatt, William C. "Complexity and Organization," in Kenneth F. Schaffner and Robert S. Cohen, eds., *PSA 1972*. Dordrecht, Holland: Reidel, 1974.

Wittgenstein, L. *Remarks on the Foundation of Mathematics*. Edited by G. H. von Wright, R. Rhees, and G. E. M. Anscombe, with English translation by G. E. M. Anscombe. Oxford: Basil Blackwell, 1956.

———. *Philosophical Investigations*. 3d ed. Translated by G. E. M. Anscombe. New York: Macmillan, 1958.

Index